THE MEN WHO MADE THE RAMS

Origins and Who's Who of Derby County Football Club 1884 to 1888

Peter Seddon

A Soccerdata Publication

Published in Great Britain by Tony Brown,
4 Adrian Close, Toton, Nottingham NG9 6FL.
Telephone 0115 973 6086. E-mail soccer@innotts.co.uk
www.soccerdata.com

First published 2013

© Peter Seddon 2013

All rights reserved. No part of this publication may be reproduced, stored in a retrieval system, or transmitted in any form, or by any means, electronic, mechanical, photocopying, recording or otherwise without the prior permission in writing of the Copyright holder, nor be otherwise circulated in any form or binding or cover other than in which it is published and without a similar condition including this condition being imposed on the subsequent publisher.

Cover design by Bob Budd.

Printed and bound by 4Edge, Hockley, Essex
www.4edge.co.uk

ISBN: 978-1-905891-77-1

FOREWORD

When I retired from full time journalism at the *Derby Evening Telegraph* in 2002, one of several projects in mind was an examination of the early years before the Rams became founder members of the Football League. That period was neglected, apart from extracting Cup details, in successive editions of the 'Complete Record' and the 'Who's Who'.

Other projects took precedence and, as the years passed, my spinal problems causing severe loss of mobility and natural indolence reduced the chances of hours in the Derby Local Studies Library.

Now, I am pleased about the way the situation developed. With no effort on my part, I can discover all I need to know about 1884 to 1888 as the result of Peter Seddon's industry and meticulous research. He is dogged and determined, seeing obstacles as challenges.

I especially admire the brief biographies of players, containing as they do much previously unseen information. In the heyday of Gentlemen v Players at cricket and amateur football teams like the Wanderers and the Corinthians, the disparate personalities in the dressing-room appeared to blend together.

This is an important addition to the annals of Derby County and I wish it well.

Gerald Mortimer
Ilkeston
September 2013

THE MEN WHO MADE THE RAMS

CONTENTS

Foreword		3
Introduction		5

PART ONE

1	The birth of Derby County – 1884	7
2	1884-85 – A turbulent beginning	15
3	1885-86 – Consolidation and a major scalp	26
4	1886-87 – Records and rifts	32
5	1887-88 – A pivotal campaign	40
6	1888-89 – Founder members of the Football League	47
7	1889 to 1896 – Coming of age	55

PART TWO

8	The men who made the Rams – Founding fathers	63
9	Who's Who of the 'Chocolate and Blue' – Players 1884 to 1888	76

Acknowledgements	154
Derby County line-ups 1884-1888	155

7th January 1885 – the Derby County team which drew 4-4 with Cambridge University Wanderers, plus Spilsbury who assisted the opposition. Back (l to r): F. H. Sugg, H. A. Morley, G. Bakewell, A. Williamson, W. A. Weston, A. Smith, L. Cooper, E. Hickinbottom. Front: B. W. Spilsbury, A. H. J. Cochrane, W. Weston, E. B. Farquharson.

INTRODUCTION

*'But sometimes during the dullest play,
Something comes back from an earlier day,
A fleeting moment, a hint of grace,
Brings back a feeling, a time, a place.'
(Gordon Jeffery, 'Men on the Terraces')*

Over the years Derby County Football Club and its loyal band of supporters has been particularly well-served in the way it has been written about. A complete 'DCFC library' would go a long way towards filling an entire bookcase. For that we must thank a succession of dedicated authors who have covered in the greatest detail almost every aspect of the club's eventful history since its 1884 formation. But note the word 'almost'....

I use that qualification for a definite reason – one that explains why I am adding 'The Men Who Made The Rams' to the already comprehensive Derby County shelves. The book is intended to fill a nagging gap – the last major untold story in the life of a celebrated football club. By its end all who played a part in the football theatre of those far-off days will finally take their due eternal bow. There was no way out – the book had to be written....for the club, its fans, football history in general, and the 'vanished men' in particular. Whilst the window on the past remained fleetingly ajar....before it was too late.

The story that follows embraces the earliest distinct period of the club's existence – namely the first four seasons 1884 to 1888 from the moment of birth to its surprise election as a founder member of the Football League. That pioneering time has never been fully chronicled. Only a handful of results have ever been captured. The long-gone players who pulled on the 'chocolate, amber and blue' have remained as shadowy phantoms – unidentified beyond the odd early star. Yet collectively they propelled Derby County into 'The League' after just four seasons of existence – the youngest of the twelve elected clubs. How they worked this apparent miracle cannot be ignored.

The general tone in previous books has been that the first four campaigns comprised mostly 'friendly games' that didn't amount to much – the inference is that apart from the FA Cup the real business only started in 1888 when the Football League began. But 'challenge matches' would be a far better term than 'friendlies' – although 'unofficial' those pre-League encounters truly mattered.

Did the players locked in robust combat really believe the contests were meaningless? Not for one moment. And what of the supporters who followed every move with the keenest eye? This was no sepia-tinted age of prancing men in curious garb – blame the 'sporting artists' for creating that quaint impression. In fact this was fast and furious football in full glorious colour – green grass and bright days, brown mud and grey days, hard knocks, red blood, real pain, and more than a few black days. And those first four seasons were the most important in the entire history of Derby County FC. They need to be captured.

But for the progress made in those early campaigns the club would no longer exist. On more than one occasion it might easily have folded before the League was formed. Clubs like Derby Midland and Derby Junction – bitter rivals of the 'Chocolates' – wouldn't have minded a bit. They resented Derby County's arrival deeply. Yet Midland and Junction fell by the wayside – now mere ghosts of the past. It was Derby County that survived as the town's only professional football club – the very same club now resident at Pride Park Stadium.

So the 'distant past' is not really too long ago. An unbreakable thread links 1884 to the present. Derby County's origins and ancestry makes the club what it has been, is now, and always will be – whatever its varying fortunes. Deep down we all need to know 'where we come from'.

The story of the club's birth and early rise is intended above all to entertain. I have tried to steer away from 'dry history' – aiming instead to put vivid life into the events and personalities which progressively nudged the club to a coming of age. Much of the narrative has all the elements of 'soap opera' – football 'then' was not so different from football 'now'... only the 'quantities' really differ, players' pay the most astonishing change.

The 'Who's Who' section of the book puts flesh and blood on the names of those early players. Turning out for little or no financial reward, a pure love of football was their primary motivation. No longer with a voice, they deserve to be remembered. If only they knew their legacy....

The book has been put together from disparate sources. Much of the narrative material has come from early newspapers – tiny print, grainy photographs, tantalising clues, and misty reminiscence. The 'Who's Who' drew heavily on genealogical records. At times the task of writing felt like attempting to complete a jigsaw without a picture....in a darkened room. But I hope the result succeeds in its stated aims in at least some small part.

If today's football enthusiasts can emerge from the reading with an enriched knowledge and a closer bond to Derby County Football Club, then something worthwhile has been achieved. If the book entertains and raises spirits then better still – the 'vanished men' will not have battled in vain. As they take their positions for one last time – please be upstanding for 'The Men Who Made The Rams'.

Peter Seddon
Derby
October 2013

CHAPTER ONE

The Birth of Derby County
1884

*'It is desired to render football worthy of the
patronage bestowed upon it by the public....'*
(Derby County FC May 1884)

On Wednesday 7th May 1884 a brief news item appeared in the *Derby Mercury*. Given no prominence it was buried deep in page five somewhat below the church news. Under the modest heading 'DERBYSHIRE COUNTY FOOTBALL' it began thus – 'We understand that the Derbyshire County Cricket Club has decided upon the formation of a football club under Association Rules in connection with county cricket.' This earliest written intimation of the new sporting arrival might justly be considered the official foundation date of the body which was soon christened Derby County Football Club.

Derby Mercury 7th May 1884 - the leaked announcement.

A day later Derbyshire County Cricket Club formally confirmed the birth. Via the 'Public Notices' column on the front page of the *Derby Daily Telegraph* the club announced that it had indeed created an association football arm. But the new entity was not yet kicking and screaming with the vigour it would eventually attain – for the moment of revelation was quiet and largely unheralded. Indeed many of Derby's 80,000 inhabitants were initially unaware that the delivery had occurred at all. Nor at that stage did it seem to matter much.

There were few hearty congratulations. On the contrary – as the club's first faltering steps were attempted, its very christening was tinged with petty controversy. A vociferous minority of vested interests in both the town and county actively resented the newcomer. After the initial notice had boldly named the offshoot 'Derbyshire County Football Club' – a seemingly innocent mirror of the cricketing parent – the founding fathers of this fledgling band were swiftly censured and compelled to settle for a less grand compromise.

Principal objector to the declared title was the Derbyshire Football Association. Founded in 1883, still finding its feet and seeking to assert its influence, the county governing body quite reasonably observed that the 'Derbyshire County' tag appeared to usurp its authority – it was presumptuous of any club, let alone a new and unproven one, to suggest that it represented the entire county strength. In any case the name was

7

potentially confusing, even downright misleading — for the DFA 'county representative elevens' were already routinely referred to in the press as 'Derbyshire County'.

The naming conundrum was quickly resolved six days after the foundation date. On Tuesday 13th May 1884 a joint sub-committee of officials from the Derbyshire FA and Derbyshire County Cricket Club met in Derby at the Bell Hotel on Sadler Gate. The primary business was to discuss terms for the DFA's use of the cricket club's County Ground in the coming 1884-85 season — but first the DFA delegation made clear its official disapproval of the Derbyshire County Football Club title. After brief but earnest discussion a compromise was reached — the cricket executive sportingly agreed to discard the 'shire' element. Thus the ancient Bell Hotel became the spiritual birthplace of 'Derby County Football Club' — and 13th May 1884 its formal christening date.

Derby Daily Telegraph 8th May 1884 - the first official announcement.

DERBYSHIRE COUNTY FOOTBALL CLUB.
THE Committee of the "Derbyshire County Cricket Club" beg to announce the FORMATION of a FOOTBALL CLUB, under Association Rules, in connection with County Cricket.
Matches of a High Order will be arranged for next season, and the most complete provision will be made for playing the game, and for the accommodation of the public.
Subscriptions 5s. per annum.
Applications for membership to be addressed to the Assistant Secretary, Mr. WM. PARKER, 4, Amen Alley, Derby.

This was Derby County's first small triumph. By stealthily agreeing to jettison the 'shire' but retaining the 'County', the cricket committee had rather duped the Derbyshire Football Association — only Notts County had hitherto secured that lofty suffix. Through 'sleight of word' the new football arm emerged as nominal representatives of both town and county in one neat package — the revised title arguably an even better one than Derbyshire County. Although the original name still appeared in isolated match reports when the season began — and was mischievously used by the club itself in some of its early advertising — it soon faded from use. Derby County it now was and would remain.

But the name that became famous in football history initially carried much less significance. Ahead of the first campaign, no heights of ecstasy or depths of abject suffering were yet shared by Derby County's first supporters. The exhortation 'Up the Rams' — latterly delivered with pride and conscious irony in equal measure — had yet to be coined. The fabled initials DCFC adorned not a single school desk — nor did they evoke stirring memories and deep emotions in the sage older ranks. Quite simply there were no memories. Derby County FC began with a blank sheet, an organisation without a football history to call its own — just one more addition to an already established crop.

From as early as the 1860s a healthy complement of football clubs had already sprouted both in and around the town — initially playing to a variety of rules but in time embracing the standardised 'Association code'. 'Derby Football Club' — generally known as Derby Town — was founded in 1869. Other town-based pioneers were Derby Derwent, Derby Trinity, St. John's and St. Andrew's — the latter said by the 1860s to be 'the first team in Derby to develop scientific play'.

The southern reaches were the true cradle of the game in Derbyshire — the gentler landscape offered more level ground on which to play. And in or close to Derby was a sufficiency of influential 'sporting gentlemen' willing to promote football, often as an adjunct to cricket. Under the benevolent patronage of three such leaders — Colonel Sir Henry Wilmot VC and brothers Walter and Henry Boden — a 'South Derbyshire Football Club' was already active by 1869 — an offshoot of the South Derbyshire Cricket Club which had been formed in 1835.

This team's influence soon extended. On 11th March 1871 the 'South Derbyshire Football Association' was formed in Derby over a post-match tea in the St. Andrew's schoolroom – the St. Andrew's side having just defeated South Derbyshire at Osmaston Park bolstered by the influential Clegg brothers from Sheffield, who encouraged the SDFA's birth under 'Sheffield Rules'. After 'the' FA (1863) and the Sheffield FA (1867) the SDFA was the third oldest Football Association in the world, placing Derbyshire at the very forefront of the game's development. In 1872 the SDFA widened its scope by truncating its name to the Derbyshire Football Association, but its influence later waned. Ultimately that first DFA was superseded by the 1883 organisation of the same name, still the governing body today.

Elsewhere in the vicinity the village of Sawley was already engaged in football combat by 1868 – and teams at Long Eaton, Ockbrook, Borrowash, Breaston and other South Derbyshire settlements all adopted the 'new football pastime' well before Derby County was thought of. The area's most prominent schools too were swift on the football uptake – Repton, Trent College at Long Eaton, Derby School, Ockbrook Moravian and Derby Whitworth all took up the 'round ball game' and graduated to association rules.

This was soon mirrored further north – as Victorian society increasingly enjoyed the novelty of 'leisure time' due to legislation bringing shorter working hours, clubs multiplied rapidly. By the early 1880s Derbyshire had countless practitioners of the burgeoning pastime by then coined 'association football'. Progressively modified and finally standardised through the 1860s and 1870s, the 'new game' was 21-years-old when Derby County first took the field – its 'association' and later 'soccer' tag tacitly supplied by the formation of the Football Association in London in 1863.

Ockbrook Moravian School 1875 – probably Derbyshire's earliest Association football image

Yet when Derby County took its opening bow in 1884 – football's laws and styles by then refined into a game eminently close to today's – no-one knew whether the newcomer would make its mark, or even if it would survive at all.

Most prominently barring the way were four established local teams which had both the potential and desire to hinder Derby County's progress right from the outset – the railway side Derby Midland (1881), church offshoots Junction Street (1870) and St. Luke's (1870), and the village side Darley Abbey (1880). Although disparate in character, these enthusiastic clubs shared a common bond – each had an established track-record and its own tight-knit group of adherents. And their supporters and management alike were united in one staunch belief – that the town of Derby already possessed quite its due quota of leading clubs.

With that in mind a committed phalanx of Derby sportsmen believed the 'upstart' newcomer might justifiably be killed off in its infancy. Yet within only weeks of its entry into the town's crowded sporting calendar, the fortunes of Derby County Football Club were being earnestly followed by at least a sector of the population – as the *Derby Daily Telegraph* archaically put it 'the bantling thrived'. Propelled by a love of football and an innate curiosity, spectators lined the ropes at the 'County Ground' in increasing numbers – by head of population the early gates of 1,500 to 3,000 the equivalent of five to ten now. Rituals firmly entrenched today were soon initiated. A few games into the club's opening season their performances were already hotly debated, players closely assessed, ideas and solutions proposed – and the first letter declaring 'if only the forward men would shoot more' appeared in the *Derby Daily Telegraph*. Evidently football mattered a great deal. And the new club had an allure which was hard to resist. Perhaps the name was the master stroke – town and county proudly united under one umbrella – for even before the first season was over the dashing outfit called Derby County seemed to matter most of all.

So the 'famous football club' had come into being. But where did it truly emerge from? What core factors led to its formation? Before progressing to the action a retrospective on the club's deeper roots is worth pursuing. For in truth the club would never have been formed at all but for a set of mounting key events and specific circumstances which provided exactly the right conditions for its successful conception. In that sense Derby County's birth was at one and the same time both 'inevitable' and 'providential' – 'written in the runes' yet almost a 'happy accident'.

The club's deepest ancestral roots lay in more primitive rites. Derby was renowned for a different brand of football more than a century before the association game arrived. 'Since time immemorial' the 'Derby Football' had been played through the streets and open country each Shrovetide. Only in 1846 was that 'big-side' mob game finally quelled – as fields had been enclosed or developed, and the town became much more populous and densely built, the boisterous inter-parish contest became an anachronism, considered both impractical and too injurious to life, limb, and property to be allowed to continue. But the celebrated 'Derby game' left an unquenchable legacy – by the time 'association' came into being Derby was already a 'football town' in the most primeval sense. With football 'in the blood' the acceptance of the 'new game' was a mere formality.

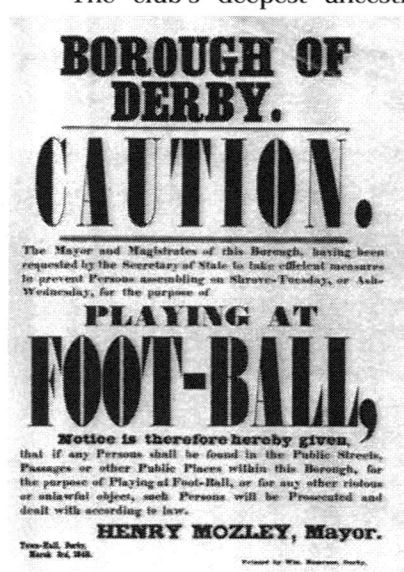

Derby Shrovetide game finally banned

Next in the timeline of key pre-requisites was the creation of the mother body – in the Grand Jury Room of Derby Guildhall on 4 November 1870 the Derbyshire County Cricket Club was formed. In its first summer it pitched its wicket in the centre of the long-established Derby Racecourse, gaining as its nominal landlord the Derby Recreation Company which leased the racecourse from Derby Corporation. 'The Racecourse' was thereafter additionally dubbed the 'County Ground' – Derby County's first home ready and waiting.

Derbyshire County Cricket Club's new pavilion 1884 - Derby County FC was formed to help pay for it.

The seniority of racing over its cricketing tenant provided a further crucial but quite incidental impetus to Derby County's formation. In 1883 the Recreation Company decided to widen the racecourse by 20 yards in front of the main Grandstand – then used for both racing and cricket viewing, but already a 'long gaze' from the cricket arena. This forced Derbyshire to shift their pitch further still from the Grandstand, rendering it no longer practicable for watching cricket. Thus forcibly displaced, the cricket committee decided in autumn 1883 to build a brand new pavilion. Sited on the opposite boundary to the Grandstand it would house both the dressing rooms and the premier spectator area, including a separate wing for ladies. The solution was perfectly sound but for one difficulty – a complete absence of ready funds. Derbyshire had ended the 1883 season several hundred pounds in debt, yet the pavilion would eventually cost £800. Allowing for fringe expenses and existing debt the ailing cricket club needed to raise around £1,200.

Individuals gave generous donations, lavish fund-raising events were planned, and the project set in motion – but by the end of March 1884 the fund remained £500 short. At this troubling juncture a timely catalyst to Derby County's formation was about to occur. On Saturday 5th April 1884 the County Ground staged the first Derbyshire FA Challenge Cup Final – the East Derbyshire side Staveley against Derby Midland. Fifteen hundred Staveley fans came by train to see the 'Easterns' triumph 2-1 – and the large crowd of some 6,000 generated healthy gate receipts of £160 10s 6d. At a time when Derbyshire's cricket crowds were often pitiful, quite often with form to match, the way forward was almost transparent. Football of the right calibre spelt cash.

Some three weeks after the DFA Cup Final – on 24th to 26th April 1884 – Derbyshire staged their long-planned three-day Grand Bazaar at Derby Drill Hall, the stallholders wearing rosettes in 'the cricket club's new colours of chocolate, Cambridge blue and pale yellow.' Barely two weeks further on these would also be the adopted colours of a new football club.

All the leading personnel connected to Derbyshire County Cricket Club attended the Grand Bazaar. The well patronised event surely provided a forum at which the idea of a football arm was first freely discussed. With the pavilion almost finished but still not fully funded the time was ripe for William Thomas Morley to make a proposal. A clerk at the Midland Railway, he forcefully advocated to his father William Morley senior – also a Midland Railway clerk and a Derbyshire CCC committee member – that the cricket club should form a football section. Morley senior sold the idea to his fellow committee members and by doing so became the 'Founding Father' of a fabled institution. The deal was done – Derby County Football Club had been brought into being to help pay for a new cricket pavilion.

The auspicious birth was 'leaked' by the weekly *Derby Mercury* on 7th May 1884 – which is where we came in. Over the coming weeks and months the club carried out a strong advertising campaign in the local press. And as the summer progressed the new organization was introduced in newspapers throughout the country – soon the whole of football was 'quietly aware' of Derby County.

From offices at 4 Amen Alley the 'secretary' William Parker offered 'membership subscriptions fixed at five shillings' – 'which we think will be thought sufficiently moderate'. Parker in fact worked under Sam Richardson, who in a matter of weeks assumed control – although Parker did become secretary some years later after Richardson had quit in disgrace. Prospective season ticket holders were further promised that 'the club will also play under Rugby rules concurrent with Association' – but the oval ball section was soon to fade. In the voice of the age – 'the Derby public place the 'globe' well above the 'egg' in their football predilections.'

The club's advertisements also stated its aims and rationale – this in a tone which thoroughly set the scene for some bitter ensuing rivalries. Consider the opening parry: 'It is desired to form a football club worthy of the patronage bestowed upon it by the public. The committee will endeavour to arrange matches with first-class clubs, thereby enabling the public to witness matches of a higher order than have hitherto been played in Derby.'

The 'higher order' line provoked great indignation among the established Derby clubs even before a ball was kicked. Derby County were 'upstarts', their tone 'pompous' and 'inflammatory', they needed 'taking down a peg'. The birth had been centuries in the making, but the 'chocolate and blue' had finally arrived on the Derby football scene – let play begin and battle commence.

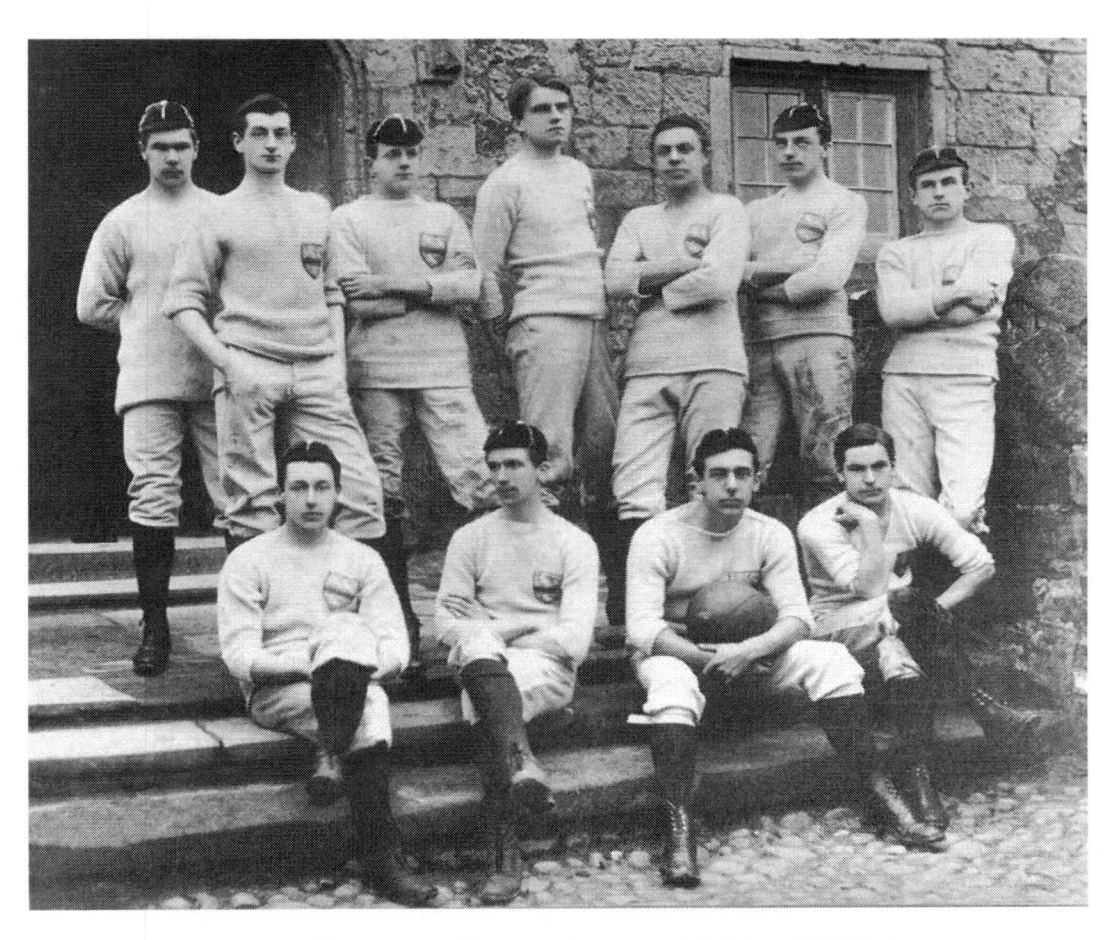

Repton School 1880-81 – Back l. to r: J. L. Mills, C. J. Bristowe, B. W. Spilsbury, H. G. Topham, J. R. B. Serjeant, H. H. Dobinson, E. M. Forbes. Front: M. A. Tweedie, A. Hanmer, T. Redmayne (capt.), H. R. Cobbold.

Established rival – Derby St. Lukes 1883-84 – Back l to r: M. Roberts (assistant secretary), F. Harvey, the Rev. F. J. Lyall (president), W. E. Parsons, the Rev. E. B. Lavies (vice-president), W. Harvey, G. Oakes (umpire). Centre: W. Twigge, A. Hall (capt.), W. Shipley. Front: G. Roberts, J. Renshaw, G. Evans, J. Walker, F. Hadfield.

Rivals in waiting – Derby Midland 1883-84 – Back l to r: A. Latham, A. H. Metcalf (sec.), H. Evans, H. R. Wignall, T. H. Haynes (sec.). Middle: J. Salt, G. F. Cooper, A. Chaplin (capt.), L. G. Wright, G. W. Wignall. Front: G. Bakewell, W. H. Owen, G. H. Strutt, C. A. Ward.

CHAPTER TWO

1884-85
A Turbulent Beginning

'One more river to cross, one more mountain to climb....'
(The players' song)

Once Derby County had been formed, and its mission statement to provide football of 'a higher order' so confidently presented, the real practicalities of the task ahead quickly struck home to the club committee. They needed to deliver. Yet all they had at the beginning of summer 1884 was a name, an enclosure on which to play, and a smart new pavilion – there were no fixtures and no players.

Finding willing opponents proved the easier of the two challenges – invitations were extended, word put about, and press releases issued. At a time when organised football was making rapid strides, new clubs being formed, and established ones seeking to prove their superiority, a healthy number of positive replies were quickly received. By mid-summer the *Derby Daily Telegraph* gave an encouraging progress report – 'we understand that a good programme of matches has already been arranged by the new club Derby County and that arrangements are well in hand.' It was otherwise observed that 'some are sides of considerable repute certain to provide the newcomers with the sternest test of their expectations.'

In arranging its first programme Derby County possessed one valuable 'intangible asset' that carried considerable weight – as an offshoot of Derbyshire County Cricket Club it inherited the ready-made history of that well-respected organ, so although a new outfit in name the club enjoyed a reflected pedigree dating back to 1870. In the passing years Derbyshire County Cricket Club and its County Ground arena had become known throughout the sporting world – an invitation from its infant football incarnation was not one to be lightly declined.

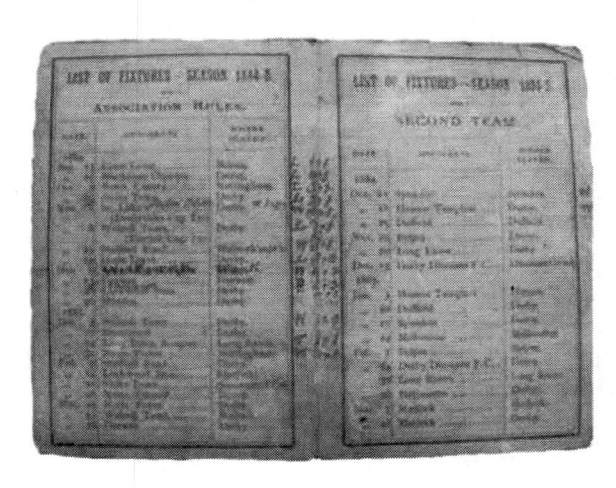

1884-85 fixture card - note the first ever win, against Repton School, pencilled in.

That a trip to Derby was considered eminently worthwhile is evidenced by the balance of home and away fixtures in the opening campaign – Derby County played 15 matches on 'alien turf' and 20 at home. This suited the committee perfectly, for away travel incurred expenditure they could ill afford. With everything thus satisfactory on the fixture front, all that remained was the fundamental matter of recruiting players, by no means an easy task.

This was laden with highly-charged conflicts of interest. By definition their targets would already be experienced players with established links to other clubs, mostly in or close to Derby – that immediately cast Derby County in the villainous role of aggressive poacher. This in turn would create instant enemies of the clubs they sought to raid. And so it proved – acrimonious fall-outs with local rivals, and ultimately the ruling Derbyshire FA, proved the prevailing theme of a stormy first season.

No players at that time were contractually engaged to a chosen club – all were nominally 'amateurs' (literally 'lovers' of the game) free to play wherever they wished. Many retained an inbuilt loyalty to a certain club, but others were motivated purely by whim or personal ambition. Some chopped and changed between several sides throughout the season, or played for multiple clubs simply to bag as many games as possible. Out of this football free-for-all, the first to pledge allegiance to Derby County was young Derby solicitor Haydn Morley – as the son of club founder William Morley and brother of its chief advocate 'W.T.' it was natural he should join the ranks. An ebullient personality, full of energy and persuasive banter, the 'Pocket Hercules' adopted the unofficial role of chief recruitment officer, promoting the ambitious new club's cause at every turn. Word rapidly spread and a network of potential players grew.

The earliest DCFC photo - the first two signings Haydn Morley (left) and George Bakewell.

During that important summer of 1884 much lobbying was undoubtedly done on Derbyshire's sundry cricket fields – Haydn Morley was a keen cricketer and many of Derby County's new recruits shared his interest. Second to join the club was speedy right-winger George Bakewell, who had already made a mark with Derby Midland. Soon to follow was the 'Mids' left-winger Charlie Ward.

Such flagrant defections deepened the already-drawn battle lines between Midland and Derby County even before a ball was kicked – in truth the two clubs had been severely at odds since the day Derby County formed, but the perceived poaching of Bakewell and Ward sharpened the rivalry beyond easy repair.

In fact sections of the Midland hierarchy were fundamentally opposed to Derby County on the purely 'political' grounds that Derby's chairman William Morley and his son 'W. T.' were long-standing employees of the Midland Railway Company – that their joint efforts should have fathered Derby County was considered by Midland devotees an almost treasonable act. The rift remained for the entire season – the clubs refused to play each other.

A Midland committeeman articulated their wider disquiet with some credibility: 'There is no wonder that many who have worked hard for many years in the interests of local football should feel sore that a new club, claiming to represent the county, has stepped in and tried to reap all the advantages by players ready-trained for them at the expense of other clubs.'

Yet in truth the Midland stance was starkly hypocritical – after they formed in 1881 one of their first acts was to engage several leading players from the established oldsters Derby Town, effectively sounding that club's death knell. Officially 'Derby Football Club' – the nearest to a forerunner of Derby County – it folded soon thereafter. And indeed most of the 'Mids' ranks had come from foreign fields. Yet this same organisation now vilified Derby County. To coin a modern riposte... what comes around goes around.

Derby County continued to hunt down local talent – several leading players were lured away from the South Derbyshire hotbeds of Sawley and Long Eaton. Others were engaged from Derby's local rivals Junction Street and St. Luke's. Hickinbottom and Cooper were prised from Darley Abbey for a 'try out' – their apparent disloyalty earning them the tags 'the Darley lightweights' and 'those two young renegades'. And amidst all these movements were accusations of dark skulduggery.

Despite vehement denials from Derby chairman William Morley, it was said to be 'common knowledge' that financial inducements had been offered by Derby County to prospective targets. Make no mistake, although 'professionalism' – playing for money – would not be legalised by the Football Association until 1885, cash or perks were a familiar part of the game when Derby County began.

When not provoking outright indignation, Derby's robust recruitment policy was always good for a mirthful anecdote. The *Derby Daily Telegraph* related: 'We hear that John Lowles who is in charge of Darley Abbey has a warning system in place to safeguard his talent. Whenever he gets wind that Derby County representatives are about to visit, he takes his players on long walks in the countryside to get them out of their clutches – nevertheless, several of the Abbots have already changed their shirt.' Later his son Harry Lowles would join the exodus. Already a familiar adage was beginning to assert itself – 'If you can't beat 'em, join 'em.'

The club also offered an open door policy to aspiring players. On 23rd August 1884 newspaper adverts began announcing that 'the ground is now open for practice daily from 5pm to 7pm, and on Tuesdays and Fridays at 6.30 for special match practice.' The new outfit meant business.

By the time of the first game in September 1884 a large pool of willing bodies had been garnered. The healthy numbers were crucial – nearly all the players had full-time jobs or were still at school or university, so allocating or indeed 'negotiating' time to play football was seldom straightforward. Along with the additional certainty of disruptive injuries, these 'other commitments' made the chances of fielding a settled side remote. With that in mind, some 30 or so core players formed the basis of the three teams run by the new club – flagship side Derby County, the well-organised reserves Derby County Wanderers, and a more loosely-structured third string as a nursery side cum general back-up, later dubbed Derby County Rovers.

Match report for the first home game.

Alas this did not guarantee that most coveted asset in football 'strength in depth' – among the lower-ranked players were some whose enthusiasm far outstripped their ability. And too often circumstances required these 'reserve men' to be promoted to the first rank. A season of mixed results was almost inevitable – and so it turned out.

The club's first ever game on 13th September 1884 proved a chastening experience. Encountering 'a higher order of football' Derby County were felled 6-0 by Great Lever at their Woodside ground near Bolton. The Lancastrians' fetching 'pink and white' attire belied a tough resolve. A team of hardened paid 'professionals' in all but name, the 'Leverites' were highly-organised and far too strong – their debutant John Goodall scored four, later to prove an irony, for the England international would eventually captain Derby County.

Despite the heavy defeat the new outfit emerged with some credit – the *Bolton Football Field* gave a measured summing up which in the course of time proved prophetic: 'The Derbyshire men are apparently athletes all, well-formed, active and smart. They certainly deserved letting down more gently. There is that about them which will ensure the new club being known to fame in the football world. All they want is practice together, for it must be remembered this was their first appearance in their present organisation, the match resolving itself more into a trial contest than a passage of arms.'

Certainly the 'first eleven' was not the strongest of Derby's debut season – but historical significance alone merits its posterity. This is the line up including principal former clubs.

Goalkeeper
L. F. Gillett
(Charterhouse School, Old Carthusians, Notts County)

Right full-back   *Left full-back*
R. L. Evans   F. Harvey
(Derby Whitworth)   *(Derby St. Luke's)*

Right half-back   *Centre half-back*   *Left half-back*
A. Williamson   H. A. Morley (captain)   W. H. Warmby
(Sawley Rangers)   *(Repton School, Derby Town)*   *(Derby St. Luke's)*

Outside right	*Inside-right*	*Centre-forward*	*Inside-left*	*Outside-left*
G. Bakewell	W. Shipley	B. W. Spilsbury	A. Smith	C. A. Ward
(Derby School, Derby Town, Derby Midland)	*(Derby St. Luke's)*	*(Repton School, Cambridge University)*	*(Sawley Rangers, Long Eaton Rangers)*	*(Derby Town, Derby Midland)*

Although the positional layout may seem unfamiliar to the modern eye, in practice a team's shape during the progress of a game was extremely fluid. Men dropped back or pushed forward as necessary – as such the pattern of play which emerged from this 'quaint' line-up was little removed from the variety of supposedly different 'systems' the game has since witnessed.

A more striking feature of this first team – and one prevailing throughout the pre-League era – is its curiously eclectic social mix, quite different from that soon to reign in football's long-term future. In the 1860s and into the 1870s organised football had been to a large extent the preserve of educated 'gents' who had embraced the game during its evolving period at the public schools and universities. But as the 1870s progressed an increasing number of 'ordinary working men' – and particularly their young sons who would ultimately form the game's first professional ranks – had also begun to join or form clubs. Churches and schools especially championed the 'healthful pastime' amid growing urban populations. So although the number of amateur gents would soon wane when professionalism took hold, by the early 1880s the game found itself in a transitional stage, a curious social limbo in which an amalgam of all the strata from 'toffs' to 'workers' played both together and in their own defined circles.

In the industrial north especially, teams were beginning to emerge made up largely of men from factory backgrounds – but even so these players were more generally of the skilled artisan type rather than the lowlier *hoi polloi*. The Derby County team reflected that – there were no 'general labourers' in their earliest sides. Even foundry workers and miners would not begin to dominate until a decade had passed. In the meantime Derby County adopted a pragmatic mixed approach reflecting both the context of the age and their declared intention of representing the town of Derby and county of Derbyshire in the broadest sense.

There was also another facet to the side's early composition – namely that Derby County considered itself above all a 'respectable' club with a responsible ethos. It sought to attract not only men to its spectator ranks, but juniors and ladies too – indeed not until 1890-91 were ladies required to pay for entry. It also courted backing from the influential business community – the very same profile which Derby County pursues today. That meant setting standards for its personnel. Barring the odd lapse the players' conduct met and often exceeded the expected level. To borrow a modern phrase – they were 'a decent set of lads'.

The spine of the first line-up – goalkeeper, centre-half, centre-forward – all honed their football talent at public school. Now in turn a civil engineer, solicitor, and Cambridge undergraduate. Soon the Old Etonian J. B. T. Chevallier – teaching mathematics at nearby Repton School – would also wear the Derby colours, as would others whose university background then marked them out as 'men of calibre' still wishing to pursue the game. Standing alongside them were a clutch of 'white collar' and professional men – Reg Evans a surveyor, Shipley in accounts, Harvey, Ward and Bakewell clerks at the Midland Railway. Completing the side were brass buffer Harry Warmby and 'sons of the soil' Smith and Williamson, both natives of rural Sawley now engaged as lace mill operatives in Long Eaton.

That disparate mix might have presaged a 'tricky dressing room'. But despite the stark differences in background between the likes of country lad 'Jammer' Smith and landed gent 'J. B. T.', all indications are that a healthy democratic air pervaded both on and off the field. This had much to do with individual character but also reflected the nature of football itself. By contrast cricket tended to the almost ritualistic practice of social apartheid between 'gentlemen' and 'players' – although by no means endemic, and often over-egged in the later telling, examples of such 'class separatism' did exist in the summer game. Its ordered structure, slower pace, remote field placing and scant physical contact created a stage for individuality, enabling those who favoured aloofness to enact it but still survive – but not so the winter game. Football was fast-paced, tightly-knit, and awash with contact – a genuine team activity requiring every man to pull together for the collective benefit of the side. Ever the great equaliser, the rough and tumble of ninety minutes 'chasing the leather' allowed little time for social division.

After two weeks in which to reflect on their Great Lever baptism, that solidarity began to emerge in the second game. Derby's first home match on 27th September 1884 ended in a narrow 4-3 defeat by the 1883 English Cup winners Blackburn Olympic, and that after Derby had hit the bar on the stroke of time. The illustrious Spilsbury scored Derby's first ever goal after four minutes and later 'shot through' his second – the game would not see nets until 1891. The more workaday Charlie Ward scored the other. This big improvement greatly impressed and indeed rather surprised the County Ground assembly. And the visitors and press alike praised the performance as 'showing much promise'. It was an important day – in their first appearance 'before the Derby public' the side had passed muster. A first hurdle of sorts had been successfully negotiated.

Certainly the Derby committee seemed confident of the way ahead – sufficiently emboldened only two games into their history to actually decline prestigious fixtures. The *Derby Mercury* reported: 'The result of Derby County's excellent play against Blackburn Olympic was that challenges were quickly received from two of the other leading clubs in Lancashire – Blackburn Rovers (Holders of the English Cup) and Halliwell – but in view of the numerous engagements which have already been entered into, it was thought advisable to decline the invitations, though they were of a very cordial character.'

Thereafter the team was further juggled through both necessity and choice, and greater attention was paid to formulating 'an effective strategy.' At last in the fifth game a first victory was secured – a 3-2 triumph at Repton School in which Chevallier bagged a brace, the match passing off with little fanfare on a Tuesday afternoon towards the close of October.

Four days later Derby St. Luke's were beaten 3-1 in a first-round Derbyshire Cup match, a large crowd of 3,000 witnessing the first home win – this has routinely been designated the club's first ever win in prior publications, the date of the Repton game having been then untraced. Despite victory in this first ever 'local Derby' it was no real grudge match – the 'Churchmen' took their origins seriously, always maintaining benevolent relations with the newcomers, the only one of Derby's big local rivals so inclined.

But there were disconcerting set-backs too, the first real crisis a 7-0 home defeat by Walsall Town in the opening round of the FA Cup. Two notable absentees on that black day were Ben Spilsbury and recently-designated club captain J. B. T. Chevallier. Each had elected to play in the Cup for their alternative clubs Cambridge University and Old Etonians, a decision rendered more pertinent since both scored in their respective victories. In contrast Derby County's crushing reverse in football's pre-eminent competition prompted the first rash of supporter letters to the Derby newspapers. Soon all the 'Monday moan-in' themes routinely delivered today had been loudly aired – 'an absolute disgrace, shoot more, better combination, feed the wings, give the reserves a chance, try more youngsters, decline to attend'.... – 'twas ever thus.

A more perceptive but acerbic analysis was given by 'Argus' of the *Long Eaton Advertiser*: 'The new organisation would probably fare better with a team playing regularly together, and on whose support they could always rely, instead of trusting so much to the periodical assistance of two or three 'cracks' by whom they are liable to be thrown over at the last moment.'

On 29th November 1884 only three weeks after the Walsall debacle Derby suffered another 7-0 home defeat which caused a different kind of stir. The assassins this time were arch rivals Junction Street, keen to assert the ambitious authority which would soon see them change their name to the grander-sounding Derby Junction. The defeat provoked a bout of politics which sorely irritated Junction and severely strained Derby County's already delicate relations with the Derbyshire FA.

The particular grouse of the Derby committee was that they had released no fewer than six of their best players to represent the Derbyshire Association XI playing Hallamshire Association on the same day as the Junction game. With the Derby men to the fore Hallamshire had been defeated 5-0. Yet in contrast Junction had refused to release any players at all, as had Midland, St. Luke's, Darley Abbey, Staveley and Chesterfield. Evidently in putting 'county before club' Derby County had come off very badly. As a consequence they asked the DFA to officially expunge the Junction result on the grounds 'we were not at full strength'. The club fondly hoped the ruling body would recognise its selfless support of the Derbyshire XI and redress the iniquity. It was a forlorn and in truth a rather naïve hope – the request was airily dismissed.

In consequence the Derby committee became much less co-operative in releasing men to play for Derbyshire. And the players too hardened their line. Secretary Richardson also omitted the Junction fixture from the list later handed to the press as the season record, effectively creating a 'phantom match' obliterated from the club's history. This and other incidents presented Derby County in a bad light, although not always fairly, for their local rivals were frequently over-sensitive, and missed no opportunity to stir up trouble for the 'upstarts'. The mounting situation gave the Derbyshire FA a dilemma. If they chose to routinely back Derby County they would alienate most of their other member clubs – so by default the DFA were pressured to take the easier option. They adopted a stern line against Derby County at every turn.

The heat thus raised, ongoing 'episodes' were not infrequent, all thoroughly dissected by the Derby newspapers. One singular complication was that the Derby County president William Monk Jervis was also president of the Derbyshire Football Association – although his vote alone carried no absolute power, this foot in both camps placed him in an invidious position. And perversely, for fear of being labelled biased, he often erred against rather than for Derby County. It seemed inevitable that something would have to give.

Derby County's first president William Monk Jervis - resigned from the Derbyshire FA amidst great controversy.

Matters on the pitch had gradually improved as a more settled side began to emerge – by the end of January 1885 Derby had lost 9 but won or drawn 13. That was encouraging, but alas January also saw the politics reach a sorry head.

Central to the animosity was a dispute between Derby County and Long Eaton Rangers concerning the agreed date for their third round Derbyshire Cup game. Rangers turned up on 'their' date to find no Derby County waiting for them. County contended this was the 'wrong' date, and produced a letter sent by Long Eaton which appeared to prove it. Yet amidst much talk of 'crossed lines' the Derbyshire FA settled firmly in Rangers' favour, disqualifying Derby County from the Derbyshire Cup in their debut season.

This humiliating decision so incensed the Derby committee that they made a pointed stand. Secretary Sam Richardson withdrew the Derby players selected to play for Derbyshire in a forthcoming fixture against Staffordshire. This with the full backing of the men concerned, among them the redoubtable Derbyshire cricketer Frank Sugg whose statement to the *Derby Daily Telegraph* pulled no punches: 'H. A. Morley, G. Bakewell and myself have decided for the future to play for our own team in preference to the Association, as we consider the Association, as at present constituted, is a complete farce.'

Sugg augmented his verbal volley with a more overt insult to the DFA. He subsequently took the field at the County Ground with his DFA representative badge removed from his shirt, cut into two, and sown onto his shorts, half on each buttock – an action hardly calculated to improve relations with the ruling body. The *Derby Daily Telegraph* conceded that Sugg's impulsive stunt had 'caused great mirth' among sectors of the County Ground gathering, but otherwise condemned the act: 'His behaviour is completely unpardonable. As Hamlet would say – 'though it make the unskilful laugh, it cannot but make the judicious grieve."

One of the judicious was Derby County president William Monk Jervis. On 30th January 1885 he resigned his presidency of the Derbyshire FA. At the same time Derby County severed its allegiance to the DFA, stating that 'from now on the club will ally itself to the national body, the Football Association in London.' Although in the course of time the rift healed, this action signalled the firm resolve of Derby County to become a club of national significance, increasingly less tolerant of the petty politics of 'local' football. For a club not yet a year old this was an audacious stand, but it won Derby valuable new admirers and key contacts among the higher echelons shaping the game.

Thereafter honours of national import seemed increasingly to graduate towards Derby County at the specific behest of FA officials. Spilsbury was selected for England – marking his debut on 28 February 1885 with a goal against Ireland. On the same day the County Ground had been chosen to stage the 6th round FA Cup replay between Notts County and Queen's Park. Derby secretary Sam Richardson made 'a magnificent job of the occasion' – a wooden stand was erected to span part of the 'rifle range end', an estimated 13,000 seeing Queen's Park progress.

So impressed were the FA by the 'big match' arrangements that they quickly appointed Derby County to stage the Queen's Park v Nottingham Forest semi-final. Yet again Richardson pulled it off, extending the wooden stand along the entire rifle range end to house 3,000 of the 9,000 gathering. This structure was subsequently retained, placing the County Ground among the elite of football arenas in the entire land. As a consequence it was to host a series of important neutral fixtures over the coming seasons, including the 1886 Cup Final replay when a crowd of 15,000 created 'a most imposing sight'.

Another significant compliment paid to the club in 1884-85 was delivered by Nicholas 'Pa' Jackson, the august founder of the celebrated amateur side Corinthians, who selected their opponents stringently. Having been held to a 3-3 draw at Derby in April 1885, Jackson pronounced his club 'most impressed', and invited Derby County to play Corinthians at Kennington Oval the following campaign. This was no mean honour, for Corinthians had use of the arena on only four dates a season – a telling measure of the great strides made by Derby County in such a short time.

When the opening season ended, the new club was able to reflect on a number of particularly gratifying results. In January 1885 they achieved a shock 6-1 victory at Nottingham Forest, the first encounter between the clubs. Derby established a first-half lead kicking with a strong wind, which a Forest spokesman afterwards blamed for their defeat. He bluffly asserted that 'if we had won the toss and had the elements in our favour first, then the result would surely have been reversed.' This was quickly declared by the *Derby Daily Telegraph* 'completely ridiculous' – having initially enjoyed a relationship of mutual cordiality, the famous Derby-Forest rivalry was thus swiftly born.

In the course of the season several valued local scalps had been taken – Darley Abbey, St. Luke's and finally Junction Street all vanquished. And in the final game the much-respected Notts County, already boasting two decades of history, were beaten 2-0. As for individual feats, player of the year honours must surely be handed to Amos 'Jammer' Smith. Missing only two games he scored 17 goals in 33 appearances, cementing his place as the club's first cult hero.

The Notts County victory must have particularly pleased Nottingham-born William Morley, for he always maintained he had founded Derby County 'along similar lines to the Notts Club.' Certainly the committee expressed a quiet satisfaction with the first season's work. On 7th May 1885 – the precise anniversary of the club's foundation – its first annual dinner was held at the Royal Hotel in Derby, where rousing speeches tinged with sensible caution were proudly delivered.

The quest to 'bring a better class of football to the town' had been 'achieved without question'. Finances had moved in the right direction and were 'now helping the cricket club'. Derby County had 'gained a distinct following', and while only a small proportion of the public actively attended football (then as now in truth) the perceived benefit to the wider community was solidly asserted in a speech by Alderman Hobson: 'Derby County is a public benefactor. The club gives a great deal of healthy and pleasant enjoyment to large numbers of their fellow townsmen and brings into the town many people from the surrounding neighbourhood, causing a large amount of money to be spent in our midst' – the adoption of a familiar business model right from year one.

The club toast was 'to a long and successful future, hoping this proves to be our worst season and not our best.' During the evening the players gave their song 'One More River to Cross' admirably led by 'Jammer'. In truth there would be many hazardous crossings yet to come – and the 'mountains to climb' – before the 'promised land' was reached. But on balance the summations were apt.

The vitriolic squabbles with jealous local rivals had been unpleasant but arguably necessary for progress to be made. So too the unseemly wrangles and bitter split with the Derbyshire FA. But both were offset by the new 'friends in high places' that the club had gained. And the supporters it had attracted. From a cold and uncertain start Derby County had not only survived, but rapidly acquired a status in English football on which to build. The club had boldly marked its local territory. And a growing following was irresistibly seduced by the sheer theatre of it all. The Derby County show was on the road.

1884-85 Results and Scorers

Sep	13	(a)	Great Lever	L	0-6		1500
	27	(h)	Blackburn Olympic	L	3-4	Spilsbury 2, Ward	
Oct	2	(a)	Notts County	L	1-3	A. Smith	2000
	25	(h)	Stoke Town	L	0-2		1500
	28	(a)	Repton School	W	3-2	Chevallier 2, Ward	
Nov	1	(h)	St. Luke's (DC)	W	3-1	Bakewell, Spilsbury, A. Smith	3000
	8	(h)	Walsall Town (FAC)	L	0-7		1500
	15	(a)	Stafford Road	W	3-0	Sugg 3	1000
	22	(h)	Great Lever	L	0-3		3000
	29	(h)	Junction Street	L	0-7		1500
Dec	6	(a)	Wirksworth (DC)	W	4-2	Ward, C. Sherwin, A. Smith, Bakewell	300
	13	(a)	Darwen	D	3-3	E. Hickinbottom 3	1000
	15	(a)	Halliwell	L	1-4	L. Cooper	
	20	(h)	Lockwood Brothers	W	2-1	Buttery (o.g.), E. Hickinbottom	1000
	26	(h)	Hendon	W	3-1	Sugg, L. Cooper, A. Smith	2000
	27	(h)	Casuals	L	1-2	Bakewell	1500
	29	(h)	Halliwell	D	1-1	E. Hickinbottom	3000
Jan	3	(h)	Walsall Town	W	1-0	Spilsbury	1200
	7	(h)	Cambridge Univ.	D	4-4	Sugg, Cochrane, A. Smith 2	
	17	(h)	Darley Abbey	W	1-0	A. Smith	
	24	(a)	Long Eaton Rangers	D	1-1	A. Smith	2000
	31	(a)	Nottingham Forest	W	6-1	Chevallier 3, A. Smith, E. Hickinbottom, L. Cooper	600
Feb	2	(a)	Blackburn Rovers	L	3-4	Nash 2, A. Smith	
	7	(h)	Stafford Road	W	8-0	A. Smith 3, Springthorpe, Chevallier, Bakewell, Morley, Nash	3000
	12	(a)	Repton School	W	4-1	Scorers not known	
	14	(a)	Junction Street (DCC)	D	0-0		500
	21	(a)	Bolton Wanderers	L	1-4	E. Hickinbottom	1500
Mar	3	(h)	Junction Street (DCC)	D	1-1	Spilsbury	200
	16	(a)	Lockwood Brothers	W	5-0	A. Smith 2, Chatterton 2, E. Hickinbottom	
	21	(a)	Stoke Town	D	1-1	Chatterton	1000
	28	(h)	Junction Street (DCC)	W	4-0	A. Smith, L. Cooper, E, Hickinbottom, Chatterton	1500
Apr	6	(h)	Nottingham Forest	D	1-1	Cubley	
	7	(h)	Corinthians	D	3-3	A. Smith, Sugg, Chatterton	1000
	11	(h)	Spital (DCC)	L	1-2	Chatterton	

FAC = Football Association Cup – The 'English Cup'

DC = Derbyshire Cup

DCC = Derbyshire Charity Cup

24

1884-85 Appearances and Goals

	Apps	Goals		Apps	Goals
Smith A	33	17	Briggs J	2	
Sugg FH	30	6	Farquharson EB	2	
Bakewell G	29	4	Flowers J	2	
Morley HA	29	1	Luntley W	2	
Hickinbottom E	26	9	Maycroft D	2	
Williamson A	23		Moore HB	2	
Cooper L	21	5	Sherwin C	2	1
Weston WA	15		Sherwin P	2	
Chevallier JBT	13	7	Shipley W	2	
Hill C	12		Springthorpe G	2	1
Ward CA	10	3	AN Other	1	
Exham PG	9		Bellamy W	1	
Chatterton W	8	6	Burgess	1	
Kelsall WL	8		Cubley FE	1	1
Nash RW	8	3	Douglas FSK	1	
Spilsbury BW	8	5	Evans H	1	
Evans RL	7		Frost J	1	
Gorham C	7		Harrison J	1	
Harvey F	7		Hodges A	1	
Gillett LF	6		Matthews J	1	
Latham A	6		Nicholls H	1	
Weston W	6		Parsons WE	1	
Hunt W	5		Peel EH	1	
Cochrane AHJ	4	1	Shepherd W	1	
Davies WT	4		Birch-Thorpe CE	1	
Parry FH	4		Wansbrough HS	1	
Warmby WH	4		Wood JB	1	
Bromage E	3				
Walker J	3				

1884-85 Season Summary

Played: 35 Won: 14 Drawn: 9 Lost: 12 Goals For: 75 Goals Against: 72
Players used: 56   Average home attendance: 1,600

CHAPTER THREE

1885-86
Consolidation and a Major Scalp

*'Hats and umbrellas went into the air, and hundreds dashed
onto the pitch to acclaim their heroes....'*
(Aston Villa knocked out of the FA Cup)

The primary aim of the inaugural season had been survival. That was achieved despite vehement opposition to Derby County's very existence. Now the committee sought to build on the club's solid foundations, assuring the growing supporter base that 'we shall endeavour to do better this time around.'

Central to their plans was the intention of putting out a more settled side. In 1884-85 a total of 56 players had worn the first team shirt, 27 of those appearing in two games or less. This frequent resort to fringe men had regularly introduced weak links to an otherwise solid base. And the newspaper reports had seldom shrunk from unmasking the perceived duffers: 'Nash was useless, but Harrison was worse than useless' – a gem of analysis from the *Derby Daily Telegraph*.

Certainly Derby needed their better players to appear more frequently. This cause was fortuitously aided by a lasting innovation for 1885-86 which encouraged the higher quality footballers to greater loyalty – in July 1885 the Football Association had formally legalised 'professionalism' in England. That enabled Derby County to legitimately reward players financially if they chose to do so. The same privilege also extended to their local rivals, but Derby's increasing crowd potential and general 'set-up' gave them an edge in offering the best incentives. That isn't to say the club yet had players who were full-time 'footballers' by profession – all for now retained their day jobs, and the majority chose to remain amateur in name at least. But the facility for pay existed – men began to see football as a second earner and possibly even a 'proper job' rather than a mere hobby. Players increasingly graduated towards the clubs whose rewards were the most attractive.

That spelled the beginning of the end for Derby's foremost local rivals – in time Darley Abbey, St. Luke's, Derby Midland and Derby Junction all failed to generate sufficient income to compete effectively on the professional stage. Each in turn was destined to fold while Derby County emerged as the dominant force and the town's sole professional club.

The appearance statistics for 1885-86 yield a telling story – this time only 29 players were used. The benefits showed marginally in the final results summary – more games won, more goals scored, and less conceded – but more importantly made the club a better-consolidated unit, improved in its organisation, and more tightly-knit. That spelt progress.

The political front too was more becalmed, although relations remained strained. Derby County and the Derbyshire FA were no longer 'daggers drawn' but kept their distance, liaising only as business dictated. Derby Midland had declared an intention to 'bid for local supremacy', but failed to put this properly to the test – yet again they avoided meeting Derby County. Nor did Derby play Junction, and there was no game against St. Luke's, the church side seemingly already adjudged too 'small fry' for the ambitious County team. The rift with Long Eaton Rangers had not healed completely, but at least the teams met. Derby had the great satisfaction of winning the sole encounter 3-1 away, the former Rangers' favourite 'Jammer' Smith being 'subjected to a great deal of chaff' by the Long Eaton faithful. Yet again Smith had a fine season for Derby – 19 goals in 30 games.

The 'Juncs' and 'Mids' doubtless felt they were making a pointed stand by snubbing Derby County, but the attitude merely damaged their own ambitions, emphasising both clubs' insularity while giving the Derby County fixture list an increasingly national rather than local flavour. Already the 'new club' were meeting equally ambitious big town opponents more frequently – Aston Villa, Preston North End, Sheffield Wednesday, Wolverhampton Wanderers, Blackburn Rovers, Bolton Wanderers, Notts County, Nottingham Forest – all were contested in 1885-86. Each became an illustrious name in football history – in contrast Junction and Midland are 'ghosts from the past'.

As such the stand-off backfired, but at the time the Midland and Junction executive seemed truly to believe there was room for more than one 'big club' in Derby, a view shared in November 1885 by the *Derby Daily Telegraph*: 'During the last year or so Derby has made enormous strides in the direction of claiming to be an important football centre. Presently it is the only provincial town to have three clubs remaining in the English Cup – Derby County, Junction, and Midland. Taking everything into account we feel sure there will be sufficient room for two first-class clubs in the town.'

The call proved incorrect – had it been right Derby as a community would have developed an immeasurably different character, one of divided team loyalties. As it is Derby County now unites the community rather than splits it – this has proved one of the club's most characteristic assets, a sure benefit to the city and county not generally articulated – a hard-won legacy of the bitter local conflicts of those earliest seasons.

As in the first campaign, the animosity of their local rivals merely steered Derby County in other directions – they continued to develop a stronger relationship with the Football Association and the country's leading clubs. After the success of the big neutral games held at the County Ground in 1884-85, the FA awarded Derby the FA Cup semi-final between Blackburn Rovers and Swifts in March 1886. After Rovers progressed they then drew 0-0 with West Bromwich Albion in the Final at Kennington Oval. A swiftly-convened FA meeting decided the replay would be staged at Derby on 10th April 1886 – Blackburn won 2-0 in front of 15,000, then one of the largest assemblies ever seen at a football match. It was the first FA Cup Final away from London – quite a coup for provincial Derby.

Once more the arrangements were brought off impeccably by Derby County secretary Sam Richardson, and his contribution to Derby's continued rise in status cannot be stressed too highly. This was a supreme irony, for unbeknown to the committee Richardson was quietly embezzling gate money for his own ends, and would continue to do so until his crime was finally exposed in the nick of time in 1890. Since his position was honorary, Richardson received little more than a token remuneration for his services – doubtless he felt Derby County's continued rise, and the big gates he was helping to generate, owed him a legitimate 'commission'.

Although the Cup Final day was a significant occasion, it was topped for Derby County supporters by the club's first real 'game to remember', a landmark victory recalled for years to come. On 14th November 1885 the mighty Aston Villa were overturned 2-0 at the County Ground in the second round of the FA Cup, a result that staggered the football world. In fact Villa had been drawn to play at home, but agreed to switch the game to Derby's 'superior enclosure' for a monetary consideration, so confident were they in securing a winning outcome.

But they had reckoned without Haydn Morley and his cunning strategy. By then Derby's regular captain, Morley called the players together a few days before the game for a blackboard session in which detailed tactics were formulated. Central to the game-plan was that Derby's swarthy centre-half Jack Flowers would man-mark Villa's star skipper Archie Hunter, a Scottish import of great repute. The rather humbler Flowers stuck to his task so doggedly that Hunter was unable to influence the game, and afterwards irritably bemoaned 'the constant attentions of that grinning organ-grinder, who followed me around like a policeman.' The County Ground crowd relished the victory – when time was called in the gathering November gloom 'hats and umbrellas went into the air and hundreds dashed onto the pitch to acclaim their heroes.'

This was the result that really put Derby County on the map, for Villa were already considered a great force in the game, and an influential voice in its administration. Thereafter Derby had little trouble gaining the most prestigious fixtures – and when the Football League came to be formed in 1888 its 'Founding Father' William McGregor, a Villa committee man, would look favourably upon Derby County as a team of the right calibre. As the Villa umpire he had witnessed the famous Cup reverse at painfully close quarters. The League story comes later – but as the Derby players might have carolled, the Villa triumph was 'one more river crossed'.

Alas Derby were knocked out of the FA Cup in the next round – losing 4-2 at Small Heath Alliance (later Birmingham City) after having beaten the 'Heathens' 6-0 only a few weeks earlier. It was a harsh illustration of the topsy-turvy fortunes of football – Derby would strive almost desperately to win the FA Cup each season thereafter, three times being losing finalists, and experiencing some heartbreaking defeats in the semis, before finally lifting the trophy in 1946.

Perhaps the players lost focus after the euphoria of the Villa triumph, for the FA Cup setback at Small Heath came in a miserly run of four defeats in a row. This began with a 3-2 loss at Blackburn Rovers at the end of November – required to leave for Lancashire by the early-morning 'newspaper train', the preparation of some of the party left something to be desired. 'Argus' of the *Long Eaton Advertiser* – a regular traveller with the team, who knew the inside track – quizzically spilt the beans: 'There were a few problems for the Blackburn game. Haydn Morley had been up all night, and so had 'Jess' Cooper, the convivial old soul making merry after being presented on Friday with £100 in connection with a benefit. Jack Flowers was also suffering – he was as stiff as an old crutch. And George Evans wasn't too well either.'

Blessedly the heavy night was an untypical aberration. Perhaps the committee 'had words', for after the losing streak ended a much better run ensued – of the 22 games remaining only 5 were lost. Although among them were some terrible defeats – 7-3 at Notts County, 6-1 at Preston North End, and 7-0 at Bolton Wanderers –

suggesting that Derby County were already acquiring a reputation for travelling badly. In contrast they lost only twice at home all season.

When 1885-86 closed Derby again had no silverware to call their own. Three trophies might have been possible, but they had not contested the Derbyshire Cup on account of the ongoing differences with the Derbyshire FA. And in the Derbyshire Charity Cup – a small invitation event run by Derby County and sponsored by the town's Star Tea Company – they had succumbed in the final to Bolton Wanderers. Nevertheless the season was again pronounced by the committee a 'satisfactory one' – in terms of general consolidation and an enhanced reputation this could not be denied. Although the bigger reverses suggested there was still much work to be done.

George Evans - leading scorer with 24 goals.

On the field new names had emerged. Nominal player of the season was undoubtedly centre-forward George Evans. Previously with St. Luke's, his 24 goals in 34 games eclipsed even 'Jammer' – who next season would return to his old Long Eaton patch to wind down his career. So despite Derby County being only two years old, an era of sorts was already beginning to pass, and a body of fondly-recalled former players gradually building.

The club now had a history and a bank of memories – the initials DCFC already resonant of a recognisable shared experience among supporters. The fortunes of 'The Chocolates' – sometimes dubbed 'The Tricolours' or occasionally 'The Peakites' but not yet 'The Rams' – now really mattered. The Derby County show was no longer simply 'on the road' – it was moving ahead and gathering momentum.

The County Ground showing the Racecourse Grandstand with the cricket field in the foreground. The photographer stands with his back towards the side touchline of Derby County's original pitch, with the 1884 new pavilion behind him, later moved to left of picture and given a second front to enable the football pitch to be moved behind it.

29

1885-86 Results and Scorers

Sep	19	(a)	Stoke	L	2-3	Spilsbury, A. Smith	
	26	(h)	Notts County	L	0-3		
Oct	3	(h)	Stafford Road	W	5-1	L. Cooper 2, G. Evans 2, A. Smith	
	10	(a)	Aston Villa	L	2-4	Scorers not known	2000
	17	(h)	Sheffield	W	5-2	A. Smith 2, Nash, G. Evans, L. Cooper	
	24	(a)	Wolves	D	0-0		
	31	(h)	Birmingham St Georges (FAC)	W	3-0	A. Smith, Spilsbury, G. Evans	
Nov	7	(h)	Small Heath Alliance	W	6-0	A. Smith 3, G. Evans 2, Nash	1000
	14	(h)	Aston Villa (FAC)	W	2-0	A. Smith, G. Evans	3000
	21	(h)	Brentwood	W	3-0	G. Evans 2, A. Smith	
	23	(a)	Sheffield Wednesday	W	8-2	Scorers not known	
	26	(a)	Blackburn Rovers	L	2-3	G. Evans, A. Smith	1000
Dec	5	(a)	Nottingham Forest	L	1-2	A. Smith	
	12	(a)	Small Heath Alliance	L	2-4	G. Evans 2	3000
	19	(a)	Blackburn Olympic	L	0-3		1500
	26	(h)	Casuals	W	2-1	E. Hickinbottom, G. Evans	2500
	28	(h)	Blackburn Rovers	D	1-1	Morley	2500
Jan	1	(a)	Bolton Wanderers	D	1-1	Knox	2000
	9	(h)	Nottingham Forest	W	1-0	G. Evans	1000
	16	(a)	Sheffield	D	3-3	Bakewell, A. Smith, "scrimmage"	
	23	(h)	Sheffield Wednesday	W	7-0	Bakewell 2, G. Evans 2, Nash, A. Smith, 'scrimmage'	
	30	(a)	Notts County	L	3-7	G. Evans, L. Cooper, Own Goal	2000
Feb	6	(a)	Preston North End	L	1-6	A. Smith	4000
	17	(a)	Cambridge University	W	1-0	A. Smith	
	20	(h)	Stoke	W	4-1	A. Smith 2, Bakewell, L. Cooper	1200
	22	(a)	Aston Villa	L	1-2	A. Smith	3000
	27	(a)	Stafford Road	W	2-0	G. Evans, L. Cooper	
Mar	13	(a)	Bolton Wanderers	L	0-7		2500
	20	(h)	Aston Villa	D	3-3	L. Cooper, G. Evans, E. Hickinbottom	2500
	27	(h)	Blackburn Olympic	W	2-1	G. Evans, J. Flowers	1000
Apr	3	(a)	Long Eaton Rangers	W	3-1	E. Hickinbottom, L. Cooper, 'scrimmage'	
	16	(h)	Notts County (DCC)	W	4-1	Knox, L. Cooper, A. Smith, G. Evans	1000
	26	(h)	Northwich Victoria	W	3-0	L. Cooper, J. Flowers, Needham	2000
	27	(h)	Bolton Wanderers	D	1-1	G. Evans	2000
May	1	(h)	Wolves	W	2-0	G. Evans, Not Known	1200
	8	(h)	Bolton Wanderers (DCC)	L	0-2		1500
	11	(h)	'Eleven of Derby'	D	2-2	L. Cooper, Bakewell	1000

FAC = Football Association Cup – The 'English Cup'
DCC = Derbyshire Charity Cup

1885-86 Appearances and Goals

	Apps	Goals		Apps	Goals
Warmby WH	36		Nicholls H	6	
Cooper L	35	10	Latham A	5	
Williamson A	35		Hill C	4	
Bakewell G	35	5	Monk I	2	
Evans G	34	24	Needham T	2	1
Flowers J	33	2	Bromage E	1	
Morley HA	32	1	Flowers G	1	
Smith A	30	19	Hickinbottom A	1	
Cooper GF	29		Hunt W	1	
Hickinbottom E	26	3	Hutchinson TEM	1	
Luntley W	19		Keys J	1	
Bestwick TH	11		Lawson EK	1	
Knox JJ	8	2	Luntley J	1	
Nash RW	8	3	Plackett L	1	
Spilsbury BW	8	2			

1885-86 Season Summary

Played: 37 Won: 18 Drawn: 7 Lost: 12 Goals For: 88 Goals Against: 67
Players used: 29   Average Home Attendance: 1,700

CHAPTER FOUR

1886-87
Records and Rifts

*'Evidently clubs must have a spare man and a few extra
goals to beat Derby County...'
(The Sportsman April 1887)*

Derby County Wanderers 1886-87 – all played for the first-team at least once. Back (l to r): J. C. Bulmer (umpire), R. Pitman, T. Brown, W. H. Levers, A. Staley, H. Lowles, G. Titterton (trainer). Middle: H. Groome, J. Keys, A. Hickinbottom, J. Henson. Front: I. Monk, T. Needham.

Derby County's enhanced reputation saw more teams keen to challenge them – in the established parlance 'to try conclusions with your good selves'. This meant a packed fixture list – between 11 September 1886 and 14 May 1887 the club fulfilled 45 engagements. In contrast to the settled side of 1885-86, reserve men were again drafted in more frequently, producing appearance figures not dissimilar to the experimental opening season. Fifty players were used – but the strength of the lower ranks had greatly improved, the Derby County Wanderers in particular becoming a solid unit in their own right with a buoyant team spirit. In consequence the changes to the first team weakened the side less than in the opening campaign – most of the draftees were now genuinely capable of filling the berth. Overall the results held up well.

But Derby's reluctance to decline invitations – and their entry into three cup competitions – sometimes created complications. On 19th March 1887 the club ended up with two designated 'first team' games on the same day, and decided to 'mix and match' by fielding a combination of reserves and first-team men in both fixtures. Although Blackburn Rovers were beaten 2-1 at the County Ground, the eleven sent to Sheffield Town were beaten 5-3, leaving the Sheffield spectators disgruntled at not having seen the 'Derbyites' at full strength, a view acidly articulated by 'Looker On' in the *Sheffield Daily Telegraph:* 'I have no desire to adversely criticise the arrangements of the Derby County executive, but I should imagine that one *bona fide* first eleven match in one day would be sufficient, and I have to say that the splitting of a first team for the purpose of carrying out multitudinous engagements is a matter to be deprecated. Use your reserves if you must, but please Derby County executive, don't fall into the reprehensible evil of dividing up your regular players for your own ends.'

Barbed words elegantly delivered – and it set a new theme for the first time. As local rivalries simmered less vigorously, Derby County were beginning to nettle other clubs beyond the county borders. Not a laudable trait, but a sure sign that they were increasingly regarded as a major club worth 'bringing down'.

This even extended to the previously impeccable relations which had existed with Corinthians. The crack amateur side had already beaten Derby County twice before Christmas, but came to the County Ground for a third meeting on 12th April 1887. Corinthians arrived with the clear expectation that their established member Ben Spilsbury – also Derby's star man – would play 'for' and not against them. But as kick-off approached Spilsbury was firmly lobbied by the Derby committee to wear the 'chocolate and blue'. Faced with this no-win dilemma Spilsbury declared he would play for neither side. Derby quickly found a replacement, but their opponents took the 'Corinthian approach' – some would say a martyr's stance – and opted to play with only ten men on a point of principle. But after being defeated 2-1 they were sorely displeased, a point tartly made for them by 'Wanderer' in the *Sportsman* – 'Evidently clubs must have a spare man and a few extra goals to beat Derby County.'

Nor was this the limit of testiness – several more out-of-town clubs strongly criticised Derby County in the course of the 1886-87 season. And naturally Derby defended their corner – it seemed that in the three years since the club had been formed, the stakes had been raised, as 'big-time football' crossed more geographic boundaries and made ever greater strides.

There were a number of factors involved in this change of atmosphere, but certainly the legalisation of professionalism in 1885 had added an extra edge. Indeed football's critics were already making the sort of observations more typically associated with recent times – 'big-time football is now nothing but business, all about money, and the players are surely getting above themselves.'

This arguably manifested itself at Derby County, for another new departure in 1886-87 was the first serious bout of 'dressing room politics'. Money and petty jealousies might well have been the root cause. Some players openly declared themselves 'professional' and took as much money as they could. Others made a point of remaining strictly 'amateur', accepting only genuine covering expenses or nothing at all. But

33

football had a third category too – the so-called *shamateur* – who professed to be 'amateur' but shamelessly accepted 'enhanced expenses' on the quiet. With all three types now in the Derby County teams the likelihood of undercurrents developing was certainly increased.

The bombshell dropped only four games into the season – on 6th October 1886 news broke in the *Derby Daily Telegraph* that captain and driving force Haydn Morley had resigned his place in the team. He was then quickly engaged by Notts County. Morley did play for Derby 'purely to fill a vacancy' on four more occasions towards the end of the season, and another four in 1887-88, but only returned fully to the Derby County fold in the 1888-89 first League season, when his football career was already winding down.

The circumstances of Morley's departure were never fully elucidated. The *Derby Daily Telegraph* intimated that he 'objected to the treatment he received from certain members of the committee.' In contrast the *Long Eaton Advertiser* suggested he had become too big for his boots and disaffected his colleagues – on 9th October the paper reported: 'Haydn Morley has resigned the captaincy of the Derby XI. It was quite time that he should do so. If a club is to make progress it is necessary that players and captain should work on amicable terms, and I am not sure this has been the case for some time. Spilsbury will now be captain.'

The jury remains out. But perhaps Morley's energetic behaviour had taxed the tolerance of the overtly conservative Derby County executive once too often. Morley's jocularly irreverent account of an incident just two months after he had left, provides an enlightening insight into the sort of boisterous scrapes that came his way – not entirely appropriate for a club captain expected to lead by example, the son of the founder too, and a respectable Derby solicitor:

'To the uninitiated who would ask how football teams train so as to arrive at that pitch of perfection necessary for the proper playing of the game, I will relate one little instance. I was touring with the famous amateur combination Casuals and staying at one of the leading Nottingham hotels. It was Saturday night, and after pantomime most of the fellows sat down to play poker. About four o'clock in the morning, the 30 or so on tour had dwindled to five, of which yours truly was one. I rose to go to bed. But the others would not hear of it. As there was still plenty of 'fizz' it was thought I ought to stay. I managed however to escape through the door, followed by a shower of knives and forks. I went up to my room, and having locked the door dragged up my bath against it, already filled for the morning's ablutions. It was as I expected. In a few minutes I heard a whispered consultation outside which I felt boded me no good. The door was tried and found locked. Then happened what I never anticipated, even from them. Four shoulders were put to the door and their full weight thrown on it. In they came – so did the door, torn bodily from its skirtings. One of the four came a little in advance and tumbled into my bath. The noise at 5 o'clock on a Sunday morning naturally aroused the sleepers, and so enraged our captain that he threatened to tender his resignation. I mopped up as well as I could, propped the door against the aperture, dragged a chest of drawers across as a barricade against further incursions, and went to bed. We played against Derby County on the Monday – and lost!'

Evidently the trashing of hotel rooms is nothing new. While Morley became a regular at Notts County, his full-back berth at Derby was filled by a new man spotted when they played Burton Wanderers in the week Morley departed – Sam Lawrence proved a steady replacement and a rather more containable character than the mischievous 'Pocket Hercules'.

No player was bigger than the club, and the real business of 1886-87 was on the whole ably completed – of the 45 games only 15 were lost. But that encouraging summary hides some remarkable statistics in what proved to be a season of records and bizarre sequences. Sam Lawrence became immediately involved in a seven game winning run which had started the week before Morley quit. On 25th September 1886 Liverpool Ramblers visited the County Ground – a recently-formed team of former public school men, aspiring to be a northern version of the Corinthians, but much less able. Derby County's 13-0 victory remains their record for a *bona fide* first-team match. Spilsbury scored four and 'otherwise used the occasion to practice his long shooting.' In the winning sequence – 5 at home and 2 away – Derby scored a remarkable 45 goals while conceding only 9.

Star of the run was Lewis 'Kid' Cooper, the former Darley Abbey forward now firmly established at Derby. Scoring in all seven – and then in the defeat and draw that followed – his nine game consecutive record still remains intact, an astonishing purple patch in which he 'bisected the posts' (still no nets) 12 times.

The County Ground regulars were delighted by this early season form. With or without Morley, and also the departed favourite 'Jammer' Smith, the results could scarcely have been bettered. So what happened next almost defied belief – the winning run was immediately followed by 10 games without a single victory. Only 7 goals were scored against 28 conceded – and this with substantially the same team that had so recently defeated all comers.

Lewis 'Kid' Cooper - scored in 9 consecutive games.

The key to this apparent mystery lay less in strategy or unexplained loss of form than in venue – of the 10 game horror spell 7 were away from home. Match reports and contemporary opinion firmly linked this familiar trouble 'on the road' to the variable quality of pitches. Derby County had developed a style of passing play – the much-admired 'combination' – perfectly suited to the more firm and level turf of the County Ground. The widely-praised surface also favoured skilled individualists like speedy winger George Bakewell, whose direct runs created countless scoring opportunities. Derby tried to 'play football' in the purest sense.

But not every side ran out to a verdant cricket outfield – nor was turf management yet an advanced science. Reports of Derby away games are spattered with telling evidence – 'quagmire', 'playing against the slope', 'full of humps and hollows', a 'perfect morass' – and naturally the tenants of these 'wretched surfaces' had adapted their play to suit, while Derby County frequently floundered. This ultimately proved a great irony – the club won nothing of significance while resident at 'the splendid County Ground', yet in the fullness of time the roles would be reversed. Derby County's two League Championship titles in the 1970s owed a great deal to their compelling form at the Baseball Ground, from where defeated visitors regularly departed bemoaning the 'absolute mudbath' which had completely ruined their game.

It is easy to be sceptical about blaming pitches for defeats, but in the pre-League era the playing surface factor seemed genuinely more than a stock excuse – straight after the ten without a win, Derby County won four in a row, all at the County Ground, and the final season tally showed they had won only three times on alien soil, compared to 21 victories on their own favoured turf.

By the end of a roller-coaster season the results ironed themselves out. Again no silverware had been lifted, but progress was evident. Particularly pleasing was a big improvement in goal difference – 111 scored against 77 conceded. The inclusion of a truly regular goalkeeper for the first time was an undoubted plus – Harry Bestwick formerly of Long Eaton Rangers fulfilled the 'custodial duties' in 38 games. A more settled half-back line also helped – Harry Warmby and Albert Williamson missed very few games. But the season's honours must be given to the arch-trickster 'Kid' Cooper – his 26 goals in 39 games an impressive haul, the best scoring tally thus far.

A few more landmarks were also established. Towards the end of the season George Bakewell became the first to achieve 100 appearances. And on 11th April 1887 Derby County faced 'international' opponents for the first time. The Scottish side Dumbarton Athletic surprised the 'more than usually curious' County Ground gathering by emerging 2-0 winners – a double shock, since the paying spectators had fully anticipated seeing the well-fancied Scottish Cup runners-up Dumbarton, rather than the town's supposedly much weaker Athletic. The apparent deception resulted in the Derby County executive being accused of 'misleading publicity'.

Of course club secretary Sam Richardson rarely missed a trick in boosting the gate – after all, it left him more leeway to afterwards adjust the returns and siphon off his cut. The wily practitioner was still at it, and three seasons into Derby County's existence, the accounts of the 'football section' of Derbyshire County Cricket Club were beginning to reflect this. No misdeeds had as yet been detected, but there was a growing disquiet that the football club wasn't making the financial contribution that its apparent success suggested it should. And once more the cricket club needed the boost – Derbyshire were experiencing terrible summers on the field, cricket crowds were low, and the overall debts were again mounting.

This concern manifested itself in embryo at the end of the 1886-87 football campaign. The honorary secretary of Derbyshire County Cricket Club – Arthur Wilson, effectively Sam Richardson's supervisor – stood down temporarily. As a matter of expediency, William Monk Jervis climbed down from the presidential chair to take firm hold of the secretarial reigns of the cricket club, vowing 'to address a growing crisis' in both the cricket and football sections. Challenging times lay ahead.

Both Derbyshire and Derby County would ultimately weather many financial storms – but others were going under at that very moment. Derby's erstwhile rivals Darley Abbey had failed to play more than a handful of fixtures in 1886-87 due to monetary constraints, and it was announced in April 1887 that 'the Abbots have completely suspended operations for want of funds'.

Given the original opposition to Derby County's birth, the Derby committee might have justifiably celebrated the mill-village club's demise. But a lot had happened in three seasons, the emphasis had shifted. Their conscience perhaps pricked, the 'big club' Derby County now had an attack of benevolence. Agreeing to host a fund-raising game at the County Ground – Derby & District XI v Darley Abbey Past Players – Derby freely released men to both teams.

A poor crowd on a wet May evening saw a turgid 0-0 draw. The gesture proved too little too late, and it was almost beyond irony that the side of former 'Abbots' included no fewer than nine Derby County players, not least star of the season 'Kid' Cooper. Like a ruthless assassin turned pall-bearer, Derby County quietly ushered Darley Abbey into its lowlier afterlife – the club continued, but merely as a village club with no professional pretensions. That made one rival slain, and several more yet to dispose of.

Of course that is the cynics view. President Jervis asserted that his club wasn't so heartless – 'Derby County has no desire whatsoever to trench our local rivals, but merely to progress ourselves, and to continue to bring a better class of football to the town and county.'

The old 'better class' jibe was perhaps unnecessary – but on the whole Derby appeared to have adopted a decent stance to the small club's difficulties. Yet as 1886-87 closed, the eclipse of Darley Abbey seemed only to accentuate the very progress of Derby County. Now a club with national ambitions, a real gulf had opened up – still only three years old, the 'new club' already had an air of sage seniority.

For the public the Abbots' decline was all part of the ongoing drama. And the theatre of football threw up fresh intrigues every year – as a summer of cricket was ushered in, Derby County enthusiasts were already pondering what the 1887-88 football season would bring. Little could they have anticipated that towards its end a new innovation called the 'Football League' would come into being – and that Derby County would be in at its start.

Fierce rivals – Long Eaton Rangers 1886-87 with the Birmingham and District Cup. Standing (l to r): T. Hardy, G. H. Smith, F. Start, G. Whittaker (trainer), J. Plackett, J. Wiseman, T. S. Vessey. Middle: J. Orchard (capt), B. Bestwick (umpire), Joseph Orchard (President), B. Stevenson. Front: F. Gelsthorpe, W. Smith, A. Smith.

1886-87 Results and Scorers

Sep	11	(a) Everton	L	1-4	Scorer not known	
	18	(h) Long Eaton Rangers	L	0-2		
	25	(h) Liverpool Ramblers	W	13-0	Spilsbury 4, Knox 3, L. Plackett 3, Bakewell, L. Cooper, Latham	4000
Oct	2	(h) Sheffield	W	7-2	L. Plackett 2, G. Evans 2, Spilsbury 2, L. Cooper	
	9	(h) Burton Wanderers (Birm. Cup)	W	6-1	L. Cooper, Spilsbury, Clifton, Warmby, L.Plackett. G. Evans	
	16	(h) Sheffield Wednesday	W	3-0	L. Plackett, Williamson, L. Cooper	
	23	(a) Notts County	W	6-3	L. Plackett 2, L. Cooper, G. Evans, Not Known	
	30	(h) Aston Unity (FAC)	W	4-1	G. Evans 2, L. Cooper, Knox	
Nov	3	(a) Cambridge University	W	6-2	G. Evans 2, L. Cooper 2, Bakewell, L. Plackett	
	6	(a) Corinthians	L	2-3	L. Cooper 2	
	13	(a) Stoke	D	2-2	L. Cooper 2	1000
	15	(a) Aston Villa	L	0-3		
	20	(h) Mitchell St. Georges (FAC)	L	1-2	Bakewell	
	22	(a) Oxford University	D	0-0	– Abandoned after 17 minutes – fog	
	27	(a) Bolton Wanderers	L	0-2		
Dec	4	(h) Aston Villa	L	0-3		2000
	6	(a) Sheffield Wednesday	D	2-2	L. Cooper 2	700
	11	(a) West Brom. (Birm. Cup)	L	0-6		
	15	(h) Corinthians	L	0-5		
	18	(h) Aston Unity	W	2-0	Monk, L. Cooper	
	27	(h) Casuals	W	3-0	Needham, Bakewell, L. Cooper	
	28	(h) Blackburn Rovers	W	2-0	Bakewell 2	
	29	(h) London Hotspur	W	2-1	L. Cooper, 'scrimmage'	
Jan	22	(h) Grimsby Town	L	1-4	A. Hickinbottom	
	24	(h) Grantham	W	5-0	Spilsbury 2, Latham, Moss, W. Smith	700
	29	(h) Derby St. Luke's	D	1-1	L. Cooper	
Feb	5	(a) Wolves	L	1-5	Scorer not known	
	12	(h) Long Eaton Rangers	D	1-1	W. Smith	
	19	(h) Nottingham Forest	W	2-1	W. Smith, Bakewell	
	22	(h) Wolves	W	3-1	W. Smith 2, Needham	
	26	(h) Cambridge University	D	1-1	L. Cooper	
	28	(h) Oxford University	W	3-0	Spilsbury 2, W. Smith	
Mar	5	(h) Bolton Wanderers	W	3-0	W. Smith, Needham, L. Cooper	
	7	(h) Notts County	D	3-3	L. Cooper 2, L. Plackett	
	12	(a) Nottingham Forest	L	1-2	Needham	
	14	(a) Grantham	W	3-2	H. Groome, Needham, Monk	
	19	(h) Blackburn Rovers	W	2-1	Spilsbury, L. Plackett	
	19	(a) Sheffield	L	3-5	Needham, Others not known	
Apr	2	(h) Stoke	W	3-1	Spilsbury, Bakewell, Monk	
	9	(h) Notts County	W	3-0	L. Cooper 2, Lawrence	
	11	(h) Dumbarton Athletic	L	0-2		
	12	(h) Corinthians	W	2-1	Jackson 2	
	16	(h) Long Eaton Rangers (DCC)	W	5-3	Keys 2, Monk, H. Groome, 'scrimmage'	
	30	(h) Small Heath Alliance (DCC)	W	3-0	L. Cooper 2, Monk	
May	14	(h) Notts Rangers (DCC)	L	0-1		

FAC = Football Association Cup – The 'English Cup'
Birm. Cup = Birmingham Cup
DCC = Derbyshire Charity Cup

1886-87 Appearances and Goals

	Apps	Goals		Apps	Goals
Warmby WH	43	1	Bassano H	3	
Williamson A	41	1	Cropper W	3	
Latham A	40	2	Pitman R	3	
Bakewell G	39	8	Brayshaw E	3	
Cooper L	39	26	Forman A	2	
Bestwick TH	38		Groome A	2	
Plackett L	33	12	Henson J	2	
Lawrence SE	28	1	Hutchinson F	2	
Clifton G	20	1	Lawson EK	2	
Evans G	16	8	Levers WH	2	
Keys J	15	2	Parsons WE	2	
Spilsbury BW	14	13	Jackson H	2	2
Monk I	12	5	Brown T	1	
Needham T	12	6	Cooper GF	1	
Smith W	12	7	Cupit S	1	
Morley HA	7		Greaves JL	1	
Groome H	6	2	Hales G	1	
Weston WA	6		Hardy T	1	
Chatterton W	5		Iliffe FE	1	
Moss G	5	1	Kelsall WL	1	
Bower H	4		Musson CW	1	
Hickinbottom A	4	1	Smith GH	1	
Knox JJ	4	4	Taylor EH	1	
Lowles H	4		Wright LG	1	
Nicholls H	4				
Staley A	4				

1886-87 Season Summary

Played: 45 Won: 23 Drawn: 7 Lost: 15 Goals For: 111 Goals Against: 77
Players used: 50   Average Home Attendance: 2,500

CHAPTER FIVE

1887-88
A Pivotal Campaign

*'Why do players want to go to the theatre the night before
the biggest game of the season? The whole thing is
a complete absurdity.'*
(Long Eaton Advertiser January 1888)

To the world at large Derby County Football Club must have appeared to be progressing remarkably well as the fourth campaign dawned. Their continued advance was indeed more than satisfactory on many fronts, but in truth an ominous uncertainty still hovered over the rising football power. The club's roots could not be ignored – the continued link with Derbyshire County Cricket Club exposed the football section to all the vulnerabilities of the 'mother body'. And the cricket arm had fared very badly both on and off the field ever since Derby County was formed. There was a real possibility that without corrective surgery the cricket club might actually 'go under', dragging the football offspring down with it.

Derby Junction - no names, but possibly the side which sensationally knocked Blackburn Rovers out of the FA Cup in January 1888.

Consider the cricket record since Derby County was formed in May 1884. Of the 33 Championship games played in the four summers 1884 to 1887 only one was won. Even the toss was lost with a regularity that defied belief – a run of 19 times out of 22 passing into folklore. And significantly the summer just departed did nothing to brighten the gloom. Derbyshire finished bottom of the 1887 County Championship table having lost every encounter.

This cumulative lack of success led the other first-class counties to express the view that Derbyshire were not worthy of their status, threatening to refuse to play against them, and calling for the club to be demoted to the second rank of counties. When sections of the sporting press and the editor of the influential *Wisden* backed the call, Derbyshire were thrust into the wilderness. From 1888 they were classed as second rank, not regaining their first-class status until 1894. In sporting terms alone, this rendered the football team the superior body.

By the time the 1887-88 football campaign began, Derbyshire County Cricket Club found itself £1,000 in debt, then a very significant sum. This placed the supposedly 'junior arm' Derby County under a great burden of pressure, for they were expected to make a monetary contribution that justified their existence. A pivotal season seemed to beckon.

Yet perversely this worked in Derby County's favour. Had Derbyshire been flying high and substantially in funds, the cricket committee might well have let the football arm wither to nothing as 'surplus to requirements'. But in fact Derbyshire had performed so badly that the football section by comparison acquired an enhanced status – it emerged as one of the cricket club's best potential lifelines. So Derby County could not be allowed to die, indeed they needed to be fully assisted and promoted wherever possible. As such it is heartening to record that Derbyshire's oft-lamented collapses on the cricket field yielded some genuine benefit still enjoyed to this very day.

When William Monk Jervis had temporarily assumed the Honorary Secretaryship of the cricket club he had vowed to turn things round. To his eternal credit he stopped the rot – within a year through a combination of voluntary subscriptions and fund-raising events he fully discharged the liability and actually created a surplus, eventually raising £2,314. And Derby County's popularity had certainly helped – most of the events and donation requests were 'cross-fertilised' in the name of both the cricket and football clubs. By the end of 1887-88 the first real crisis had been averted. Alas there would be more to come.

This final *pre-League season* was also pivotal in other ways – that as yet unborn italicised phrase yields the clue, heralding the 'Football League' soon to be created. Little had they known it as the season began, but Derby County needed to sustain their upward momentum not just for pride, but for prizes as yet unimagined to come their way.

Once again the season was one of mixed results but overall satisfaction. It began horribly with a 1-0 defeat by Grimsby Town and an 8-0 trouncing from Preston North End. Both games away from home – the travel hoodoo persisted. Just as well that the fixtures were heavily skewed towards the County Ground – more than ever the attraction of the venue for visiting clubs paid crucial dividends. Derby played 23 at home and 15 away.

The supremacy battle with local rivals remained only partially settled. Darley Abbey and St. Luke's had been seen off – no longer on the Derby County fixture list and demoted to 'small fry'. But Junction and Midland remained very capable, so too Long Eaton Rangers, and in the north-east of the county Staveley fully believed themselves the best team in Derbyshire – the 'Easterns' had after all won county trophies. But they had not yet played Derby County.

In the event, the season's local encounters could hardly have been improved upon. At last the stand-off with Midland was ended and the clubs met for the first time. Three games were played – Midland took the honours in the first but Derby won the others. Derby also won the sole encounter with Junction – this a timely scalp, since earlier in the season Junction had acquired renewed celebrity by beating the mighty Blackburn Rovers in the FA Cup quarter final. That result on 28th January 1888 had staggered the football world and given Junction adherents something to crow about. At the call of time on the Arboretum Field 'grown men cried with joy, some prostrating themselves on the ground in a paroxysm of delight.' Blackburn unsuccessfully demanded a replay complaining that the pitch had been unfit – this gave rise to the first (and worst?)

football riddle to do the rounds in Derby: 'Why are Blackburn Rovers like a set of church bells? Because they are always a-pealing!'

Derby did suffer a stumble at Long Eaton Rangers in the Derbyshire Cup. Having re-entered Derbyshire FA competitions after two seasons' absence – the unseemly rift with the county administration now much-healed – they were surprisingly beaten 4-1. But this setback was more than compensated by two meetings with the elusive Staveley, which the press sensationally billed 'Champions of Derbyshire' fixtures.

Founded in December 1871 in a tough colliery village, Staveley had become 'a power in the land' before Derby County was even conceived. Known for their 'robust approach' – most of their players were colliers or ironworkers – they had been adorned by rivals with the colourful nickname 'The Old Foot and Mouth'. Their sloping Recreation Ground did no favours to 'scientific play' – and their fiercely partisan supporters had acquired a gruesome reputation. The 'chalk and cheese' clubs had judiciously avoided each other thus far – engaging only in periodic posturing – but on 15th October 1887 the sides were thrust head-to-head in the first round of the FA Cup on Staveley's notorious incline.

Into this inhospitable arena – replete with 500 followers from Derby – stepped the illustrious Derby captain Spilsbury, leading a team especially determined to assert itself. But an early exit beckoned – with only ten minutes remaining Derby trailed 1-0. Then centre-forward Isaac Monk enjoyed his finest hour – completing a last-gasp double to send Derby County through. Later in the season Staveley sought to avenge the defeat, but were beaten 2-1 at the County Ground.

The twin victories acquired a defining symbolism – Derby County were now tacitly considered the best team in Derbyshire. Thereafter Staveley faded. The *Derbyshire Times* observed that 'this season in some peculiar manner Staveley has drafted itself into a club of only mediocre pretensions.' It was the beginning of the end – in January 1892 the same newspaper dramatically presided over their lingering demise: 'It would take all the pen, ink and paper in the whole universe to attempt to describe the present form of the Staveley Football Club in anything like a favourable manner, and still a failure would result. From an eminence of football glory the old club has drifted slowly but surely to the bottomless depths of despair, and the name that once caused brave hearts to beat anxiously is now dying an ignominious and shameful death.' Unable to survive in the professional sphere, the club was dissolved for want of funds soon thereafter. Although later re-forming in a different guise, the 'Old Foot and Mouth' lay dead – in Derby County's eyes, another rival dispatched.

Cambridge University man Spilsbury had certainly not been cowed by the Staveley reputation – a week after the Cup victory, in the first detailed published interview given by a Derby County player, 'the indefatigable fellow' modestly showed his mettle: 'Yes, I'm pretty well marked, but I don't mind a bit so long as a man will come at me fair and square. It's those confounded low down and foul challenges that I particularly object to, but as a rule I can generally take care of myself in this respect.'

Despite such fighting talk, the FA Cup run came to a sad and controversial end. Becoming ever more professional in the wider sense, Derby County had this season put themselves in charge of a regular trainer. Derby native Joe Edwards – later to train Arsenal for three seasons – was a renowned athlete famous for his winning performances in the annual Sheffield Handicap races, and considered 'a fitness fanatic'.

After Derby had advanced to a 5th round away tie at Crewe Alexandra on 7th January 1888, Edwards was determined to keep his men together, out of trouble, and well-prepared – today's routine 'bonding exercise'. On Friday night, with the blessing of the executive, the team went to the Grand Theatre then slept at the Bell Hotel under Edwards' watchful eye. Next morning they caught the 8.50 train from Derby to Crewe. Leaving no stone unturned, Edwards had arranged for beds to be made available at a Crewe establishment – the players were ordered to take an hour's pre-match nap.

Crewe were considered a rough bunch and their preparation was less subtle. On a tight and inhospitable ground, Derby's in-form centre-forward Reverend Gwynne was nobbled early on by an ungodly kick to the kidneys – the cleric continued but was severely hampered. Spilsbury too was subjected to those 'confounded low-down challenges' he so reviled, and proved thoroughly ineffective. The team failed to perform collectively and Crewe went through 1-0.

It was the bitterest disappointment so far for fans and club alike – this had been 'our year for the Cup.' Crewe's bruising tactics were roundly criticised, but the compounded controversy centred on Derby's 'over-elaborate preparation.' Full-back Arthur Latham later recalled the 'being put to bed' episode as 'a rather strange innovation I had not encountered before or since.' But the *Long Eaton Advertiser* used less charitable terms: 'Why do players want to go to the theatre the night before the biggest game of the season? Then up next morning travelling – from what we hear of the arrangements the whole thing is a complete absurdity.'

A voice born of the abject despair known to every fan – as has since been shrewdly articulated in these tortured words: 'It's not the losing we really mind, we can take the disappointment, it's the hope that kills us, year after year, that faint flicker of possibility, always dashed.' Derby County would come to know that feeling well.

But in the season's overall doings the Crewe defeat really did little damage to Derby's steady rise. Normal service was resumed, replete with the odd little rituals which lent quaintness to proceedings. After a 4-0 win at Leek the players 'were entertained to tea by a lady friend of Mr. Jervis.'

The season lingered on, ending late in May with a creditable 0-0 draw against Preston North End, a testimonial to club secretary Sam Richardson – heaps of praise were lavished on Richardson for 'the sterling job he has done with both football and cricket' – still his creative accounting had not been spotted.

Again Richardson had 'run the show' at the big neutral fixtures still periodically held at the County Ground – and since October 1887 the arena had been even better equipped to host such occasions, as at that date the pavilion and pitch had been moved. Until then the pavilion had faced the racecourse grandstand, and Derby's regular pitch was in front of it, within the cricket outfield itself. Crowds inevitably encroached into the infield and square, so that when cricket commenced the wicket was already irreparably damaged, one of the reasons Derbyshire cricket suffered such criticism.

Occasionally Derby moved behind the pavilion when the pitch was unfit or needed a rest. There was plenty of surrounding land at the racecourse complex. This led to an inspired solution. Cricket committee man James Ragg offered to move the pavilion at his own expense on the one condition that the football club would sharpen its act by appointing a full-time paid secretary, which they did after a year's deferral – another sound progressive move. The new location was at the side of the boundary at the Rifle

Range end, almost at right-angles to the racecourse grandstand, where it remained for almost 70 years.

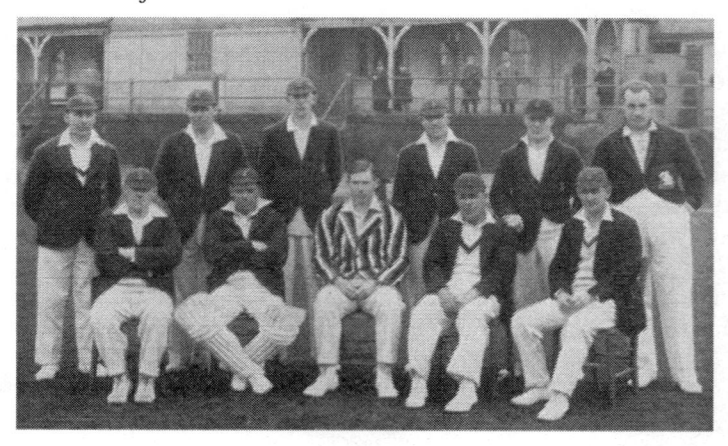

But Ragg's cleverer innovation was in adding a 'second front' to the rear of the pavilion with a balcony and raised platform designed 'to accommodate the best-paying football patrons'. This double-faced structure enabled Derby's pitch to be moved – it was marked out in front of the added 'rear' facade, placing it outside the cricket boundary altogether. Beneficial for cricket and for Derby County too – the new position 'offering a much more pleasing aspect, and altogether more commodious viewing conditions for all spectators than has hitherto been the case.' This was important symbolically as well – a first step towards Derby County splitting from the cricket club and acquiring their own dedicated ground.

Derbyshire County Cricket Club 1931 - interesting for its background shot of the second front added to the pavilion when it was moved in 1887. From the balcony and raised platform Derby County fans watched the team on their new pitch, re-sited outside the cricket boundary.

Those key moves were yet to come. For now, and considered in the light of future events, the 1887-88 season had shifted Derby County closer still to becoming a truly big name – more significant happenings had occurred in this one campaign than in any of the three previous. Viewed with hindsight, even relative minutiae shifted the club imperceptibly towards its modern guise. At home to Notts County on 31st March 1888 the team wore white shirts for the first time – a temporary courtesy to Notts whose own shirts were then also chocolate and blue. Derby prevailed 3-0 – and white would later become their colour.

But the final key happening of this pivotal season was hardly minutiae – though at the time it was not considered momentous. On Tuesday evening 17th April 1888 the four year old club was elected as one of only twelve founder members of a new national football body. Derby County's steadily accumulated persona had paid dividends – they were considered one of the 'twelve most prominent clubs in England'. The initial proposal for a name was the Association Football Union – after some debate it was christened The Football League.

The mechanics of the election, and its ultimate significance, follow hereafter. In the meantime just four days later on 21st April 1888 the newly-empowered Derby County beat fellow League members Wolverhampton Wanderers 3-1 at the County Ground – a nice one for the trivia buff – not their 'first League game', but their first 'against League opposition'. On that pivotal note an eventful campaign of triumph, tribulations, and above all continued survival may fittingly be closed.

1887-88 Results and Scorers

Sep	17	(a) Grimsby Town	L	0-1		
	24	(a) Preston North End	L	0-8		
Oct	1	(h) Walsall Swifts	W	3-0	Staley, Warmby, Spilsbury	2000
	8	(h) Derby Midland	L	1-2	Spilsbury	3000
	15	(a) Staveley (FAC)	W	2-1	Monk 2	
	22	(h) Bolton Wanderers	W	3-0	Wilshaw 2, Spilsbury	1000
	22	(a) Ashbourne St. Oswald's (DC)	L	0-3	– Tie later awarded to Derby:	
					– Ashbourne fielded ineligible players	
	29	(h) Preston North End	L	1-5	Williamson	4500
Nov	5	(h) Ecclesfield (FAC)	W	6-0	Spilsbury 3, Needham, Williamson, Bakewell	2000
	8	(a) Rotherham Town	D	1-1	Scorer not known	
	19	(h) Leek	W	2-1	Wilshaw, Latham	
	26	(h) Owlerton (FAC)	W	6-2	Spilsbury 3, Needham 2, Nash	2000
Dec	3	(h) Aston Villa	L	0-3		
	10	(h) Eckington (DC)	D	1-1	Chatterton	500
	17	(h) Staveley	W	2-1	Bakewell, Wilshaw	1500
	24	(a) Sheffield Wednesday	L	0-8		2000
	24	(h) Eckington (DC)	W	7-2	Gwynne 4, Needham 3	800
	26	(h) Casuals	W	5-1	Wilshaw 2, Selvey 2, Warmby	2000
	27	(h) Blackburn Rovers	W	2-0	Bakewell, Chatterton	3000
Jan	7	(a) Crewe Alexandra (FAC)	L	0-1		4000
	14	(a) Long Eaton Rangers (DC)	L	1-4	Gwynne	
	21	(h) Warwickshire	W	4-1	Bakewell 2, Gwynne 2	1200
	28	(a) Gainsborough Trinity	L	2-4	Scorers not known	
Feb	4	(a) Derby Midland	W	3-1	Chatterton 2, L. Plackett	3500
	11	(a) Aston Villa	L	0-5		2000
	18	(a) Notts County	W	3-2	Spilsbury 2, A. Goodall	
	25	(h) Grantham Town	W	2-0	Needham, Gwynne	
Mar	3	(a) Leek	W	4-0	Bakewell 2, Lees, Pearce	300
	10	(a) Bolton Wanderers	D	5-5	Pearce 2, Needham 2, A. Goodall	2000
	17	(a) Everton	D	1-1	Bakewell	5000
	24	(h) Derby Midland (DCC)	W	3-1	Bakewell 2, Needham	2000
	31	(h) Notts County	W	3-0	Williamson, Selvey, Needham	2000
Apr	2	(h) Derby Junction	W	2-1	Needham, Selvey	5000
	3	(h) Burnley	W	1-0	Selvey	
	14	(h) Sheffield Wednesday	D	2-2	Needham 2	1000
	21	(h) Wolves	W	3-1	L. Plackett 2, Williamson	
	28	(h) Mitchell's St. Georges (DCC)	L	2-3	Selvey, 'scrimmage'	
May	21	(h) Preston North End	D	0-0		4000

FAC = Football Association Cup – The 'English Cup'
DC = Derbyshire Cup
DCC = Derbyshire Charity Cup

1887-88 Appearances and Goals

	Apps	Goals		Apps	Goals
Warmby WH	35	2	Birch-Thorpe CE	3	
Bakewell G	32	10	Booth HD	3	
Needham T	31	14	Keys J	3	
Roulstone W	31		Lowles H	3	
Williamson A	30	4	Weston WA	3	
Latham A	28	1	AN Other	1	
Lawrence SE	28		Bingham A	1	
Bestwick TH	23		Bosworth J	1	
Plackett L	21	3	Cooper GF	1	
Selvey W	19	6	Cooper L	1	
Spilsbury BW	13	11	Cooper W	1	
Wilshaw S	12	6	Groome A	1	
Goodall A	10	2	Groome H	1	
Monk I	9	2	Hall J	1	
Staley A	9	1	Hardy T	1	
Lees J	8	1	Henson G	1	
Marshall J	8		Hodgkinson G	1	
Chatterton W	7	4	Locker W	1	
Gwynne LH	7	8	Ottewell F	1	
Pearce C	5	3	Parsons WE	1	
Pitman R	5		Radford J	1	
Storer W	5		Sinton J	1	
Morley HA	4		Smith W	1	
Nash RW	4	1			

1887-88 Season Summary

Played: 38   Won: 20   Drawn: 6   Lost: 12   For: 83   Against: 72
Players used: 47   Average Home Attendance: 2,300

CHAPTER SIX

1888-89
Founder Members of the Football League

'I beg to tender the following suggestion...that ten or twelve of the most prominent clubs in England combine to arrange home and away fixtures each season...'
(William McGregor, March 1888)

Derby's first ever home League game, against West Bromwich Albion on 15th September 1888. Standing (l to r): William Morley (founder), J. Marshall, H. Dakin (trainer), A. Latham, W. Chatterton (groundsman), I. Monk, A. Ferguson, W. Roulstone. Sitting: A. Williamson, G. Bakewell, L. Cooper, A. Higgins, H. Plackett, L. Plackett.

With the inauguration of the 'new idea' known as the Football League, the landscape of English football changed for all time in 1888-89. The world's first League for professional football teams captured the affections of clubs and supporters alike and was soon imitated at all levels of the game. In time the concept also spread abroad, creating the template by which football became the huge global phenomenon we know today. Viewed with the benefit of more than a century's hindsight, it seems astonishing that such a simple system of pre-arranged 'home and away' matches between a closed group of clubs had not been conceived in football previously, especially as English cricket had already adopted its own County Championship competition on just those lines. But like most 'obvious' good ideas it required a visionary figure to set the ball rolling – the Aston Villa committee man William McGregor.

McGregor had first mooted what he termed 'a fixity of fixtures' late in the previous season. On 2 March 1888 he tentatively canvassed five clubs by letter inviting their opinion – at this stage Derby County not consulted. His reasons for the overture were essentially financial. The countless matches of previous seasons had been played with no lack of competitive edge, but the fixture programmes hitherto had been largely randomly arranged by club secretaries on a more or less chaotic basis. Only the English Cup and other localised cup competitions carried any official recognition and were properly ordered – the remaining balance of 'friendly' or 'ordinary' games was of mixed quality, and the *ad hoc* invitations to 'try conclusions with your good selves' something of an unseemly scramble, as clubs sought to bag 'big matches' ahead of their rivals. As a result, gates had fluctuated wildly, and cancellations or the fielding of weakened sides due to fixture clashes – often with 'more important' cup encounters – were far too frequent. In consequence most clubs struggled to establish reliable income flows and led a very precarious existence.

William McGregor - Founding Father of the Football League.

By bringing a group of clubs together, with an English Champions prize to aim for, McGregor envisaged heightened competition and greater public interest, resulting in bigger gates and richer clubs. Moreover, now that since 1885 professionalism had become well-established, the better income flows generated by the League matches would enable clubs to reliably pay their players regular wages. In turn the most talented players could be premium earners and become the first true stars of the new 'modern game'. It was both a simple model and a complete game-changer, if not at first a universally popular one.

On the face of it, a young organisation like Derby County were not obvious invitees to the inner ring, but after getting to know of McGregor's proposal the club hierarchy quietly looked on and kept an open mind. This in stark contrast to a good number of clubs who spurned the League idea out of hand, not least the Southern amateur sides who considered the monetary element entirely foreign to their ethos. In any case McGregor didn't want the amateurs – they weren't invited.

Although his proposal letter had gone to only five clubs – Blackburn Rovers, Bolton Wanderers, Preston North End, West Bromwich Albion and his own Aston Villa – he soon arranged a follow-up meeting 'open to all' which was held at Anderton's Hotel in London on 23rd March 1888. Blessedly the Derby County committee saw fit to send an onlooker to assess proceedings – respected Derby accountant and committee member Joseph Handford Richardson (1854-1906) of Park Lane House, Littleover. As such, Richardson proved to be a key unsung figure in Derby County history, for the 'outside observer' reported back favourably and at the same time evidently made the right impression on McGregor and the other League backers.

For when the Football League was officially established on 17th April 1888 at the Royal Hotel, Manchester, J. H. Richardson was recorded present as a *bona fide* delegate – Derby County had been admitted to the privileged fold, thereafter forever designated one of only twelve 'founder members of the Football League', and the youngest of them too. The historic original dozen were all from the Midlands or the North – Accrington, Aston Villa, Blackburn Rovers, Bolton Wanderers, Burnley, Everton, Notts County, Preston North End, Stoke, West Bromwich Albion, Wolverhampton Wanderers....and Derby County.

How a club only four seasons old came to be part of that defining group is worth closer examination, for had Derby been overlooked they might easily have slid into oblivion, denying generations of Derbyshire football enthusiasts the myriad of seasonal dramas which have become the club's rich heritage. Arguably other Derby clubs born earlier also had valid credentials – Derby Junction and the railway side Derby Midland the foremost achievers. Not forgetting other contenders scattered around Derbyshire – in particular Long Eaton Rangers and the uncompromising Staveley were both senior in years to Derby County, and had an established renown to boot. Chesterfield too had spawned several clubs of note from as early as the 1860s.

Yet none of these potential aspirants fitted McGregor's ideal – they were either too parochial, considered financially unviable, or not sufficiently representative of the industrial heartlands the Villa man envisaged forming his ranks. In contrast Derby flew the flag for both a burgeoning industrial town and an entire county hinterland. Indeed the very name Derby County had an all-encompassing and impressive ring to it – and in four pre-League seasons the club had countered its lack of years with a fierce ambition which now bore fruit.

The 'Chocolates' had progressed remarkably quickly and taken some big scalps, not least that of Aston Villa in the celebrated Cup match of 1885-86. Played at the County Ground, this had proved particularly significant, since the Villa umpire that day had been none other than William McGregor, no doubt quietly impressed with the Derby County set up. Certainly the club had been generally remarked upon in influential circles as 'one to watch' – put simply Derby County had forward potential, while their local rivals were suffering various degrees of decline. As the story of the first four seasons has already illustrated, those discomforts were in great part caused by Derby County's very existence – the trials and tribulations of those formative pre-League campaigns now paid real dividends.

Not that membership of 'The League' was initially considered the great prize that the passage of time has revealed. Its inception attracted little fanfare – cynics and in particular the press considered the new venture might easily fizzle out. One reporter quickly dismissed it as 'just a money-making circus' – a criticism still levelled at top-class football in its present guise. Certainly no one could have dreamed how big 'The League' would become...the first and ultimately the most prestigious League in world football. Tellingly though, some clubs denied entry did sense an early malaise once it sunk in that they had been condemned to watch from the sidelines – the *Athletic News* reported that 'the supporters of Nottingham Forest are pardonably sore about their exclusion.'

As the 'ins' and 'outs' quickly became distinct camps, petty squabbles soon surfaced about who should or should not have been among the twelve, it being the general consensus among the disgruntled that 'matters other than football prowess have had an undue bearing'. This was more than sour grapes, for there in truth lay the core reason for Derby County attaining their coveted status – three non-playing factors in particular gave the club a defining edge.

Not least was that their County Ground home boasted facilities far better than virtually every rival enclosure – apart from a proven capacity for healthy gates, most visiting clubs admired its 'splendid level playing surface on some of the finest turf in England.' Secondly – and this cannot be overstated – the Midland Railway Station lay right in the centre of England at the heart of the established and still growing transport network, making Derby easily accessible for visiting teams and supporters. This was absolutely vital – in contrast 'difficult accessibility' was said to be a prime reason why the more geographically remote club Sunderland were not among the original twelve. Thirdly – and here pure self-interest showed its hand – the Derby committee was composed of thoroughly affable men whose hospitality knew no bounds. Their post-match dinners at The Midland or Bell Hotel had garnered quite a reputation among visiting sides. Collectively these fringe factors rendered a trip to Derby one that other clubs eagerly anticipated – Derby County were a club of the right calibre run by men of 'the right sort'. Perfect candidates to be 'in'.

Certainly those clubs jealous of Derby's inclusion were soon able to add weight to their own case. Advocates of selection by 'form above facilities' were quickly able to point an accusing finger at Derby County, for the inaugural League season proved extremely challenging, serving up a torrid experience that might easily have seen Derby excluded from the League after the very first campaign.

Nonetheless they started brightly – on 8th September 1888 Derby travelled to play Bolton Wanderers at Pike's Lane and emerged 6-3 winners in their first ever League match. All their goals came from established local captures – a brace each for George Bakewell, Lewis Cooper and 'Lol' Plackett – those early 'poached' signings which had so upset their rivals now surely vindicated.

Pikes Lane where on 8th September 1888 Derby County played their first League game, a 6-3 win over Bolton Wanderers.

All looked promising – and before their first home League match on 15th September 1888 the team posed proudly in their 'chocolate, amber and blue' for a historic photograph. But a hopeful 3,000 then saw the 'Tricolours' lose 2-1 to West Bromwich Albion – and thereafter Derby failed to win any of their next nine games, a sorry sequence which included eight consecutive losses. Derby lay bottom of the table as the year turned, and only towards the end of the campaign did the team show anything like consistent form – a run of five wins and a draw in the final eight games undoubtedly saved them from holding up the entire pile.

Despite the overall disappointment of the season's progress, crowds at the County Ground had held up well – a high of 5,000 watched the Preston game, with a final average around 3,000, this being 500 up on 1887-88. The figures sound low by current standards, but by percentage of the town's population equated to 10 to 15,000 today – as such the Derby County following had clearly not rejected McGregor's League concept. In fact they had embraced it in growing numbers and were eager for more.

But at the end of the inaugural 'fixture calendar' the first ever final 'League ladder' could not disguise the truth – Preston North End were hailed Champions having remained unbeaten, while Derby County had won only seven of their 22 games and finished tenth of twelve. As one of the bottom four clubs they were obliged under the initial rules to seek re-election – other keen candidates might well have replaced them, but again Derby appeared to benefit from accrued goodwill – still held in favour by their fellow members, they gained 8 votes, sufficient to get a second chance. The significance of this proved immense in the fullness of time – having survived the first Football League season, Derby County have remained valued members of its expanded ranks to this very day.

The club also played a reduced programme of friendly games in 1888-89, but at a stroke the results mattered much less, and don't bear fully recording. Of three meetings with Derby Midland two were lost. But Derby County's superiority was now inbuilt – they were members of The League. The FA Cup remained a great prize as ever – but again 'the little tin idol' eluded them. Having knocked out Derby Junction, they were beaten 5-3 at Aston Villa in the second round.

Perhaps the best indicator of the changed balance of power which League membership engendered is illustrated by a request Derby County made to the Derbyshire FA – in fact it was more of a command – that 'none of our players shall be selected for Derbyshire representative games on League match days.' The Derbyshire FA 'tipped their cap' and meekly agreed – the master-servant relationship now reversed. A symbolic signal that Derby County had completed the most important journey in their entire history – now the second and longer voyage was under way.

Still alive but destined to fold – Derby Midland 1888-89. Standing (l to r): W. Storer, H. Storer, A. Staley, A. G. Aitken (Hon. Sec.), G. A. Gilbert, T. Brown, A. Kingscott (umpire), W. Rose, H. Garden. Seated: J. Flowers, T. Daft, G. Evans (Vice-Captain), E. Hickinbottom (Captain), G. Holden, S. Meads, G. Smith.

Football League results and scorers 1888-89

Sep	8 (a)	Bolton Wanderers	W	6-3	L Plackett 2, L Cooper 2, Bakewell 2	3000
	15 (h)	West Bromwich Albion	L	1-2	H Plackett	3000
	22 (h)	Accrington	D	1-1	Higgins	3000
	29 (h)	Preston North End	L	2-3	H Plackett, Wright	6000
Oct	6 (a)	West Bromwich Albion	L	0-5		1500
	13 (a)	Accrington	L	2-6	Higgins, L Plackett	3000
	20 (h)	Everton	L	2-4	Chatterton, Bakewell	2000
	27 (a)	Everton	L	2-6	Needham, L Plackett	5000
Nov	3 (a)	Wolverhampton Wan.	L	1-4	Lees	6000
	24 (h)	Blackburn Rovers	L	0-2		3000
Dec	8 (a)	Preston North End	L	0-5		4000
	22 (h)	Notts County	W	3-2	Bakewell, Higgins, ano	2500
	26 (h)	Bolton Wanderers	L	2-3	Higgins 2	3500
	29 (a)	Aston Villa	L	2-4	Spilsbury, Bakewell	4000
Jan	12 (h)	Wolverhampton Wan.	W	3-0	L Cooper, L Plackett, Higgins	2000
	19 (a)	Burnley	L	0-1		3000
	26 (h)	Stoke	W	2-1	L Plackett, L Cooper	2500
Mar	2 (h)	Burnley	W	1-0	L Cooper	3000
	9 (h)	Aston Villa	W	5-2	Higgins 4, L Cooper	3000
	16 (a)	Notts County	W	5-3	Bakewell, Higgin, L Cooper 2, Lees	5000
Apr	6 (a)	Stoke	D	1-1	L Plackett	4000
	15 (a)	Blackburn Rovers	L	0-3		4000

Final Table 1888-89

	p	w	d	l	f	a	w	d	l	f	a	pts
Preston North End	22	10	1	0	39	7	8	3	0	35	8	40
Aston Villa	22	10	0	1	44	16	2	5	4	17	27	29
Wolverhampton Wan.	22	8	2	1	31	14	4	2	5	20	23	28
Blackburn Rovers	22	7	4	0	44	22	3	2	6	22	23	26
Bolton Wanderers	22	6	0	5	35	30	4	2	5	28	29	22
West Bromwich Albion	22	6	2	3	25	24	4	0	7	15	22	22
Accrington	22	5	3	3	26	17	1	5	5	22	31	20
Everton	22	8	0	3	24	17	1	2	8	11	30	20
Burnley	22	6	3	2	21	19	1	0	10	21	43	17
Derby County	22	5	1	5	22	20	2	1	8	19	41	16
Notts County	22	4	2	5	25	32	1	0	10	15	41	12
Stoke	22	3	4	4	15	18	1	0	10	11	33	12

1889-90 – blue shirt with amber patch and chocolate shorts! Back (l to r): W. Chatterton, A. Williamson, A. Latham, A. Goodall, H. Dakin (trainer), A. Ferguson, W. Roulstone, J. C. Bulmer (umpire). Front: G. Bakewell, A. Higgins, J. Goodall, S. Holmes, L. Cooper, R. Millarvie.

1890-91 – red shirt. Back (l to r): C. Holloway (umpire), B. Chalmers, W. Hopkins, A. Goodall, D. Haddow, A. Ferguson, W. Roulstone, J.C. Bulmer (umpire). Front: G. Bakewell, J. McLachlan, J. Goodall (capt.), S. Holmes, J. Nelson.

Derby County Reserve 1892 with the Derbyshire Challenge Cup, Grantham Charity Cup, and Derbyshire Charity Cup: Back (l to r) – J. C. Bulmer (umpire), W. Roberts, W. Rose, C. Bunyan, H. Garden, J. Hemstock, W. Storer, A. Staley (trainer). Front: C. Butterworth, G. Dunn, H. Rose, A. Hardy, L. Cooper.

1891-92 – players only, back (l to r): J. Methven, J. Robinson, J. Staley. Middle: S. Mills, J. Cox, E. Hickinbottom, W. Roulstone, J. McMillan. Front: J. McLachlan, J. Goodall, W. Storer.

CHAPTER SEVEN

1889 to 1896
Coming of Age

'Come! Rouse up supporters, for football is nigh,
"Play up Derby County" must soon be our cry,
Let us heartily welcome our old trusted band,
And rejoice that again autumn days are at hand.'
(Theodora Cecilia Wilson (aged 21) September 1892)

Derby County's lifetime in the Football League has been so completely covered in other publications that a repeat here would be superfluous. In particular *The Derby County Story, Derby County – The Complete Record,* and *The Who's Who of Derby County* can all be thoroughly recommended for taking the club's eventful story right into the present age.

One of the two main aims of this book has been fulfilled in its first part – to chronicle the club's pre-League era in greater depth than previously presented in other works. The second part – the 'Who's Who' sections which follow this chapter – aims to put flesh and blood on the pre-League characters who first breathed life into Derby County.

But before proceeding to 'The Men Who Made The Rams' a broad summary of the club's continuing progress as far as 1896 will bring the formative period to a logical stopping point – by then Derby County had separated from Derbyshire County Cricket Club, moved home, and become a Limited Company, effectively signalling the club's coming of age and the dawn of a second era.

The close association with the cricket club had undoubtedly helped Derby County take its first steps, but it had also been fraught with difficulties. Ground-sharing created conflicts, likewise running two sets of accounts under one umbrella – the waters became muddied. Once Derby County found their feet it seemed logical to break away.

Another financial crisis precipitated the parting. In 1889 adverse balances in both sections led the cricket executive to examine the books more incisively than ever before – finally the fraudulent deeds of Secretary Sam Richardson were exposed. Early in 1890 he fled to Spain amid revelations that he had embezzled around £1,000 from both the cricket and football sections. Richardson admitted before departing that he had systematically robbed both clubs over a number of years. The chastening news prompted a great deal of turmoil and soul-searching among club officers – in April 1891 after a full year of uncertainty the cricket committee finally issued a significant statement:

'After the present football season, the football club will be separated from the cricket club, as the system of running them in conjunction with one another has been found of late years not to pay. The committee are prepared to let the ground at a fixed rent for football because they consider it will be better to have a fixed sum coming in than having to depend upon whatever profits might be made.'

So 1891-92 began with a newly-independent Derby County continuing to play at the County Ground. But the split seemed to magnify the complications inherent in playing at what remained first and foremost Derby Racecourse, bringing a change of home ever closer. The Derby Recreation Company – which leased the entire racecourse complex from Derby Corporation, and was nominal landlord of the cricket club – increasingly placed obstacles in Derby County's way. The Company was so fiercely protective of racing that it took to cancelling football fixtures both the week before and after race meetings. Their logic was that if people got their sporting fill from attending football, they would give racing a miss, thereby reducing the racing income. The *Derby Daily Telegraph* labelled this 'an artificial rationing of sport' and a 'completely absurd notion' – but all the same it denied Derby County full control of their own affairs.

On 19th March 1892 they repaired for the first time to Mr. Ley's 'Baseball Ground' – a 1-0 defeat by Sunderland. Ley's sports arena had staged baseball since 1890 – introduced after the well-known Derby industrialist had visited America. But the ground was already an established football venue too – Derby Midland had played there throughout 1890-91. In 1892-93 Derby County were nudged into using Ley's ground a second time – on 12th November 1892 they beat Burnley 1-0. Otherwise life continued at the County Ground in relative but uneasy harmony with the Cricket Club and Recreation Company – until the situation reached a head in 1895. Because of a scheduled race meeting Derby were prevented from fulfilling an attractive Easter fixture against the crack Corinthian amateurs. Embarrassing and irritating in equal measure, it proved the final straw – for 1895-96 Derby County 'accepted Mr. Ley's kind offer' and decamped fully to the Baseball Ground.

In response to Derby's commitment to lease his ground, Francis Ley had generously spent over £7,000 in preparing it for big-time football. By moving wooden stands from the County Ground he increased the Baseball Ground's capacity from 4,000 to 20,000 for Derby's first 'permanent' game there. On 14th September 1895 a crowd of 10,000 saw Derby beat Sunderland 2-0. Before the season ended the Derby directors also added the Railway Stand, increasing capacity to 27,000.

This was now a genuine football enclosure – the turf may not have been 'the finest in the land', the surrounds were industrial, and the space a confined one, but the move gave Derby County their own home at last, albeit for now as tenants. It proved a wise move – not least because of its location in a vibrant and expanding community which had sprung up outside the town centre, but close to it. By retaining established support and gaining new, the average crowds improved markedly. Moreover the ground generated atmosphere – the Baseball Ground remained Derby's home for 102 years.

But relocation was by no means the only change precipitated by the separation from the cricket club. Having already experimented with new colours in 1890-91 – navy blue shirt with cardinal sleeves – the Derby County first team permanently jettisoned the 'chocolate, amber and blue' parent colours in favour of their own new identity. In 1891-92 they adopted cardinal and white halves. Other 'red' combinations were also tried, but by 1895-96 the club had settled for white shirts with black shorts – aside from the odd departure this has remained the club strip ever since. The team was also by 1896 routinely dubbed 'The Rams' – a folkloric moniker bestowed by the press which first the public and later the club warmly embraced as an official nickname.

But far more significant was another change which occurred only two months after the cricket split. In June 1891 news broke that those bitter rivals Derby County and Derby Midland had amalgamated. This unlikely alliance was not a choice on Midland's part, but a situation forced upon them by the insurmountable problems arising from professionalism. Midland had agreed to pay their better players purely to keep up with other professional sides. But this increasingly strained the club's resources – and greatly troubled the directors of the Midland Railway Company on moral grounds. Paying football players in the Midland name sat uneasily on their conscience – as did the common practice of presenting good players with a ready-made railway job. When Midland FC emerged from the 1890-91 season more than £100 in debt, the railway company's directors issued an ultimatum – either revert to amateurism or wind up completely.

The amateur option met with almost universal opposition – it was considered as good as a death sentence anyway. So when Derby County offered a surprise amalgamation deal the Midland committee swiftly agreed. As the *Derby Daily Telegraph* dryly observed – 'extremes do sometimes meet'. In truth it was more absorption than amalgamation. Derby agreed to discharge the Midland debts up to £100 – but also acquired their players. Among them were familiar names like Ernest Hickinbottom who returned willingly to the Derby fold. Other Midland stalwarts took a hard line and defected instead to Junction rather than join 'the enemy'. And some of the younger 'Mids' were yet to make their mark. Two campaigns after the deal one Midland 'orphan' was given his Derby County first team debut – the pale 18-year-old tried in an emergency on 3rd September 1892 blossomed into the legendary 'Destroying Angel' Steve Bloomer, worth the merger in his own right.

But it was not all one way traffic. Although Derby Midland Football Club ceased officially to exist, the game continued to be played at the Midland Railway on various levels – and now their primary team drew on Derby County's reserve pool, effectively becoming a nursery club for their new masters. The amalgamation markedly sharpened the Derby second string in particular. In 1891-92 the former Derby County Wanderers, now re-christened Derby County Reserve, bagged a hat-trick of important local trophies – the Derbyshire Challenge Cup, Grantham Charity Cup, and Derbyshire Charity Cup. Buoyed by this achievement, the Derby County Reserve then adopted a grander-sounding title – in 1892-93 they took the new name Derby Town in honour of a 'sadly demised forerunner'.

A further landmark in 1892-93 was the implementation of a more organised training regime throughout the club. The minute book stated that 'all players not in regular employment shall meet every morning at 10am and take such exercise and practice as the trainer directs.' Hitherto they had met a couple of times a week in somewhat looser fashion.

As Derby County continued to thus evolve into a 'modern professional football club' both on and off the field, the *Derby Daily Telegraph* articulated the perceived importance of the Midland absorption: 'The result of this unlikely union between the two clubs is apparent to all. The marriage of resources has placed our native town in the very front rank of the football world.' And Derby County had gained a more primeval satisfaction too – the disposal of yet another local rival. Now of their original Derby enemies only Junction remained.

Team strengthening apart, the extinction of Midland also had a big financial and administrative impact. Management of the merged clubs was jointly vested in a combined committee of sixteen elected by guarantors of not less than £5 to the club funds. More than £600 was quickly subscribed from business and supporters, and some good Midland men joined the administrative fold. One was Sawley man Arthur Kingscott – later a celebrated referee and important FA administrator. Although employed at the railway and nominally a Midland man, his Derby County sympathies were well-established – in the opening season he had helped steer fellow Sawley natives 'Jammer' Smith and Albert Williamson into the Derby ranks. Now he delivered again, this time recommending the untried Steve Bloomer for a chance in the first team.

Arthur Kingscott - able administrator inherited from Derby Midland.

The replenished coffers also enabled Derby to compete more vigorously for new signings – and importantly to retain them. In June 1891 concurrent with the merger young full-back Jimmy Methven arrived in town from Edinburgh St. Bernard's, immediately signing a professional contract. He remained at Derby County as a player and manager for over 30 years. A wave of other Scottish imports followed, and with both John and Archie Goodall now also in the side the first truly memorable team began to take shape. In the course of time the Derby County of the mid- to late-1890s would be recalled as one of the finest in the club's history.

In 1893-94 Derby County finished third in the League, their highest position to date. But this came at a cost – players' wages had stretched resources to such an extent that the club again found itself in financial difficulty. The directors sensed a real possibility that the club would fold. But here the accrued support and goodwill of the Derby people now paid genuine dividends – they could not see the club perish. A series of fund-raising events culminated in the Drill Hall bazaar held over four days in March 1894, which alone boosted Derby's ailing finances by £1,000.

Yet with the off-field crisis averted, another developed on it. In 1894-95 Derby surprisingly finished second from bottom in the League, by now expanded to 16 clubs. Under prevailing rules they were required to 'play-

17-year-old prospect in Derby Midland colours 1891-92: Steve Bloomer.

off' in a 'Test Match' to avoid relegation to the 'Second Division' – the League extension formed in 1892-93. Trailing 1-0 to Notts County with only five minutes remaining their fate looked sealed. But after a desperate final push two last-gasp goals from Bloomer and McMillan saw Derby County retain their top flight place. Played at the Walnut Street home of Leicester Fosse – later Leicester City's Filbert Street – the game passed into legend, the 'ecstatic celebrations' of players, fans and officials acknowledging its significance.

The preservation of such a hard-earned status proved a pivotal moment in the club's history. In 1895-96 Derby finished League runners up to Aston Villa and reached the FA Cup semi-final – and despite not bagging the major prizes (that gnawing 'hope' still not yet fulfilled) they were considered by informed opinion to be 'generally the most attractive side in football at the present time.'

The same campaign also delivered a seasonal bonus. On Christmas Day 1895 a cash-strapped Derby Junction played its last ever game. The *Derby Daily Telegraph* wistfully declared that 'having ascended like a rocket, the Juncs fell to earth like its stick, and the grand old team has decided to throw up the sponge.' Six hundred fans witnessed the poignant death throes at the Vulcan Ground – barely a stone's throw from their Baseball Ground rivals the 'Juncs' were defeated 8-1....by the Derby County reserves. Less than eight years earlier Junction had been 90 minutes from an FA Cup final, but after this telling indignity they disbanded and never played again – 'the growing popularity of Derby County having diminished our receipts almost to vanishing point.'

As 1895-96 closed, the rise of 'The Rams' and their now sole domination in the town must have given immense satisfaction to founder William Morley and the rest of the club executive – in just twelve years they had elevated Derby County from a mere idea to a position of high prominence. Their rocket was still rising. Amidst this sentiment of quiet pride and no little relief the club's rulers seemed innately to sense that the formative journey was almost complete – crises had been averted, rivals slain, survival assured, and many 'rivers crossed'.

From that lofty vantage point the executive decided that one more act would signal the club's coming of age. In July 1896 it was announced that procedures had been put in motion to make Derby County a Limited Company. It would be run by a President (William Monk Jervis), two vice-presidents (Arthur Wilson and William Thomas Morley) and a board of 9 Directors, with a share capital of £5,000 in 5,000 shares of £1 each. The formal incorporation of Derby County Football Club (Limited) was completed on 14th August 1896. This committed the club to be run on sounder business lines than ever before – at least in principle. In truth the ride would seldom be smooth – and at every bump thereafter supporters would always blame 'the board'. But no one could accuse the new directorate of 'limited' aspirations – clause three subsection two of the 'Memorandum and Articles of Association' stated Derby County's intentions:

'To promote the practice and play of football, cricket, baseball, lacrosse, lawn tennis, hockey, bowls, bicycle and tricycle riding, running, jumping, physical development and the human frame.'

Billy Clark - first designated manager

As a mission statement it left little in doubt – the 'upstarts' now ruled the roost. Concurrent with this, the

59

constitution also listed a first designated manager in W. D. Clark – otherwise William Dickinson Clark (1864-1939). Poached from Burton Wanderers, 'Billy' Clark had first arrived in June 1895 as 'Club Secretary'. His duties already extended to team affairs, but he was given the grander title 'Manager' in the Limited Company prospectus. Although required to balance the books, results on the field were his primary responsibility, albeit the Board retained an influence on team selection. His reward for this newly-created modern role was 'a private office and £100 per annum plus reasonable expenses' – for which he was expected to 'devote his attentions full-time to club and team affairs'.

Thus transformed for 1896-97 the club embarked on another season's trail. Billy Clark again managed the side to good effect – Derby finished third in the League and reached another Cup semi-final. That made Clark a wanted man – in June 1897 he resigned to become manager of Leicester Fosse. Countless such ups and downs of 'the modern game' would follow – many of a financial nature – but at this juncture it could not be denied that the foundations of a great football club had now been firmly laid down. After three losing FA Cup Final appearances and numerous defeats in the semis, Derby County would finally lift the trophy in 1946 – a number of the pre-League players lived to see the day. The League Championship title was gained in 1972 and 1975 – alas none of the 'Chocolate and Blue' then surviving.

But what does remain is the dimmed but dauntless spirit of those early times. Derby County Football Club today is the sum of all its history – its ancestry matters, its unique DNA is firmly implanted. They say that 'the past is another country' – but it is seldom as far removed as we might imagine. The pre-League pioneers may have faded from life, but a handful of their descendants still alive both met and knew the 'phantoms' before they passed. While researching this book I learnt that the 'handshake link' with Derby County's very first player remained a remarkably short one – Haydn Morley's daughter Grace Nora Pritt, born in 1919, still living.

With each passing season '1884 and all that' recedes further into the 'distant past' – but for a fleeting moment the window remains open. It is not quite too late to reel in the years and reclaim a 'lost' age for posterity. I hope this book can capture at least a modicum of that sentiment. The part-one historical narrative is now complete. But the 'vanished men' deserve to be recorded as individuals too – they created an institution. What follows is a varied cast – first the administrators and then the players. Of the latter, some were extraordinary characters in their own right, others more workaday yet occupying the same coveted stage. But all share a bigger commonality – in pulling on the chocolate and blue shirt they are collectively 'The Men Who Made The Rams'.

1895-96 – in civvies – back (l to r): J. Robinson, W. D. Clark (manager-secretary), J. Methven, J. Goodall, G. Kinsey, J. Miller, W. Leach (trainer). Middle: J. McMillan, J. Stevenson, A. Goodall, J. Cox, J. Leiper, J. Staley, J. Paul, H. McQueen. Front: S. Bloomer.

1895-96 – the completed outfit – back (l to r): J. Methven, A. Staley (trainer), J. Leiper. Middle: W. D. Clark (manager-secretary), J. Cox, A. Goodall, J. Robinson, G. Kinsey, J. Staley. Seated: J. Goodall, J. Paul, J. Miller, J. Stevenson, H. McQueen. Reclining: S. Bloomer, J. McMillan.

Derby County's new home – the Baseball Ground 1895.

Early action at the Baseball Ground – note the high fences to stop baseballs being hit into Ley's foundry.

CHAPTER EIGHT

THE MEN WHO MADE THE RAMS

*Mr. Morley and those who acted with him realised that
football had a great future before it, and in founding Derby
County they determined that Derby should not be left behind.'
(Derby Daily Telegraph, February 1912 on the death of William Morley)*

When Derby County was formed in May 1884 it was a collective effort which both brought the club into existence and thereafter nurtured its rise and progress. Five men in particular played leading roles. The founder William Morley and his son William Thomas Morley were the prime movers in creating the club. But their ambition could readily have been thwarted at source without the support and approval of the first President William Monk Jervis and the first Honorary Secretary Arthur Wilson, both already figures of authority within the parent organisation Derbyshire County Cricket Club. As such both men deserve their billing among the 'Founding Fathers'. As too does the club's first long-standing day-to-day secretary Samuel Richardson, who did so much to advance the name and reputation of Derby County whilst at the same time almost condemning the fledgling club to oblivion through his 'creative handling' of the club's finances. Yet little knowledge of this long-demised quintet has survived into the modern age – that a brief summary of their lives be therefore put on record seems the least they deserve, for without their vision, dedication and dogged determination, Derby County Football Club would simply not exist.

WILLIAM MORLEY
'FOUNDING FATHER' OF DERBY COUNTY

Among the extended ranks of early administrative figures connected with Derby County Football Club, none deserves the tag of founder more than William Morley, the club's first Chairman. Indeed he had the singular satisfaction of being dubbed the 'Founding Father' within his lifetime, and he died knowing that his creation had become an established force in top-class football. After receiving a suggestion from his son William Thomas Morley that Derbyshire County Cricket Club should establish a football offshoot, he presented the idea to the cricket club committee towards the beginning of May 1884. Already a highly-respected member of that committee for some seven years, Morley applied the wisdom and experience of his then 62 years to significant lasting effect. His credibility and ever-youthful enthusiasm proved sufficient to win over his fellow committee men in the face of some scepticism, and by 7th May 1884 he had turned the mere idea of a 'football arm' into visible reality. When Derby County was founded, Morley was a long-serving senior clerk in the Secretary's

63

Department of the Midland Railway. That is as much as has generally been revealed about him, but there was a great deal more to the 'Founder of the Rams'.

First the shocking truth – he was neither a native of Derby or even Derbyshire, but born instead in the adjacent county of Nottinghamshire. In fact in Nottingham itself, in the fullness of time home to Derby County's greatest football rivals Nottingham Forest. But no matter – although Morley was certainly an admirer of Notts County, and indeed stated that he modelled his Derby club on that pioneering side, at no time did he ever profess allegiance to the 'Red' side of that city, seeing fit to vacate it early enough in life to become a fully-fledged honorary Derbeian.

William Morley was born on 12th August 1821 to the moderately prosperous publican – later parish clerk and registrar – Thomas Morley and his wife Elizabeth Fox in Old Sneinton, then an outlying village of Nottingham not far from where both Notts County and Nottingham Forest later established their homes. William was educated at one of the principal private schools in Nottingham, emerging at the age of 15 with a sound range of knowledge and skills. He then entered the counting house of Messrs D. S. Churchill and Co., hosiery and lace merchants, as a trainee, and progressed well.

In all probability he would have remained in Nottingham for life had it not been for a tragedy that befell the curiously named Mr. Daft Smith Churchill, principal of the firm. In that respect the genesis of Derby County is linked by fate to the legendary shipwreck of the *S.S. Forfarshire* which occurred in treacherous conditions off the coast of Northumbria on the night of 6th September 1838. The ship had left Kingston-upon-Hull bound for Dundee with Mr. Churchill among the 63 passengers and crew. After it foundered on rocks in heaving seas, nine were saved with the assistance of celebrated rescue heroine Grace Darling, daughter of the keeper of a nearby lighthouse.

With her father the gutsy 24-year-old rowed from Longstone Lighthouse to aid those in distress – a number of others secured their safety by their own efforts, but Daft Smith Churchill was not among the survivors. Denied of his guidance, the firm of D. S. Churchill entered a steady decline and was ultimately liquidated in 1842. As a consequence William Morley was made redundant and for three long years was unable to find a suitable position. Only in 1845 did his fortunes, and indeed his entire life's course, change. In November of that year 24-year-old Morley moved to Derby to take up a 6 months trial position as a clerk in the Secretary's Department of the recently formed and quickly expanding Midland Railway Company, which had established Derby as its headquarters.

What an opportune move it proved – and a seminal one for the yet to be conceived Derby County. Impressing his seniors, Morley was kept on by the Midland Railway and grew with the company, rising to Chief Clerk in the Secretary's Department and staying for 56 years – he retired on 31st December 1901 at the age of 80, described as 'the oldest railway servant in the kingdom'. But such was his renowned vitality he had been mischievously dubbed 'Young Morley' by his colleagues.

Outside of work Morley had a broad range of interests – a highly accomplished vocalist and solo violinist, music was a lifelong passion. He was often in demand for concerts, and when Derby Market Hall was opened with great ceremony in 1866 Morley conducted the orchestra. He was said to be 'very well-read', but also appreciated more vigorous activities, maintaining a fervent interest in sports throughout his life. That he had a tough side was evidenced by an observation on his prowess as a boxer – 'in his younger days he had the gloves on with many professional and amateur celebrities, and could hold his own in his light-weight class with all save the first-rankers.' But his was a determination devoid of natural venom, his character remaining balanced by a natural geniality and strong religious conviction. He was a worshipper at St. Peter's Church and Churchwarden there in the 1890s. In politics he was a Conservative but seldom took actively to the political platform. He was a member of Derby Conservative Club and an almost daily visitor there during the last 10 years of his life.

Nor was his personal life compromised – on 17th June 1848 he married local girl Ann Slater. The couple raised a family of 7 sons, two of which died before him. One son William Thomas Morley succeeded his father as a long-serving chairman of Derby County, and another Haydn Arthur Morley was the first to sign for the club when they were formed.

After the death of his wife on 12th July 1900 Morley was increasingly cared for at home by his unmarried niece Anne Harrison. Although in his will Morley described himself as 'Gentleman' he was essentially a man of the people, a stolid townsman with the common touch, whose position at the Midland Railway gave him useful access to influential contacts yet kept him connected with the more prosaic world of Derby's ordinary working men. This made for a good balance on the first Derby County committee – Morley as Chairman nominally sporting the 'Derby' colours, while 'country squire' William Monk Jervis added the 'County' flavour as the club's first President.

Nevertheless Morley lived quite comfortably, graduating to grander homes as his career progressed and his family grew. Most of his abodes are recorded – 10 Midland Place (1850s), 43 Regent Street (1860s), 62 Wilson Street (early 1870s), 'Bingham Lodge' on London Road (1880s), 15 Hartington Street (1890s) and finally 5 Leopold Street (1900s). All in his adopted Derby – but between 1871 and 1880 he enjoyed an interim sojourn in nearby Repton, where his wife's family had connections and some of his sons were educated. Whilst there Morley took a keen interest in village life and sport – a co-founder and vice-chairman of Repton Cricket Club and for 5 years a churchwarden.

Morley served as Derby County chairman for the first seven years of the club's existence, handing over the reigns to son 'Willie' in 1891 only when the club had become firmly established as a genuine force in the top echelons of 'big-time' football. He continued to attend the Rams' games to a grand old age, and enjoyed the satisfaction within his lifetime of being acknowledged in print as not only 'the founder of Derby County' but 'a veritable legend among football administrators'.

When his time finally came, fulsome tributes poured in from many quarters. After a prolonged bout of bronchitis he died at his home 5 Leopold Street, Derby, on 21st February 1912, aged 90, his estate amounting to £1,689. Sundry obituaries were united in painting a picture of a genuinely popular man, not always the case for football club chairmen. One stated: 'He enjoyed the goodwill of all he came into contact with through his unfailing courtesy – his good temper and juvenility was proverbial, his young looks and buoyant stride well known around the town. He illustrated in truly delightful fashion the value of personal cheerfulness, his sprightly manner and well preserved figure were wonderful to contemplate, but more remarkable still was his unwearying geniality'.

He was buried at Derby's Uttoxeter Road Cemetery in a grave principally that of his mother-in-law Mary Slater. Her daughter Ann – William's wife – shares the resting place, and Morley himself was interred there last. Sadly he is recorded on the stone slab only in the most cursory terms, his surviving family electing to make no mention of his Derby County credentials or professional achievements.

Moreover the ravages of time have since rendered his name barely discernible, while the gravestone itself is increasingly threatened by encroaching undergrowth which might ultimately claim it forever if left unchecked. That is surely less than 'Young Morley' deserves. But if one monument to such an accomplished figure lies crumbling and forgotten, there is another much bigger one which has lasted better. The football club he created is his greatest legacy. Through good, bad and indifferent times it has remained a constant pulse in the life of both the City of Derby and the County of Derbyshire.

'R.I.P. William Morley 1821-1912
Founding Father of Derby County Football Club'

WILLIAM THOMAS MORLEY
AN ARDENT ADVOCATE

Although William Morley senior secured the formation of Derby County, the idea was not entirely his own. The crucial offstage advocate was William's son William Thomas Morley – 'Willie' to the family. Whilst resident at Repton early in 1884 he first suggested to his father that the precarious financial position of Derbyshire County Cricket Club might be ameliorated by the formation of a properly organised football club under the same umbrella. That the idea came to fruition is a matter of fact – but if the more youthful 'Willie', then aged 35, had not presented it to his father so forcefully, the conservatively inclined elder statesmen of Derbyshire County Cricket Club may never on their own account have mustered the courage to embrace football. An early reminiscence certainly makes it clear that both the initial lobbying and continued interest of 'W. T.' was acknowledged as a vital factor – 'the idea for Derby County really germinated in the brain of W. T. Morley – he had quite a genius for the task, and applied to it altogether congenial and exceptional powers.'

William Thomas Morley was born in Derby in 1849, the eldest child of William and Ann Morley. After a sound education at the Litchurch Lodge School he followed his father into the service of the Midland Railway Company, entering in 1864 and advancing to a senior clerical position. He served 50 years before retiring in 1914 aged 65.

His suggestion of forming a new football club was not motivated entirely by benevolent feelings towards the ailing cricket club – there was a vital pre-requisite, namely that he liked football and what it stood for. The formation of the Football Association in 1863 fell within Morley's formative teenage years – he had earlier been exposed to the evolving sport in his schooldays, took readily to it, and in due course performed at various times for sides of modest stature. Indeed 'W. T.' embraced sport and outdoor pursuits of most kinds, enjoying the company and manly banter that went with it. He 'pulled a fine oar' with Derby Rowing Club, was co-founder of the Derbyshire Golf Club, and keenly associated with one particular activity at which Derby teams excelled – in May 1900 elected a vice-president of the National Baseball Association.

Like his father he was also musically talented, being a fine vocalist and for 30 years choirmaster of St. Osmund's in Derby. But his tastes were not entirely high-brow. He needed little encouragement to deliver comic ditties at sundry functions, and in the 1870s had been a wise-cracking 'corner man' with a popular troupe of minstrels called the 'Gentlemen Niggers', a name at that time not deemed shameful.

W. T. Morley became a member of the Derby County committee soon after the inception of the club, and became steeped in all aspects of its often troublesome affairs. Serving initially as vice-chairman to his father, he eventually became chairman in 1891 when Morley senior stepped down. 'W.T.' then filled the role for over 30 years. When he finally retired from the board in February 1923 aged 73 he had known Derby County 'chapter and verse' for the entire course of its almost 40 years existence – what a story he could have told if only he had left his memoirs.

In his personal life he married Hannah Jane Smith at Repton on 4th September 1879 – born in 1848 the daughter of well-known Repton farmer Seth Smith, she was considered 'the first female who really followed Derby County seriously, travelling with them wherever they went, and genuinely respected for her knowledge of the game.' The couple settled initially in Repton, living for quite some time in the 1880s with Hannah's bachelor brother Richard William Smith at the family farm on Long Street (now High Street). As such it was in Repton that Derby County FC might be said to have been notionally 'conceived'.

In the 1890s William and Hannah graduated back to Derby, settling ultimately at 'West Holme' 1085 London Road. After suffering the loss of his wife in 1921, Morley left the Derby County board two years later and retired initially to the Isle of Wight. He spent his summers there but generally wintered at the Welsh seaside resort of Barmouth, in his final few years making it his permanent home. He died there at 'Allt Fawr' on 10th July 1939, having attained the same 90 years as his father, at that time considered a rare double feat. He was buried at St. Helen's Church, Sea View, back on the Isle of Wight.

W. T. Morley undoubtedly ranks alongside his father as a hugely significant character and 'guiding light' from the 'birth, rise and progress' era for Derby County. The club have much to thank him for.

'R.I. P. William Thomas Morley 1849 -1939
His Idea Bore Fruit'

WILLIAM MONK JERVIS
A PRESIDENTIAL AIR

Just as club founder and Chairman William Morley provided the stolid townsman's touch, in suitably balanced contrast The Honourable William Monk Jervis added a distinct 'county' air, even an aristocratic one, to the running of Derby County. As its first President, his impressive family lineage, sound business brain, and affable personality, all coupled with an ardent love of sport, greatly benefited the club in its formative period.

A noted ancestor was the illustrious Admiral Sir John Jervis – later Earl St. Vincent – whose victory over the Spanish fleet at Cape St. Vincent in 1797 earned him a reputation second only to Nelson at that time. William Monk Jervis acquired a certain amount of reflected glory from such a pedigree, and his respected standing in social circles certainly helped advance Derby County's cause – he was a man few would choose to ignore, bringing to Derby County the sort of cachet which often eluded clubs from similar provincial towns.

But Jervis was far more than a mere figurehead – at crucial moments for both the football and cricket clubs he made it his personal quest to raise and inject much-needed funds into the ailing operations, on several occasions making generous donations from his own pocket. It was afterwards stated that his efforts had 'more or less saved both Derbyshire CCC and Derby County FC from the brink of oblivion.'

William Monk Jervis was born into grand surroundings at 19 Seymour Street near Mayfair in London on 25th January 1827, the son of William Jervis and his wife Sophia Vincent. He lost both parents before entering his teens. Educated at Eton and then Trinity College, Oxford, he emerged with sound degrees set at a legal career. In 1853 he was admitted to the Inner Temple as a barrister-at-law, but was never regularly in practice, instead devoting much of his life to civic duties and charitable causes.

He spent time in London, Staffordshire and Kent before graduating to Derbyshire in the 1860s and adopting the county as his own – although sometimes declaring himself 'strictly speaking a man of Staffordshire'. This was because the ancestral family seat was Meaford Hall near Stone, birthplace of the famous Admiral, and where Jervis spent some of his boyhood.

In his youth he was considered a promising cricketer, playing for Oxford University in 1848 and later MCC and the Gentlemen of England. Already past his best when Derbyshire was formed in 1870, he played for them only once, at home to Lancashire in 1873 when aged 46. Otherwise he devoted himself to the club's administration – Derbyshire's President from 1871 to 1886, and temporary Honorary Secretary in 1887 in a time of crisis.

In 1884 his willingness to also patronise football had been a vital pre-requisite to Derby County's formation – Jervis backed the idea when his opposition could readily have killed it. He was made Derby County's first President, and also accepted the first Presidency of the Derbyshire Football Association, although resigning that post within two years due to conflicts of interest. He was besides President of Derbyshire Golf Club, a vice-President of Derby Town Rowing Club, and a Director of the Derby Recreation

Company which ran the Derby Racecourse, the latter office not always sitting easily with his Derby County credentials.

Described as a man of 'great energy and sagacity' Jervis had countless interests beyond sport. Qualifying as a magistrate for Derbyshire in 1872 he served on the Bench for over 30 years. Among countless other offices he was a patron of Derby Sketching Club, governor of Derby School, and manager of Derby Ragged School. He was also for some time in the Third Staffordshire Militia, attaining the rank of captain in 1870.

Jervis was thrice married and twice a widower. In 1864 to Harriet Wilmot Sitwell who died in 1875. Secondly in 1876 to his cousin Mary Maude Jervis – she died in 1879. And finally in 1882 to widower Mary Stepney who survived him. None of the marriages produced children. His third wife was particularly sympathetic to his various sporting causes, said to be 'the moving spirit at the three great bazaars which gave such aid to the cricket and football clubs.'

With a penchant for tweeds and in later life wielding a walking cane, Jervis was something of a dandy who became a familiar figure in and around the town. When his end came the *Derby Daily Telegraph* said 'the news of his death will be received with unfeigned regret by an exceedingly large circle of friends.' Following a bout of influenza he died at his home Quarndon Hall on 25th March 1909. Aged 82 he was buried in Morley churchyard in a brick-lined grave.

Whilst on the face of it 'not at all the football type', varied fulsome obituaries acknowledged that Derby County owed Jervis a genuine debt of gratitude. One commented: 'The news will come as a great shock to the town and neighbourhood. Throughout his long and honourable life Mr. Jervis was ardently devoted to outdoor sport, and always manifested the warmest possible interest in Derby County's welfare.'

'R. I. P. the Hon. William Monk Jervis 1827-1909
a sporting gentleman'

SAMUEL RICHARDSON
'SPANISH SAM' – FROM HERO TO VILLAIN

Of all Derby County's early administrators none proved more colourful a character than Sam Richardson. As honorary assistant secretary of both Derbyshire County Cricket Club and their newly-formed football section, he was entrusted by senior honorary secretary Arthur Wilson to administer and oversee the financial affairs of both arms, a role which he fulfilled with conspicuous vigour and great enthusiasm, but largely unsupervised.

He was trusted because he was 'known'. Richardson was both a respected tradesman and one of the most prominent names in the early annals of Derbyshire County Cricket Club – the side's first captain, honorary assistant secretary from 1880, and manager of a large tailoring shop in Derby. Yet in time that trust proved ill-judged, for despite doing a great deal to advance the cause of both cricket and football, Richardson succumbed to temptation, systematically embezzling funds for his own ends. As a result, serious losses were made, and his actions might easily have sounded the death knell for Derbyshire's cricket side, and with it Derby County, within just a few short years of the football club's formation.

As it was, Richardson's shameful misdemeanours were uncovered just in time. In 1890 he fled to Spain under an assumed name, and both cricket and football clubs were able to recover sufficiently to carry on – but it was a close run affair.

Samuel Richardson was born in Derby on 24th May 1844. He gained proficiency at cricket, and in the late 1860s when in his early twenties represented the long-established South Derbyshire Cricket Club. During Richardson's spell their home was the Racecourse Ground on Nottingham Road, later christened the County Ground, still home to Derbyshire cricket, and where Derby County played their home fixtures for their first decade. So Richardson had known his territory for some years, and with that came the boldness of familiarity which ultimately proved his undoing.

In the wake of the success of the South Derbyshire Cricket Club, the foundation of a 'bigger' club was proposed. In consequence the Derbyshire County Cricket Club came into being in November 1870, Richardson sitting on the committee which presided over the birth.

And when Derbyshire's initial first-class match was played against Lancashire at Old Trafford, Manchester, commencing 25th May 1871, it was the former South Derbyshire representative Sam Richardson, the wicket-keeper in that opening game, who was honoured to be elected Derbyshire's first ever captain.

Having thus cemented his place in the club's historical record, Richardson proved a competent cricketer rather than an outstanding one – yet he remained Derbyshire's captain until 1875. His first-class career spanned 1871 to 1878, but his appearances were sporadic and unspectacular – in all he played only 14 first-class matches and scored 202 runs at an average of 8.8. His highest score was a modest 25, and as a bowler he took one wicket for 43 runs in 56 balls.

But rather more 'spectacular' was Richardson's involvement with Derbyshire as an administrator. He was appointed Assistant Secretary in 1880, and when Derby County formed in 1884 his role was extended to cover football affairs. Yet even by then the cricket club was deep in financial crisis, one of the very reasons the football section was formed. And by 1890 both cricket and football sections had suffered greatly. The troubles appeared to coincide with Richardson's tenure, and attendant close scrutiny proved the two events to be firmly connected, for in 1890 an audit of the club accounts by Derbyshire's celebrated Australian player Frederick 'The Demon' Spofforth revealed that Richardson had quietly embezzled the substantial sum of almost £1,000.

Sam Richardson had seen it coming, for he had already resigned a few months earlier, on 22nd October 1889. But now faced with evidence, he admitted his guilt, confessing that he had routinely robbed the cricket club over a period of ten years. Nor had he confined his activity to the summer game, for since 1884 he had dipped into the Derby County takings too. It had proved an easy trick to work – among various ruses Richardson's favoured methodology was to understate the size of the crowd in order to syphon off gate receipts for his own ends. This was by no means uncommon in Victorian sport, the very reason why turnstiles with more secure counting mechanisms soon became standard.

If the affair proved embarrassing for Richardson, the shame was no less keenly felt among club committee members, for the scandal had unfolded right under their noses. Honorary secretary Arthur Wilson bore a particular burden of responsibility, for Richardson was in his charge. Perhaps distracted by his own busy professional life, Wilson largely left Richardson to his own devices, and assumed all was well. Indeed as late as the Annual General Meeting of Derbyshire County Cricket Club in March 1889, Wilson spoke in glowing terms of Richardson's credentials. Seconding a proposal that he be re-elected assistant honorary secretary, Wilson said: 'Mr. Richardson has been the backbone of the club since it started. We all owe a deep debt of gratitude to him.' This was met with a rousing 'Hear, Hear' and further backed up by another member of the finance committee who testified to 'the excellent manner in which Mr. Richardson has performed his duties.'

Yet by the cricket club's next AGM in 1890 the phrase 'deep debt' came back to haunt Arthur Wilson. Richardson had by then fled to Spain, and reflecting on his crime – for that it surely was – Wilson admitted: 'Richardson has had an extraordinary power, almost an imperial power, over the destiny of Derbyshire cricket.' And again, at the Derby County AGM in September 1890, Arthur Wilson displayed heartfelt regret. Revealing that the annual football accounts showed £140 and 5 shillings in ticket money 'not accounted for' he apologised to the cricket club's football counterparts in contrite terms: 'We are sorry Richardson treated you as he did us, and we only hope you will go on for another year and that things will turn out better.' Thus was enacted the climax to the first of the many financial scandals that have befallen Derby County over the passing seasons – blessedly they survived this initial fiasco to live another day, but only just.

As for Sam Richardson, the 'moments of weakness' changed his life's course. It seemed at first that he might brazen out the scandal by staying in Derby after he had resigned his post, and indeed his erstwhile colleagues may have tolerated his continued presence with a touch of pity, and not pressed charges. He had after all done a great deal of good work for the cricket and football club, effectively unpaid, so perhaps the benefit of the doubt was due. But Richardson quickly realised that he had spurned all possibility of a 'second chance', for further misdemeanours were soon to be revealed.

Since 1884 he had been the manager of the Derby branch of Messrs S & A Thompson clothiers and tailors, trading as S. Richardson & Co. from substantial retail premises at 40 Babington Lane. Early in 1890 they too had discovered that Richardson wasn't all he seemed – the tailor's 'cut' had included a portion of the takings. Faced with this further humiliation he decided to flee the town. He left Derby by the 2.05pm train to Nottingham on Saturday 18th January 1890. By 12th February – his whereabouts at that stage unknown – a warrant was issued by Derby magistrates for 'the arrest of Samuel Richardson on a charge of embezzlement from Messrs Thompson & Son'.

In fact the 45-year-old abscondee had fled rather further than Nottingham. He had crossed the Channel, journeyed through France, and pushed onward to the Spanish capital Madrid, where legal sanctuary was then guaranteed. There the interest in Samuel Richardson's story might readily have ended. But over time his new life eclipsed his old – he spent a further 47 years in Madrid, surviving to the ripe age of 93, remarkably with William and W. T. Morley the third nonogenarian from the earliest rank of Derby County officials. So the story bears concluding.

Previous allusions to Richardson's life in Spain have tacitly suggested he was an exile in lonely isolation, yet that was far from the case. For much of his time there he was supported by a loyal cast of females – in 1866, aged 22, he had married Derby-born Mary Ann Archer, and by the time of the flight to Spain in 1890 the couple had six daughters. In time Richardson's wife and several children – plus Haydn Morley Richardson an illegitimate grandchild fathered by Derby County captain Haydn Morley – joined him in Spain, the entire family adopting the name Roberts to cover their tracks. Thus the former Derbyshire cricketer and Derby County secretary Sam Richardson became John Roberts.

Secure in his new identity he fell back on tailoring. This had a great bearing on his new life in Spain, for he opened an English-style outfitters in the centre of Madrid and made a great success of the business. Indeed he received the official patronage of the Spanish monarch Alfonso XIII (1886-1941), supplying personal clothes to the royal household and winning lucrative contracts for ceremonial dress and uniforms. This placed Richardson's business well to the fore, and he grandly styled himself 'Court Tailor to the King of Spain'.

Richardson continued in tailoring well into his eighties. But his good fortune was destined to falter – his last few years witnessed more barren times. Political events in Spain had conspired against him when in 1931 his most valued customer King Alfonso was forced from the Spanish throne. Like Richardson before him, Alfonso fled into exile, living in the 'Grand Hotel' in Rome until his death.

Nor did the onset of the Spanish Civil War in 1936 help Sam Richardson's cause, and he lived out his final days in relative hardship. The last few months of his life were spent in Madrid's Anglo-American hospital, where he died on 18th January 1938 at the age of 93 years and 239 days. That made him the last survivor of Derbyshire's inaugural first-class cricket team – he was also decalred by the Spanish press 'Madrid's oldest British inhabitant'.

There ends the colourful story of a cricketer who yielded to temptation and was 'caught out'. So Derbyshire's first captain, and the man who 'kept the books' for Derby County, lies at peace in a Madrid cemetery far from the place of his birth. The death certificate names him John Roberts, but in the Derby County annals Samuel Richardson will always be 'Spanish Sam', who ran off with the takings and never came home.

'R.I.P. Samuel Richardson 1844-1938
May God Forgive Him'

ARTHUR WILSON
HE WEATHERED THE STORM

In addition to founder William Morley, the earliest written allusions to the formation of Derby County Football Club credit two men above all for piloting the new organisation through its turbulent infancy. One is the club's first President William Monk Jervis, and the other its first Honorary Secretary Arthur Wilson. In accepting ultimate responsibility for overseeing the financial affairs of both the cricket and football club, Arthur Wilson had burdened himself with an onerous task, and one not fully remunerated at that. When his assistant Sam Richardson defrauded the clubs of significant monies, that task was made more difficult still. The consequent deficits might have caused lesser men than Wilson to throw in the towel and disband operations. Derby County would then have had a very short life indeed. So it is to Wilson's credit, and a mark of his determined character, that he simply refused to accept defeat.

Arthur Wilson was born on 18th December 1843 in Mitcham, Surrey, into comfortable surroundings. Mitcham was at that time a hotbed of cricketing activity, so he was drawn early to the summer game. At the age of only 15 he played for the village club, being noted for his unerring enthusiasm rather than great ability. Educated at Rugby School he was considered good enough only for the fourth eleven, never winning his colours. This relative failure in the sporting arena actually had a beneficial consequence, for it led Wilson and a fellow 'duffer' A. G. Guillemard, to form their own cricket club in 1862, when still in their late teens. 'The Butterflies' was open initially only to Old Rugbeians who had never represented the school First XI – that elite breed already had their own club called The Pantaloons, which Wilson considered too exclusive. Soon after he went up to Oxford University, widening his circles, membership of The Butterflies was thrown open to the alumni of five other Public Schools – Eton, Harrow, Winchester, Charterhouse and Westminster – as a consequence Butterflies CC proved a great success, and members of the Pantaloons defected to it, resulting in that club's abandonment, whereas Butterflies remains in existence today. Arthur Wilson's pioneering foray into cricket 'management' led him later to repeat the success when in 1878 he provided the inspiration for the founding of the Derbyshire Friars Cricket Club.

These activities may seem remote from the doings of Derby County, but in fact have a sound bearing – namely that from a tender age Arthur Wilson had garnered a good track record in club administration, with all its attendant difficulties and keen rivalries. He was imbued with a certain resilience even before graduating. Moreover his involvement with Butterflies rendered him countless sporting contacts among former Public School and Varsity men – this proved advantageous when the earliest Derby County sides made overtures to recruits from those very ranks, or sought fixtures against the leading amateur clubs from the south. In short, Wilson brought a touch of 'class influence' to the Derby County committee, something that Chairman and founder William Morley possessed only to a much lesser degree.

Wilson went from Rugby School to Christ Church, Oxford, where in due course he took his MA degree with a view to entering the medical profession. Unfortunately badly failing eyesight compelled him to relinquish that intention, and through a subsequent romantic attachment his life took a turn which brought him to Derby, where on 22nd November 1870 he married Miss Matilda Davenport of Wilderslowe House, Osmaston Road. A Derby native of some standing, his bride was the daughter of a member of a well-known firm of silk throwsters with connections to an old Derby family. This brought Wilson into association with the management of a factory in Spa Lane, Derby, who engaged him for a position there. For some twenty years the couple resided in the outlying town of Melbourne, raising a family of three girls and three boys, but finally settled back in Derby at 30 Ashbourne Road.

Armed with the requisite experience, Wilson first took office at Derbyshire County Cricket Club in 1882 when he succeeded Walter Boden as Honorary Secretary. Apart from a short break in 1887 – when William Monk Jervis took the reins in the midst of a crisis – he stayed in that role until 1889. Thus his tenure spanned the entire formative period for Derby County – he was an enthusiastic backer of the formation of the club in 1884, and joined the committee as Honorary Secretary.

That he was let down badly by his more 'hands-on' assistant Sam Richardson – the embezzler of club funds – is in no doubt. Perhaps Wilson's public school ethos led him to believe that 'fair play' would always prevail, but Richardson didn't 'play the game'. Wilson was culpable of a degree of naivety in his lack of supervision, but nothing more sinister. Indeed the most important factor in the whole sorry affair was Wilson's reaction to it, for he refused to believe that either the cricket or football club was done for, instead taking steps to recruit a first paid secretary. Undoubtedly Wilson's never say die spirit and buoyant mood even in time of crisis helped to weather the storm.

Wilson's family too were most supportive. His wife and daughters were keen helpers at the sundry Grand Bazaars which raised emergency funds for the oft-styled 'Derby County Cricket and Football Club'. His daughter Theodora in particular became an avid Derby County supporter, penning occasional verse in praise of her sporting heroes. She remained a spinster.

There is no evidence that Wilson had ever excelled at football – cricket was his first love – but whilst at Rugby School he had embraced that establishment's pioneering ethos that the pursuit of organised sports had a beneficial effect on character development. As such, even the more robust football – coined by one contemporary writer 'the rude and manly game' – received Wilson's hearty patronage, despite his monocle, waxed moustache and passionate love of music seeming to mark him out as 'not the football type'. But his contribution was certainly recognised by his peers, evidenced by a fulsome tribute which appeared in the *Derby Mercury* after his passing:

> 'He was a very fine specimen of the best class of English sportsman – an educated gentleman who believed that the future of the country lay in the development of the sporting instincts of its classes. He gave his wholehearted support to every movement which was calculated to bring out in young men and the people of the race generally

their sense of sporting excellence, and during the whole of his life he gave to football and cricket his very best energies.'

Nor were his energies confined to sport. From the late 1890s he was a member of Derby Town Council, like most of the early Derby County officers a staunch Conservative in politics. He was also a governor of Derby School and a member of the Derby Board of Guardians. But above all a thoroughly popular character said to possess 'a considerable gift of humour and a wide knowledge of men and affairs.'

It is to be regretted that his end was premature. After a chill developed into pneumonia he passed away peacefully at his residence 30 Ashbourne Road, Derby, in the early afternoon of 7th November 1906, at the age of 62. Among the tributes paid was one which best epitomised the crucial part he played in safeguarding the very existence of the 'Derby County Cricket and Football Club':

'Of all the men that have been associated with the club, none have ever displayed more energy and enthusiasm and a greater determination not to be depressed by passing difficulties than Mr. Wilson. Indeed it is not too much to say, that but for him the club would at more than one crisis in its career have had a hard struggle to maintain its existence. It goes without saying that his infectious enthusiasm will be much missed by his colleagues who were associated with him in the management of club affairs.'

'R.I.P. Arthur Wilson 1843 -1906
steadfast to the cause'

CHAPTER NINE

Who's Who of the 'Chocolate and Blue' Derby County 1884 to 1888

'Oh! for the touch of the vanished men....
....and the cheers of the crowd that are gone.'
(Anonymous couplet Derbyshire Times, 1892)

The mini-biographies which follow have been created from many sources – extensive use of genealogical records and original newspapers the most useful. All players who made at least one first team appearance in the pre-League era 1884 to 1888 are included. Where any of these also played in the League era, those statistics have been added. Early players like Steve Bloomer who appeared only in the League age are not included – the *Who's Who of Derby County* by Gerald Mortimer has already covered them comprehensively.

Many players have been identified with absolute certainty. A few remain complete mystery men and have been labelled as such. In a number of cases the evidence threw up more than one possible candidate – rather than 'take a best guess' these entries are tagged 'inconclusive'.

Photographs of the earliest players are difficult to source. Of those located, many have come from early printed sources of variable quality – some players were captured only in old age, others via school photographs, but the majority are contemporary with their playing years. Overall it was felt better to include 'any' available image rather then none at all. If readers have further photographs or extra information, the publisher and author would be pleased to hear.

BAKEWELL George
Outside-right

Born: Queen Street, Derby, 13 May 1864
Died: 'Tower House', Cambridge Road, Ely, Cambridgeshire, 25 January 1928
Career: Derby School, Derby Whitworth, Derby Midland, Derby County 1884, Sheffield Wednesday, Notts County

The son of master baker George Bakewell senior, his father was able to send George to Derby School, where he made a mark as both footballer and athlete. Winning many prizes in local sprint races, he employed his lightning pace on the wing, defecting from Derby Midland to become Derby County's second 'signing' after his old Whitworth team-mate Haydn Morley had become the first. Noted for 'right-angled crosses on the run', he played in the opening fixture and soon became a crowd favourite dubbed the

'Demon of the Wing' – in time made captain and seldom absent in the first four seasons. Bakewell was so well respected by the County hierarchy that in June 1888 when still a player he was elected to the club committee. Despite playing one game for Sheffield Wednesday in March 1885, and one for Notts County in March 1887, he was loyal to Derby into the League era, scoring twice in their opening League game – and the first Derby player to reach both 100 and 150 games for the club. When eventually lured to Notts County in July 1891 he played five League games there. He came 'very close to England honours' but never got beyond representing the North in the trial games against the South. Beginning work in his teens as a railway clerk at Derby station, he had a chequered employment history – at times assisting his father, rejoining and again leaving the Midland Railway, having a brief abortive interlude as a law student, then in 1887 setting up his own bakery shop on Normanton Road, only to close it down in 1891. After his football days ended he termed himself 'out of work' or 'retired'. This reflected wider troubles – indeed it is painful to reveal that the 'idol of the crowd' had 'feet of clay' and suffered a turbulent personal life encapsulated by three court appearances. In 1897 his wife Florence was granted a separation order on grounds of persistent cruelty, being given custody of their three young sons. Regular insobriety was cited as a problem. They later reunited but parted again following a 1900 case in which Bakewell was found guilty of severely thrashing his sons aged 9 and 6. And in 1915 a court in Brentwood, Essex, ordered him to pay maintenance in support of an illegitimate child. Adding to his woes, his youngest son Horace died aged 23 when his ship *HMS Indefatigable* went down at the Battle of Jutland in 1916. Bakewell then lived alone in Derby, but moved away and faded from the scene. As the saying then went, he had 'fallen on evil times' – the former Derby School boy had been working as a labourer when he died aged 63 in the Infirmary wing of the Ely Poor Law Institution. No newspaper appears to have reported his passing – a poignant end to a man who despite his failings remains a stirring presence in Derby County's early history.

Appearances: Pre-League: 135 apps 1884-85 to 1887-88, 27 goals. League era: 54 apps 1888-89 to 1890-91, 10 goals. Total: 189 apps 1884-85 to 1890-91, 37 goals

BASSANO Henry
Right-back

Born: Derby, 1865
Died: Boundary House, Uttoxeter Road, Derby, 1 November 1928
Career: St. Luke's, Derby County 1886, Derby Midland

When St. Luke's regular full-back played against Derby County in January 1887 he was labelled 'very safe and worked like a Trojan.' A few games later he appeared for Derby only for another reporter to observe that 'he is hardly class enough for the County'. Although none of his three senior games were lost, Bassano proved merely solid but uninspiring, and the regular berth was ultimately regained by the rather classier Arthur Latham, an experienced back who had been deputising at centre-half. Bassano was also tried out by Derby Midland but again could not break through. He resumed with 'Saints' and otherwise assisted Derby County Wanderers. Bassano enjoyed Italian lineage – 'via the early 16th century musician Jeronimo di Bassano from the Venetian town of Bassano del Grappa'. After two of Jeronimo's sons were recruited by Henry VIII as court musicians, the Bassanos established themselves as one of the oldest musical families in England. The Derby link was forged when descendant Christopher Bassano married and settled there in 1709. Henry was the son of electrical manufacturer George Henry Bassano whose experiments with audio technology led to his invention circa 1906 of the 'Bassanophone', a pioneering disc gramophone. Henry pursued a similar business with only sporadic success. His 1892 marriage produced a son, but after losing his wife he remarried a widowed licensee in 1912 – together they ran the Lord Raglan in Clover Street until her death in 1925. He had been living at 658 Osmaston Road when he died aged 63 in the infirmary wing of Boundary House Institution, the former Derby Union Workhouse.

Appearances: 3 apps 1886-87, 0 goals

BELLAMY William
Outside-right

Born: Long Bennington near Newark, Lincolnshire, 1856
Died: Derbyshire Royal Infirmary, Derby, 4 March 1946
Career: Derby Town, Derby Midland, Derby County 1884

In the early 1880s 'Billy' Bellamy was a stalwart of Derby Town, the nearest club to a genuine forerunner of Derby County. He had already transferred his allegiance to the railway side Derby Midland when he made his sole appearance for Derby in November 1884, a controversial 7-0 loss to Derby Junction. 'Mids' colleague 'Harry' Evans also made his only Derby County appearance in the same game. Bellamy was a real crowd-pleaser – 'a very clever dribbler with peculiar abilities as an artful dodger, his trickiness sent the crowd wild with delight.' The son of agricultural labourer turned railway worker Robert Bellamy, he followed a migratory route typical of the time, leaving rural Lincolnshire for a job in Derby with the Midland Railway, giving long-service as a clerk in the Superintendent's Office at Derby Station. In 1886 he became one of the first Derby County players embroiled in a personal scandal, all gleefully reported by the press, when he was made to pay £50 compensation – over half his annual salary – to a jilted Leeds girl in a 'breach of promise' case. Extracts from his countless fervent letters to 'my idol' were read out in court and printed in the Derby papers, where he was jocularly dubbed the 'railway clerk lover'. Perhaps cowed by the experience, he married only when into his forties – and after losing his wife in 1916 remained solo. In later years he became a noted bowls enthusiast, still an active player in his mid-80s. He was 89 when he fell and broke a leg, but insisted on getting about before the fracture was diagnosed several weeks later – he had been living at 49 Wilfred Street when he died of pneumonia accentuated by the fall.

Appearances: 1 app 1884-85, 0 goals

BESTWICK Thomas Henry
Goalkeeper

Born: Long Eaton, Derbyshire, 30 August 1864
Died: 3, Breedon Street, Long Eaton, Derbyshire, 30 July 1946
Career: Long Eaton Rovers, Long Eaton Rangers, Derby County 1885

Son of lace draughtsman Thomas senior, 'Harry' Bestwick made his name with Long Eaton Rangers before joining Derby County in 1885-86. Despite some torrid days – twice letting in seven in his debut season – he became the club's first truly regular keeper, surviving long enough to play a single game in the League era. A tribute recalled: 'He always kept goal in long trousers and was a good keeper, often conspicuous by throwing himself at the uprights in endeavouring to stop dangerous shots, and taking ugly risks.' The first Derby custodian to reach 50 appearances, he might have made his century, but commitments as a lace designer and mill manager hastened his withdrawal from serious football. A lifelong resident of Long Eaton, after retiring from work in the 1920s he gained distinction in the game of bowls with Long Eaton West Park, winning his county badge for both Derbyshire and Nottinghamshire. At 70 he was invited to tour America and Canada with the England bowling team but decided not to go. A further passion was sea angling – he recorded in his 'catches book' that in Filey on a single day in 1939 he landed 100 cod at the age of 74. Bestwick reached 80 still very active, but then suffered ill-health. He died aged 81 leaving a widow and two sons, living just long enough to know that Derby County had won the FA Cup.

Appearances: Pre-League: 72 apps 1885-86 to 1887-88, goals conceded 134. League era: 1 app 1888-89, goals conceded 0. Total: 73 apps 1885-86 to 1888-89. Goals conceded 134

BINGHAM Albert
Inside-left

Born: Derby, 21 August 1865
Died: Breadsall Hospital, Derby, 14 October 1933 (Estate value £728. 13s 11d)
Career: Derby County 1887

On Christmas Eve 1887 Derby County were committed to two fixtures both considered first-team status. Reserve player Bingham made his sole full appearance in a makeshift forward-line at Sheffield Wednesday. Only nine Derby men were able to travel, so two were borrowed on arrival at the ground. The 8-0 defeat was hardly surprising. The result back at the County Ground was rather better – Eckington Works were beaten 7-2 in a Derbyshire Cup replay dubbed 'Gwynne's game'. Albert Bingham was the son of architect-builder Henry Bingham. An artistic bent led him to become a lithographic draughtsman for the well-known Bemrose printing and design firm. He died aged 68 at the Isolation Hospital in Breadsall, leaving an only daughter and a modest estate.

Appearances: 1 app 1887-88, 0 goals

BIRCH-THORPE Charles Edwin
Half-back

Born: Bedworth, Warwickshire, 5 October 1865
Died: 20 Mill Hill Road, Derby, 27 February 1951 (Estate value £792. 14s)
Career: Derby Whitworth, Derby County 1884, Darley Abbey, Midland Railway Managers XI

C. E. Birch-Thorpe played in Derby's first ever home game while still only 18, although quite 'by accident'. The step-son of Derby County committee member Albert Thorpe – manager of Weston's Elastic Manufactory – he happened to be on the spot when the initial selection Frank Sugg cabled to say he had missed his train. Thereafter Thorpe appeared for Darley Abbey before becoming an enthusiastic member of the Derby County Wanderers, adding only three more first-team games in 1887-88. The son of plumber Edwin Birch, he lost his father in infancy. After his mother re-married, Charles acquired the name Thorpe, but later styled himself Birch-Thorpe. He began as a clerk with the Midland Railway at 15, and retired 48 years later in a senior well-paid position, Superintendent of the Season Ticket Department. Married with one son, both he and his wife were keen vocalists, regularly performing at local gatherings. Charles was also a leading light in the lively Macaw Minstrels troupe with several others from the Derby County Wanderers, and a founder member of Derby Operatic Society. He continued to play football into the 'veteran' stage, in 1898-99 captaining the General Managers' team which won the Midland Railway League. He stayed involved with Derby County as a shareholder and keen follower. He was on the committee of both Derby Swimming Club and Harriers Athletic Club and an enthusiast of golf, tennis and angling. His only son William Noel Birch-Thorpe, a gunner in the Royal Field Artillery, was killed aged 24 in France in February 1918. In contrast Charles lived beyond Derby County's 1946 FA Cup win – he died aged 85 at his Derby home. His wife lived a further nine years.

Appearances: 4 apps 1884-85 to 1887-88, 0 goals

BOOTH Herbert Drewry
Half-back

Born: Derby, 1864
Died: 41 Regent Street, Derby, 12 January 1932 (Estate value £604. 10s)
Career: Derby Midland, Derby County 1888, Derby Midland

The son of Derby coal merchant William Booth was a clerk with the Midland Railway and playing for the strong works side when Derby County gave him a try. He assisted the reserves but played three consecutive games in the first team towards the end of 1887-88 – deputising twice for Walter Roulstone and once for Albert Williamson. Despite two wins and a draw, the regular half-backs were so reliable that Booth had little chance of breaking through, and he rejoined Derby Midland for the few seasons prior to their absorption by Derby County. He lived in the family home in Regent Street in the Litchurch area and remained a bachelor. In common with a small group of other Derby reserves he was a keen vocalist, singing at various gatherings around the town, particularly those for the Conservative cause at the Beaconsfield Club. He became head of the family, and died aged 67 taking his rare 'unbeaten record' with him.

Appearances: 3 apps 1887-88, 0 goals

BOSWORTH
Goalkeeper

Born: Inconclusive
Died: Inconclusive
Career: Derby Midland, Derby County 1888

Kept a clean sheet in his only game – the last match of 1887-88 against the mighty Preston North End, a benefit for Derby secretary Sam Richardson. Bosworth was then more regularly assisting Derby Midland. Although listed in the line-up as J. Bosworth, this could be an error for the G. Bosworth more regularly listed as a local keeper. Alternatively there may be two Bosworth custodians active at that time. Either way, conclusive donation of the jersey is not possible on current evidence.

Appearances: 1 app 1887-88, goals conceded 0

BOWER Henry
Full-back and half-back

Born: Chesterfield, 1864
Died: 'At sea', last address 317, King Street, Dukinfield, near Manchester, 26 October 1915 (Estate value £215. 10s 8d)
Career: Chesterfield Spital, Derby County 1886, Chesterfield Spital, Hyde

Derby County had increasingly begun to raid Derbyshire's northern outposts when early in 1886-87 they tried out the Chesterfield Spital full-back 'Harry' Bower (often styled Bowers), son of iron-moulder Thomas. Doubtless he thought the task easy, for his first two games were won 7-2 and 6-1 against quality sides Sheffield Town and Bolton Wanderers. After his debut a report described him as 'lumps in front of Hales' – the one-gamer from Breaston who he had replaced – but added a telling rider: 'At the same time he is only a second-rater, and not up to County form'. Indeed the two defeats which followed proved his final outings. The *Derbyshire Times* acidly asserted after the second that 'as cover for Latham, Bower proved a very feeble substitute'. Misfortune continued to plague him – after relocating to the Manchester area as an engine fitter, he played in the Hyde side which lost 26-0 at Preston North End in the 1887 Cup. Bower perhaps sensed the worst – with the score only 3-0 he departed the field 'injured' after 17 minutes. Bizarrely the Hyde goalkeeper that day was widely praised for 'keeping the score down' – the former Chesterfield keeper Charlie Bunyan who later signed for Derby County. Others with Derby links played in the same game – not least the Rams' future star John Goodall, who pulled the strings for Preston. Bower married a divorcee in 1894 but the couple later split in acrimonious circumstances luridly reported in the press. He seems never to have remarried. The sad headlines continued to the last – his death aged 51 was recorded 'at sea' in circumstances not fully explained.

Appearances: 4 apps 1886-87, 0 goals

BRAYSHAW Edward
Full-back and half-back

Born: Sheffield, 6 October 1863
Died: Wadsley Bridge, Sheffield, 20 November 1908
Career: Walkley All Saints, Bethel United, Sheffield Wednesday, Derby County 1887, Sheffield Wednesday, Grimsby Town, England (1 cap).

After regular right-back Arthur Latham was moved to centre-half midway through 1886-87, Derby cast around for a good replacement. 'Teddy' Brayshaw of Sheffield Wednesday was one of the men tried – the 'fearless full-back with a huge return' made his debut under the name E. 'Brown' before fully identifying himself. His first three games all ended in victory but proved the limit of his stay. He played once for England at centre-half and in the 1890 Cup final for Wednesday alongside former Derby favourite Haydn Morley. After 'retiring' through injury in 1891 he made a comeback in 1892-93 with Grimsby Town. His life was beset by periodic troubles from a young age – when only four his Police Detective father Richard died. After marrying he ran a public house in Sheffield and later worked as a joiner, but was also one of the first well-known footballers whose stormy private life got into the papers. Under the lurid headline 'Ted Brayshaw's Domestic Relations' the *Sheffield Telegraph* revealed that in August 1891 he had deserted his wife Clara 'entirely without provocation' and then 'gone missing'. A bitter court case ensued. It proved the start of a sad decline for the former England man – his later life said to be 'marked by poverty, misery and despair'. He was admitted to Wadsley Bridge Asylum in Sheffield in 1907, and died there a year later aged 45.

Appearances: 3 apps 1886-87, 0 goals

BRIGGS John Morley
Forward

Born: Alvaston, Derby, 1865
Died: 'Alvaston Grange', Alvaston, Derby, 27 October 1924 (Estate value £6050. 11s 4d)
Career: Osmaston Rectory School, Alvaston and Boulton, Derby Whitworth, Derby County 1884

John Briggs was a reliable member of the tight-knit group who represented the reserves – Derby County Wanderers – in their own full fixture list. His first-team debut was in a prestigious home fixture against Casuals during the stretched Christmas period in the opening season. He played once more but was otherwise unable to supplant the likes of Spilsbury, Bakewell and 'Jammer' Smith. The sixth son of gentleman-farmer Robert Briggs of Alvaston, he attended Osmaston Rectory School in Derby prior to qualifying as a solicitor. Well-known in legal circles throughout the Midlands, he remained a bachelor living in the family home Alvaston Grange. He was a good club cricketer for Alvaston, in company with Rams colleagues Percy Sherwin and more occasionally Haydn Morley, a fellow solicitor. At his death aged 58 his financial legacy somewhat outweighed his sporting one.

Appearances: 2 apps, 1884-85, 0 goals

BROMAGE Enos
Goalkeeper

Born: Mickleover, Derby, 30 April 1864
Died: Derbyshire Royal Infirmary, Derby, 25 March 1947
Career: Derby Junction, Derby County 1885, Derby Junction, Derby County 1889

Between spells with Derby in both the pre-League and League eras, Bromage kept goal for Derby Junction, which was certainly his first love – the club was founded by his father, brickyard owner Henry 'Harry' Bromage, patriarch of a dynasty which ultimately supplied several Bromages to both Derby and other clubs. Enos had been the Junction centre-forward, but ironically took to goalkeeping after 'injuring his eye' in a nasty collision. He made his Derby debut towards the end of the opening season, but in two pre-League campaigns made only four appearances, otherwise staying loyal to 'Juncs'. The Derby County committee were encouraged when he agreed to play in the last two games of the inaugural Football League season. This turned to delight when he joined Derby more formally for 1889-90 as regular replacement for the departed Joe Marshall. Their belief that they had made a great capture seemed vindicated – of the first eleven games only three were lost. And when Bromage missed the next two, his replacement Reuben Pitman was beaten ten times. Back came Bromage for three good wins on the trot, but his next two outings left a stain on his career. A 5-0 defeat at Preston in January 1890 was directly followed by a loss at Everton in the Cup which remains Derby's heaviest ever. Bromage was said to be 'completely beset by nerves' as Everton completed an 11-2 rout – he was never selected again. Away from football Bromage worked in the family brickmaking business, but later moved to Littleover and found employment as a dairyman. Married with one daughter, he had been living at her home 1 Thornhill Road when he died aged 82. Only a year previously Derby had finally won the FA Cup competition which had given Enos Bromage his most torrid ordeal.

Appearances: Pre-League: 4 apps 1884-85 to 1885-86, goals conceded 6. League era: 18 apps 1888-89 to 1889-90, goals conceded 50. Total: 22 apps 1884-85 to 1889-90, goals conceded 56.

'BROWN'
See HILL Charles

One of a number of pseudonymous appearances in Derby County's early days. The 'Brown' who appeared 'out of the blue' on 29 December 1884 is thought to be Trent College goalkeeper Charles Hill, who became Derby's most regular keeper of the opening season.

'BROWN' E.
See BRAYSHAW Edward

Against Wolverhampton Wanderers on 22 February 1887 Derby County's debutant right-back was identified only as E. 'Brown'. When playing again five games later the mystery man was unmasked as the Sheffield Wednesday and England back of the same initials Edward Brayshaw. It proved a brief dalliance – after only three appearances Brayshaw again hooked up with Wednesday.

BROWN Thomas
Full-back and half-back

Born: Darley Abbey, Derbyshire, 1865
Died: Darley Abbey, Derbyshire, 1904
Career: Darley Abbey, Derby County 1887, Derby Midland

In common with a number of others, Tom Brown's career embraced Darley Abbey, Derby Midland and Derby County. He was a regular in the Derby County Wanderers side in 1886-87, but was promoted only once, when Derby had two designated first team fixtures on a single day. Almost the full Wanderers side was sent to Sheffield Town, where they met with a 5-3 defeat. By 1887-88 Brown was registered as a professional with Derby Midland, who in 1891 would be absorbed by their foremost rivals Derby County. The son of bobbin turner Arthur Titus Brown, Thomas was still an infant when his father died. He was afterwards brought up by relatives in Chesterfield, but returned in his teens to work in Darley Abbey as a cotton mill hand. He was later a warehouseman and a maltster's clerk. Married with three children, he died aged 39 in his home village.

Appearances: 1 app 1886-87, 0 goals

BURGESS
Left-back

Born: Inconclusive
Died: Inconclusive

One-gamer Burgess was listed as 'borrowed on the ground' for the 3-3 draw at Darwen on 13 December 1884 when Derby County arrived a man short. This was because Harry Warmby failed to turn up to travel, opting to play instead for St. Luke's. Nothing more concerning the identity of Burgess has come to light.

Appearances: 1 app 1884-85, 0 goals

'CAMERON' R. T.
See JACKSON Harry

The pseudonymous R. T. 'Cameron' listed at home to Blackburn Rovers on 19 March 1887 – described only as a 'well-known forward from a neighbouring town' – was by his second outing unmasked as Notts County centre-forward Harry Jackson. In the pre-television age – when the faces of opposition players were not widely familiar – pseudonyms could prove effective in maintaining anonymity at least in the short term. The subterfuge was generally used by a player 'trying out' – largely to prevent news reaching his own club until necessary. In practice the press were seldom slow to reveal all.

CHATTERTON William
Forward

Born: Thornsett, Birch Vale, Derbyshire, 27 December 1861
Died: Flowery Field, Hyde, Cheshire, 18 March 1913
Career: Derby County 1884

Best known as one of Derbyshire's finest cricketers, 'Chatty' assisted Derby County through to the first League season, one of four Test cricketers to appear for them. He also acted as the club groundsman during the same period. A versatile and speedy forward, with a healthy goals ratio, he was considered an even better rugby player – 'one of the fastest three-quarters of his day' – assisting the short-lived Derby County Rugby Club and later Cheshire and Burton-on-Trent. But cricket dominates – he was just 18 when he moved south to accept his first professional engagement at Christ's College, Finchley. Proving effective, he came to Derbyshire's attention, playing for them from 1882 to 1902 and captaining the side between 1887 and 1889. 'One of the most graceful batsmen of his era', he scored 10,914 runs in 289 first-class matches, also taking 208 wickets. In his one Test innings in South Africa in 1892 he scored 48 and finished as the tour's chief run-maker. Later as a coach in Durham and Cambridge he counted the sons of gentry amongst his charges, and in 1901 created a new cricket pitch at Sandringham on the instructions of the newly-crowned King Edward VII. This stood in stark contrast to Chatterton's humble background – the son of millworker Daniel Chatterton, he was working at the age of 10 in a printworks, and by 1881 was carrying cotton at Newton near Hyde. In the 1890s he ran the Victoria Inn near Derby station, when he was also on the referees' list for Football League games. It was said that he 'fell on evil times' when his cricket days ended – he had a wife and daughter but was living in his father's house at the time of his death aged only 51. Even so the *Derby Daily Telegraph* laced his laudatory obituary with unashamed affection: 'With all his faults and failings it was impossible not to like his engaging personality and breezy originality of manner. He has been called to his last account amidst the sorrowful regrets of all who knew him. We wish no more than for his epitaph to read – 'After life's fitful fever he sleeps well'.'

Appearances: Pre-League: 20 apps 1884-85 to 1887-88, 10 goals. League era: 5 apps 1888-89, 1 goal. Total: 25 apps 1884-85 to 1888-89, 11 goals

CHEVALLIER John Barrington Trapnell
Centre-forward

Born: Aspall Hall, Aspall, Suffolk, 10 January 1857
Died: Aspall Hall, Aspall, Suffolk, 17 February 1940 (Estate value £10,049 16s 9d)
Career: Eton College, Swifts, Cambridge University, Old Etonians, Derby County 1884, Ipswich Town

Son of a landed clergyman, the Etonian J. B. T. Chevallier belonged to the unpaid 'gentleman amateur' breed ubiquitous in football in the 1860s and 1870s. He played into the transitional 1880s, but after professionalism was legalised in 1885 football increasingly became the province of the lower echelons. As such Chevallier and his ilk add a curious mystique to the early Derby ranks. At King's College Cambridge he gained a first class BA in mathematics (1880) and won his football blue. Twice an FA Cup winner with Old Etonians in 1879 and 1882, and a runner-up in 1881 and 1883, he was described as 'a hard-working forward, possessing both weight and pace, energetic and very useful to his side.' After becoming an assistant master at Lancing College (1880 to 1883) he moved to Repton School (1883 to 1885) and first appeared for Derby County in their opening home game. Although named official captain for the season, teaching duties severely limited his appearances. Some sources credit Chevallier with a 'final touch' on his debut, but he first scored conclusively in Derby's first ever win, at Repton on 28 October 1884, when he bagged a brace. He bettered this on 31 January 1885 in Derby's inaugural encounter with Nottingham Forest, plundering a hat-trick in a sensational 6-1 away win. In the season's final game at home to Notts County, he was again on the mark in a 2-0 victory, thus helping claim two coveted local scalps which cemented Derby's reputation in their first campaign. But departure was imminent. During the close-season he inherited the family estate and cider-making business at Aspall Hall, where he established himself as a fruit grower and innovated the newly-styled Aspall 'cyder'. A man of great energy and fine repute, he also continued tutoring into the next century, taking in boarders at the Hall. Yet he still found time to become a noted breeder of Red Poll cattle, a Suffolk JP, President of the Suffolk Chamber of Agriculture and a director of the Mid-Suffolk Light Railway. He is credited besides with one appearance for Ipswich Town in April 1886. He was aged 40 when in 1897 he married Isobel Amy Cobbold, twelve years his junior – the couple had three daughters. When Chevallier died aged 83 his obituary noted the celebrated statesman and soldier Lord Kitchener as his first cousin. J. B. T. Chevallier seems light years away from today's professional game, yet he played a key part in Derby County's important early steps, not least in raising the club's profile in influential circles. Curiously his name lingers on modern lips to this very day – his trademark 'Aspall Cyder' is a leading brand.

Appearances: 13 apps 1884-85, 7 goals

CLIFTON George
Half-back

Born: Long Eaton, 1865
Died: 20, Richmond Avenue, Breaston, Derbyshire, 2 February 1947 (Estate value £851. 2s 10d)
Career: Long Eaton Rangers, Derby County 1886, Long Eaton Rangers, Derby County 1888

One of the Long Eaton Rangers clan who so ably assisted Derby County in their first few seasons. Clifton got his chance early in 1886-87 after Haydn Morley, Jack Flower and 'Jesse' Cooper all defected from the Rams. He scored on his winning debut – in the pivotal midfield role which was then 'centre-half' – playing 20 games there before versatile former full-back Arthur Latham replaced him. Although resuming with Long Eaton he also played once for Derby in the opening football League season. The son of master shoemaker James Clifton, he was twice married to brides some years his junior. A lace threader in his playing days, he subsequently had contrasting interludes as an Eastwood policeman and landlord of the Royal Oak in Clay Cross near Chesterfield, but later returned to the lace trade in Breaston. One of the few pre-League players to live beyond Derby County's 1946 FA Cup triumph – he died a year later aged 81.

Appearances: Pre-League: 20 apps 1886-87, 1 goal. League era: 1 app 1888-89, 0 goals. Total: 21 apps 1886-87 to 1888-89, 1 goal.

COCHRANE Alfred Henry John
Forward

Born: Moka, Mauritius, 26 January 1865
Died: 'Elm Hurst', Batheaston, Somerset, 14 December 1948 (Estate value £13,383. 4s 2d)
Career: Repton School, Oxford University, Derby County 1884

'Useful and never showy' the fresh-faced undergraduate A. H. J. Cochrane played four times in the opening season when home from Oxford, where he gained his degree at Hertford College. Born in Mauritius – where his father the Revd. David Crawford Cochrane was chaplain to the Bishop – he was brought up in

Etwall, Derbyshire, after his father became vicar of the parish and Master of Etwall Hospital. With three of his brothers Alfred attended Repton School where he was captain of football and excelled at cricket. He later wrote a *History of Repton Cricket*, contributed numerous sporting articles to *The Times*, and was a governor of Repton for over twenty years. He was unusually a right-hand batsman and left-arm medium bowler – in 28 first-class cricket matches 1884-88 he averaged only 10.51 with the bat, but took 103 wickets at a decent average of 18.99. All but six of his games were for Oxford University, but he appeared four times for Derbyshire in 1884 and 1886 – one of the elite 'Derby Double' group to play for both Derbyshire and Derby County. After graduating he joined the administrative staff of the Armstrong engineering works at Elswick, Newcastle on Tyne, rising to become the Armstrong Whitworth company secretary. In 1895 he married Ethel Noble, daughter of Armstrongs' future chairman Sir Andrew Noble – the couple remained childless and lived in some style at the Manor House, Jesmond, with a complement of servants. In the January 1910 General Election Cochrane stood as the unsuccessful Conservative and Unionist candidate for the Tyneside constituency. He fared better as a writer – his *Early History of Elswick* (1909) reflected an interest in antiquity, but he also produced poetry and light verse, some in humorous vein. One stanza 'to a sweetheart' quizzically confessed 'I once admitted to my shame, that football was a brutal game, because she hates it'. His *Later Verses* were published in 1919. Cochrane's enduring legacy to Repton was the school song 'To the Founder' which he penned in 1907 to mark the school's 350th anniversary. One of the most intriguing characters to wear a Derby shirt, he was living near Bath when he died aged 83. His wife lived until 1961 – his poetry remains in print.

Appearances: 4 apps 1884-85, 1 goal

COOPER George Frederick
Half-back

Born: Derby, 25 July 1859
Died: City Hospital, Derby, 1 February 1939 (Estate value £3,883. 2s)
Career: Derby Midland, Derby County 1885, Derby Midland

Known by his family nickname 'Jesse', great surprise was expressed when he defected from Derby Midland at the start of 1885-86, it being observed that 'no man was considered more loyal to the Mids than Jesse Cooper' – a perfect illustration of the pulling power of Derby County, and why such animosity was engendered between the newcomers and older-established Derby clubs. Cooper was a regular throughout the second season but in 1886-87 renewed his allegiance to Derby Midland, playing only twice more in a County shirt when asked to help out. He was labelled 'one of football's true Greathearts who made every game a Waterloo', while Midland team-mate L. G. Wright observed that 'few opponents cared to run against him a second time – his bones left painful memories.' The son of a pattern maker on the railway, Cooper was an iron moulder, one of the breed of 'ordinary working men' who later came to dominate football, but were less ubiquitous in the pre-League era. He married and had ten children, progressively moving home before settling in Pybus Street. He spent his entire life in Derby and died there aged 79.

Appearances: 31 apps 1885-86 to 1887-88, 0 goals

COOPER Lewis
Forward

Born: Shottle Gate, Belper, Derbyshire, 1864
Died: 26, Lichfield Drive, Alvaston, Derby, 12 February 1937 (Estate value £484. 12s 10d)
Career: Darley Abbey, Derby County 1884, Grimsby Town, Derby County 1888

Cooper's boyish looks when he began with Darley Abbey earned him the lifelong nickname 'Kid'. After he joined Derby County in December of their opening season, the *Derby Daily Telegraph* labelled him 'a young renegade' for deserting the 'Abbots', but he still assisted them in odd games, most pointedly against Derby County when both he and Ernest Hickinbottom asked for permission to play with their old club. In time he became a Derby County stalwart and a real crowd favourite dubbed the 'Prince of Artful Dodgers' – small in stature, known for his tricky skills and quick feet, he adapted to most forward positions, and was always a source of goals, notching 26 in 1886-87, when he was on the mark in 9 consecutive games – 12 goals in all – a successive scoring sequence which remains a club record. Derby were disappointed when he accepted professional terms with Grimsby Town for 1887-88, but after failing to settle he resumed with Derby after one season. In fact he played in Derby's final game of 1887-88 – a testimonial played in May after the regular season had concluded – and in the next campaign scored twice in their opening League game. Before he bowed out in March 1892, his long service was marked by a benefit game in November 1891 against Birmingham St. George's, when he scored in a 7-2 victory. The son of carpenter Francis Cooper, the family moved to Derby when Lewis was an infant. He grew up in a row of cottages named 'Folly Houses' – still standing on the banks of the Derwent near Darley Park. After marrying he worked at Haslam's Foundry for over 50 years, living in Leyland Street before retiring to Alvaston. In 1934 he was one of the few players from 1884-85 who attended Derby County's Golden Jubilee Dinner – 'Kid' Cooper died three years later aged 72.

Appearances: Pre-League: 96 apps 1884-85 to 1887-88, 42 goals.
League era: 54 apps 1888-89 to 1891-92, 26 goals. Total: 150 apps 1884-85 to 1891-92, 68 goals

COOPER W
Right-back

Born: Inconclusive
Died: Inconclusive

Cooper was one of two men 'found on the ground' after Derby County turned up two short on Christmas Eve 1887 for a game at Sheffield Wednesday. Not surprisingly the home side ran out 8-0 winners. The selection difficulty arose because Derby had to play a Derbyshire Cup replay against Eckington on the same day. Nothing further is known of stand-in W. Cooper.

Appearances: 1 app 1887-88, 0 goals

CROPPER William
Centre-forward

Born: Brimington, Derbyshire, 27 December 1862
Died: Clee Park, Cleethorpes near Grimsby, Lincolnshire, 13 January 1889
Career: Spital, Eckington Works, Derby County 1886, Staveley

'Will' Cropper made three consecutive appearances in 1886-87 but otherwise played for north-east Derbyshire teams, ultimately joining Staveley in October 1888. One admirer rated him 'speedy on the ball, a clever dribbler, difficult to stop, and a splendid shot at goal noted for his low lightning-like shooting' – but he never scored for Derby. Cropper was better-known as a cricketer – after making his Derbyshire debut in 1882 he scored 1,636 runs in 60 first-class matches and took 171 wickets, batting right-handed and bowling left. He was also a valued club cricketer for Brimington and others – when assisting Bolton in July 1886 he took eleven wickets in the game. The son of mason and master builder John Cropper, he remained single and became a bricklayer in his father's thriving business, said to be 'much-liked by all classes'. Fate seemingly favoured Cropper when on Saturday 23 January 1886 he should have played for Eckington Works against Derby Junction but failed to turn up – ten minutes into the game his 18-year-old replacement suffered a kick in the stomach and died on Sunday morning. But perchance Cropper's end was pre-ordained. On Saturday 12 January 1889 playing for Staveley at Grimsby Town he suffered a kick in the stomach ten minutes into the game and died on Sunday morning. He had remained overnight in Grimsby's clubhouse under watchful care – but internal poisoning caused by a ruptured bowel ended his life aged 26. Much sympathy was aroused and in death he gained the sobriquet 'Poor Will Cropper'. An obituary said –

'Cropper was a gentleman in the true sense of the word and a man who might always be looked upon as a staunch and true friend. He gained a reputation for kindness and other endearing qualities and will be sorely missed.' A large sum was raised by public subscription for an elaborate gravestone crafted in white Sicilian marble by Belper sculptor James Beresford – the enduring monument to one of Derbyshire's most tragic sporting lives stands in Brimington Cemetery. The notion that his accident gave rise to the phrase 'to come a cropper' is fanciful – it is a much earlier horse-riding term coined by the hunting community.

Appearances: 3 apps 1886-87, 0 goals

CUBLEY Francis Edward
Full-back

Born: Derby, 1865
Died: City Hospital, Nottingham, 1 November 1950 (Estate value £289. 15s 10d)
Career: Derby Town, Derby Whitworth, Derby Diocesan, Derby County 1885

One of three brothers who attended Derby School, Frank Cubley played a single game as an emergency stand-in 'found on the ground' when Frank Sugg failed to arrive. He marked the occasion by scoring in a 1-1 draw with Nottingham Forest. Thereafter he reverted to his level, a good local club player occasionally assisting Derby County Wanderers. The son of painter and decorator William Cubley, he began work as an ironmonger's clerk, but after marrying Lily Evelina Wade in 1892 moved to Nottingham where he set up a window cleaning business. The couple's only daughter died in childhood. After losing his wife in 1946 he had been living at 142 Russell Road when he died in hospital in Nottingham aged 85. Older brother Lawson was the superior footballer, and would surely have played full-back regularly for Derby County had he not removed to Hull to pursue his career as a naval architect and ship's draughtsman. Lawson also became a prominent figure in rugby football, a vice-president and secretary of Hull Football Club, still a famous name in Rugby League. Frank outlived him by 13 years.

Appearances: 1 app 1884-85, 1 goal

CUPIT Sampson
Goalkeeper

Born: Stretton, near Alfreton, Derbyshire, 1859
Died: Vancouver, Canada, 22 March 1913
Career: Derby County 1887

The adage that 'goalkeepers are different' might have been created for Sampson Cupit. He appeared only once – listed as Sergeant Cupit – when in March 1887 Derby County found themselves committed to two first team fixtures on the same day. Rather than face the might of Blackburn Rovers at the County Ground, Cupit took guard at Sheffield Town, where a mixed selection was defeated 5-3. Cupit stood at something of a disadvantage, for his army record indicates he was not quite 5 feet 5 inches tall. The son of engine tenter Thomas Cupit, he joined the army in 1877 as a general labourer, serving in Gibraltar and Egypt but mostly based in England. By 1881 he was with the 95th Regiment in Aldershot, where he married, and a year later his daughter Annie was born in Gibraltar. In Derby he was at Normanton Barracks, playing football and cricket for the 45th Regimental Depot. Cupit left the army in 1899 ranked Quartermaster Sergeant – after a brief civilian stint in Nottingham as stock-keeper to the Robin Hood Rifles he moved to Canada and involved himself in real estate. On a return visit to England in 1909 he crossed the Atlantic on the ill-fated *Lusitania*. His death in Vancouver aged 54 was not quite unique in the Rams' early annals – fabled forward Benjamin Ward Spilsbury also died there.

Appearances: 1 app 1886-87, goals conceded 5.

DAVIES Walter Thomas
Full-back

Born: Wrexham, 1863
Died: 86, High Street, Coedpoeth, near Wrexham, 8 January 1931 (Estate value £258)
Career: Wrexham Victoria, Wrexham, Wrexham Olympic, Derby County 1884, Wrexham Gymnasium, Wales (1 cap, 0 goals)

The first Welshman to play for Derby County took part in Wrexham's underdog victory over Druids in the 1883 Welsh Cup Final, and was already capped for Wales when he gained employment in Derby late in 1884. In all likelihood this was engineered by the club to secure his services, since Derby's initial full-backs Reg Evans and Frank Harvey had both severed their involvement by early-December. The 'well-built Welsh international of some renown' was given an experimental run – yet despite 'showing well' an alarming 17 goals were conceded in his 4 games. Three defeats and a draw materialised before a regular full-back slot was given to Willie Weston. The son of Samuel Davies a master stonemason, Walter became a tailor, and it is likely his employment was created by Derby County secretary Sam Richardson, who managed a large outfitter in Babington Lane. Alas the English sojourn failed to endure, and by 1886 Davies was back in Wrexham playing for junior club Wrexham Gymnasium. Married with a son and daughter, he continued in tailoring, and died close to his home town aged 67.

Appearances: 4 apps 1884-85, 0 goals

DOUGLAS Reverend Francis Sandford Keith
Right-back

Born: Lambeth, Surrey, 13 July 1857
Died: Sao Paulo, Brazil, 9 April 1892
Career: Spondon, Derby County 1884

The 'gentleman cleric' Reverend Douglas played only a single game but a significant one. At the age of 27 he helped Derby County to their first ever victory – 3-2 at Repton School on Tuesday 28 October 1884. Douglas was then captain of Spondon. During his time in Derby between 1884 and 1886 he threw himself into the sporting arena – a vice-president of the Derbyshire Football Association, member of the Derby County rugby side and a capital addition to Spondon Cricket Club, having played once for Cheshire in 1881. The second son of Scottish-born timber merchant and landowner John More Douglas and his high-born wife Eliza Helen Charnock Sandford, he began life in London and spent much of his boyhood living in some style in Harrow-on-the-Hill, attending Harrow School as a home boarder. When his parents moved to Glasgow he attended lessons at Glasgow University aged only 16 – his maternal grandfather Sir Daniel Sandford had been Professor of Greek there. This proved a traumatic interlude – in 1874 when enacting a skirmish scene at Paisley Theatre Royal the young student caused a fellow actor's death through discharging a stage firearm close to his face. At first charged with 'culpable recklessness' he was later exonerated. He suffered more ill-fortune the following year when after the family had removed to Chester his father died there. Francis subsequently resolved to enter the Church – after gaining his BA at Oxford in 1883 he was ordained in 1884 and licensed to Spondon House School near Derby. While there he married Agnes Mary Duncan in Chester – the couple had 3 children. Reverend Douglas left Spondon in 1886 for a curacy in Bridgnorth, Shropshire, but soon departed for Brazil. He was chaplain at Santos and then Sao Paulo, where he died during a severe yellow fever outbreak aged 34.

Appearances: 1 app 1884-85, 0 goals

EVANS George
Centre-forward

Born: Handsworth, Birmingham, 27 June 1864
Died: 'Clifton', Kidderminster Road, West Hagley, Worcestershire, 23 May 1947 (Estate value £9,580. 4s 2d)
Career: Derby St. Luke's, Derby Midland, Derby County 1885, Derby Midland, West Bromwich Albion, Newton Heath

'Man of many clubs' George Evans migrated to Derby in the early 1880s to work, and had already assisted two of the town's leading sides when Derby County secured his services at the start of 1885-86. Their judgement proved sound – after scoring nine in his first nine games he ended up top scorer, eclipsing even 'Jammer' Smith to finish on 24 goals in 34 games. He was again scoring well in 1886-87 before re-joining Derby Midland in mid-campaign. Evans became their vice-captain, but after two seasons took up the professional challenge. He moved to West Bromwich Albion in May 1889 before spending the 1890-91 season with Newton Heath, later to be Manchester United. Never a first-team regular at either club, he left Manchester in December 1891 to return to his West Midlands roots. The son of engine fitter Emanuel Evans – also licensee of the 'Frighted Horse' on Soho Road, Handsworth – he was a brass turner by trade but altered course after his marriage in 1892 to Elizabeth Ruth Bettany, daughter of a successful china dealer. They had seven children, unusually losing a son in each of the World Wars. By his forties, living in West Bromwich, Evans styled himself licensee and 'glass, china and earthenware dealer'. The couple did well and retired to Hagley, where George died at home aged 82. His wife lived to be 93.

Appearances: 50 apps 1885-86 to 1886-87, 32 goals

EVANS Henry
Forward

Born: *Codnor Park Farm, Stoneyford, Derbyshire, 8 July 1857*
Died: *'The Beeches', Spondon, Derbyshire, 30 July 1920 (Estate value £15,624. 11s 9d)*
Career: *Derby Town, Derby Midland, Derby County 1884, Queen's Park, West of Scotland*

'Harry' Evans was a stalwart of Derby Town from the late 1870s but left them in 1881 to captain newly-formed Derby Midland. Indeed he was instrumental in the club's foundation. Broad-shouldered and standing over 6 feet he cut a fine figure, doing his best work at centre-forward. Derby County secured his services only once, in a controversial 7-0 defeat by Derby Junction in November 1884. Evans also played cricket 5 times for Derbyshire between 1878 and 1882, taking 19 wickets at an average of 13.26 including a hat-trick. He might readily have achieved more at both sports, but business took much of his attention. The son of farmer Thomas Evans, he started as a clerk with the Midland Railway in 1873 and made great strides. After leaving Derby for Glasgow in 1885 he continued his career rise. He also assisted the great Scottish amateur side Queen's Park and qualified by residence to turn out for the West of Scotland XI. He returned to Derby in 1905 on being appointed Chief Goods Manager of the Midland Railway, living in some style at 'The Manor House', Borrowash, and finally 'The Beeches', Spondon. Only a year after retiring through ill-health he died there aged 63, leaving a wife and two daughters. He is buried in Spondon churchyard. His older brother Thomas also played cricket for Derbyshire, and was several times full-back for Everton in the pre-League era.

Appearances: 1 app 1884-85, 0 goals

EVANS Reginald Lawton
Right-back

Born: Burton-upon-Trent, Staffordshire, 8 March 1866
Died: 44 Crewe St., Derby, 12 April 1928
Career: Derby Whitworth, Ordnance Survey, Derby County 1884

Full-back Reg Evans played in the historic first game at Great Lever on 13 September 1884. A few games later 'his kicking was very strong and sure'. But after being labelled 'very weak' in a win at Wirksworth in December, he bowed out after just 7 appearances, ultimately replaced by Willie Weston after several new candidates had been tried. Evans was one of the 'white collar' group who agreed to assist Derby County early on but did not always sustain the association, either through questionable ability or working commitments. Son of engineman William Evans, he moved to Derby in childhood and attended the football-oriented Whitworth School. He worked for the Ordnance Survey and was playing for their football XI in Derby as early as 1882, ultimately qualifying as a land surveyor. He joined the Midland Railway in 1896 and retired in 1925 having spent his final two years based at Euston Station. Married with family, he lived in Crewe Street for some thirty years, and died there aged 62.

Appearances: 7 apps 1884-85, 0 goals

EXHAM Percy George
Half-back

Born: Cork, Ireland, 26 June 1859
Died: 'Laurel Hill', Repton, Derbyshire, 7 October 1922 (Estate value £9663. 7s)
Career: Repton School, Cambridge University, Derby County 1884

Derby's first Irish-born player 'George' Exham made his debut in the opening home game against Blackburn Olympic whilst a teacher of maths at his old school Repton. He remained there for the rest of his life, known affectionately to the boys as 'Pat'. Said to be 'not a showy player but extremely useful', he appeared nine times for Derby all in the first campaign. The son of Cork solicitor Richard Kenah Exham, he entered St. John's College, Cambridge, in 1878 and emerged with his BA in 1882. He made the St. John's football XI but was considered a better cricketer, representing Cambridge and in 1883 playing one County game for Derbyshire – one of the elite group to bag the 'Derby Double' of at least one game for both Derbyshire and Derby County. He also played for the MCC, Gentlemen of Derbyshire, and once for Dorset – a right-hand batsman, his average from 10 first-class innings was 8.8, with a top score of 43. A lifelong bachelor, he became a legendary figure at Repton – in advancing years he garnered a reputation for falling asleep in the middle of teaching a lesson, or by all accounts anywhere, but had been far more lively at games, his ability as a cricket coach being much valued – he was said to be greatly admired by Repton pupils for his ability to break the tiles on the pavilion roof with his on-drive. He died at his Repton home aged 63.

Appearances: 9 apps 1884-85, 0 goals

FARQUHARSON Edward Barkly
Goalkeeper

Born: Kussowlie, West Bengal, India, 20 July 1865
Died: Arrah, West Bengal, India, 29 September 1889
Career: Derby School, Hendon, Derby County 1884, Sandhurst College

Standing at almost 6 feet 2 inches E. B. Farquharson kept goal twice in the first season – both draws – at a time when a number of goalkeepers were being tried. Having already done well for Derby School – sometimes playing centre-forward – he briefly attached himself to Hendon during their Christmas tour of the Midlands in 1884, as did a number of other Old Derbeians. While playing in goal for Hendon 'against' Derby on Boxing Day 1884, he greatly impressed and appeared for Derby soon afterwards – but the Committee ultimately settled on Charles Hill as first-choice keeper. Farquharson besides had other commitments, passing direct from Derby School into the Royal Military College at Sandhurst. He was born in India to Captain Charles Elliott Farquharson of the 21st Hussars, later Governor of Derby Gaol. In February 1885 Edward was gazetted to the 1st Battalion of the East Surrey Regiment, joining them in Ranikel, a hill station in Bengal. Attaining the rank of Lieutenant, he was considered an officer of much promise, but met an unusual end while acting as 'aide-de-camp' to the Lieutenant Governor of Bengal. He was on his way to accept the adjutancy of his regiment when he fell from a train at Arrah and never recovered consciousness. After the news reached Derby the bells of St. Luke's were rung half-muffled the following Sunday. Although only 24 he was not the first Derby County player to perish – 'poor Tom Hardy' preceded him.

Appearances: 2 apps 1884-85, goals conceded 5.

FLOWER George
Half-back

Born: Darley Abbey, 1856
Died: Boundary House, Uttoxeter Road, Derby, 19 December 1933 (Estate value £201. 15s 1d)
Career: Derby County 1885

Although a stalwart of the local football scene, George Flower made only one appearance for Derby County, the opening day loss at Stoke in 1885-86 when he played alongside kid brother 'Jack' nine years his junior. The son of cotton worker John Flower, he made the short move from Darley Abbey to work as an engine and boiler fitter in Derby's burgeoning locomotive industry. A sister Annie maintained a football link – she married into the Hickinbottom clan from Darley Abbey which gave Ernie and brother 'Sammy' to Derby County. A father of seven, George died aged 77 in Boundary House Institution, the former Derby Union Workhouse turned hospital.

Appearances: 1 app 1885-86, 0 goals

FLOWER John
Full back or centre-half

Born: Darley Abbey, 17 June 1865
Died: 18, Sidney Street, Derby, 24 September 1934 (Estate value £420. 2s. 1d)
Career: Darley Abbey, Derby Midland, Derby County 1885, Derby Midland, Derby Railway Veterans

'Jack' Flower – often called Flowers – had already given sterling service to Darley Abbey and Derby Midland before their predatory rival came calling. His first Derby County outing was the unexpected 6-1 victory at Nottingham Forest in January 1885, filling in for Willie Weston at full-back. In 1885-86 he bagged the regular centre-half slot, missing only four games, but then returned to Derby Midland, his place being filled by George Clifton from Long Eaton Rangers. Son of cotton spinner John Flower, he began work in a Darley Abbey mill, but soon moved to Derby as an engine fitter and machine minder with the Midland Railway, then a familiar route. One of his games for Derby County was with older brother George, and he once featured for Derby Midland among the singular bunch of Flower, Rose, Garden and Bloomer. Described as 'tall, powerfully built, and singularly agile', his most memorable match in a Derby shirt was the shock Cup victory over Aston Villa in 1885-86. Detailed to shadow Villa's famous captain Archie Hunter, he did the job so effectively that the irritated Scotsman openly bemoaned 'the constant company of that grinning Italian organ grinder', a reference to Flower's swarthy complexion and jet black hair. Flower gave a pithy riposte – 'I may not be able to play football but I can sometimes stop those who can'. Married with six children, Jack Flower retained a passion for the game into his senior years – aged 66 he played for Derby Railway Veterans in a 'walking football match' against their Crewe counterparts. He died at home aged 69 just nine months after his brother George, and only a few days before Derby County's Golden Jubilee Dinner which he had hoped to attend.

Appearances: 35 apps 1884-85 to 1885-86, 2 goals

FORMAN, Arthur
Full-back and half-back

Born: Chellaston, 27 March 1866
Died: 'Kingswood', Devonshire Avenue, Beeston, Nottinghamshire, 9 May 1931(Estate value £3095 6s. 8d)
Career: Aston-on-Trent, Derby County 1886

The oldest of three Forman brothers to play for Derby County – the only sibling trio in the club's entire history. But while Frank and Fred went on to star for Nottingham Forest and England, Arthur's career was rather more modest. Educated at the village school in Aston and then St. Anne's in Derby – as were his football brothers – Arthur started with the Aston side before becoming a reliable member of the Derby reserves pool. He was twice selected for the first team in 1886-87, neither outing routine – the first a record 13-0 win over Liverpool Ramblers and the second at Sheffield Town when Derby were obliged to fulfil two first-team fixtures on the same day. A rather mixed side lost 5-3, Forman being handed the captaincy. Son of farmer Ralph Forman – later manager of a Chellaston gypsum mine – and his French-born wife Elise, he became a clerk with the Midland Railway, rising to head of an accounts section. When he retired in 1930 he was earning £500 per annum, but had little time to enjoy the fruits of almost fifty years service. He died aged 65 just five months later, leaving a widow and family.

Appearances: 2 apps 1886-87, 0 goals

FROST J
Half-back

Born: Inconclusive
Died: Inconclusive
Career: Derby County 1884

Frost played once in the opening season away at the Wolverhampton side Stafford Road. Fielding a much-changed side in response to the previous week's chastening 7-0 defeat by Walsall Town, Derby tried a number of reserves and emerged 3-0 winners. This was a period of experimentation in team selection, and Frost never appeared again. He remains one of the few Derby players whose identity cannot be reliably pinned down – a prime candidate is draughtsman John Edward Frost, but several possibles cannot be conclusively distinguished.

Appearances: 1 app 1884-85, 0 goals

GILLETT Leonard Francis
Goalkeeper

Born: 101A, Friargate, Derby, 21 January 1861
Died: Austin's Close, Harbertonford, near Totnes, Devon, 23 November 1915 (Estate value £14,994. 18s)
Career: Charterhouse School, Old Carthusians, Oxford University, Notts County, Ockbrook & Borrowash, Derby Midland, Derby County 1884

One of two players to serve on the committee in the opening season, Derby County's first goalkeeper stood between the posts for only six games. In the inaugural fixture he let in six, and was beaten seven times on his farewell, a chastening 7-0 Cup defeat by Walsall Town which precipitated several changes. Afterwards Gillett bemoaned that in letting in the first he had knocked his head against the post and was thereafter 'in a spin' – the first creative excuse in the club's goalkeeping annals. In total the ball eluded him 23 times – although in truth he was little protected, the team not yet fully organized. In fact the *Derby Daily Telegraph* observed: 'Gillett, though an indifferent kicker, is a cool and quick goalkeeper'. He came with an impressive pedigree – Charterhouse School XI (1879), FA Cup winner with Old Carthusians (1881), Oxford University 'Blue' (1882) and seven games for Notts County in 1882-83. That he had let in 14 for Notts was perhaps glossed over by the Derby committee – they needed a 'keeper and Gillett was available. Indeed he had been filling in at full-back for Derby Midland and Ockbrook and Borrowash, where in one game 'his cool play seemed to puzzle the opposing forwards'. The eldest son of mining engineer Francis Calvert Gillett, he was born in Derby but brought up at 'The Lodge' Risley and 'The Manor House' Borrowash. After gaining his BA at Pembroke College, Oxford, he emulated his father by qualifying as a civil and mining engineer, taking over the family practice and continuing a valuable consultancy to the Midland Railway. After marriage his last residence in Derby was Evington House (later the Evington Club near Village Street) from where in 1895 he set up a football and cricket club christened the Old Normanton Athletic Club. In 1898 he retired aged 37 able to live off family income, moving to North Wales and finally Devon, where he resided in some splendour in a large country mansion. Derby County's first custodian died there aged 54 leaving a widow. His eldest son Private Richard Francis Gillett was killed in World War One within a year.

Appearances: 6 apps 1884-85, goals conceded 23

GOODALL Archibald Lee
Centre-forward and centre-half

Born: Belfast, Ireland, 3 January 1865
Died: High Road, East Finchley, Middlesex, 29 November 1929 (Estate value £50)
Career: Liverpool Stanley, Everton, Preston North End, Derby County 1888, Aston Villa, Derby County 1889, Plymouth Argyle, Glossop North End, Wolverhampton Wanderers, Ireland – 10 appearances 1899-1904

The 'different as chalk and cheese' brothers John and Archie Goodall were legends at Derby in the League era, but younger sibling Archie also had a previous spell in the final pre-League season. His arrival in February 1888 coincided with Derby's strong finish to the campaign – playing at centre-forward, only one of Goodall's ten games was lost, and he exerted a marked influence. He then slipped away, but returned in 1889 – this time with 'Johnny' – converting to the pivotal midfield role then termed 'centre-half'. Full of energy and hard as nails, his mastery of the ball was unquestionable, unlike his robust approach, which opponents routinely complained overstepped the mark. Small and stocky, he was described as 'strong as a horse, highly intelligent, and clever in his ways' – but another observer labelled him 'a tremendous worker whose enthusiasm ran away with his judgement'. That fiery temperament and tendency to recklessness also prevailed off the pitch, resulting in several serious run-ins with the Derby County committee, the odd confrontation with supporters, periodic brushes with the law, and a veritable legion of 'high-spirited antics' and impulsive behaviour. But none of it fuelled by 'over-indulgence', for Goodall was a lifelong teetotaller. When running the Plough Inn during his long stay at Derby he dryly commented – 'I want the money and the other fools want the beer'. The son of Scotsman Richard Goodall – a soldier in the British army – and his wife Mary Lee, he was born in Ireland when his father was briefly posted there, but the family soon moved to Scotland. Growing up in Kilmarnock, both brothers had marked Scottish accents, yet by virtue of birth Archie played for Ireland and John for England. Goodall had been an iron turner when he arrived in Derby, but later as 'part of the deal' was both 'mine host' and a joint proprietor with his brother of a tobacconists and sports goods shop in Babington Lane.

His marriage in 1889 to Mary Ann Duthie ended tragically – in January 1890 when expecting their first child she fatally swallowed a quantity of Archie's liniment, the court delivering a verdict of suicide. His second marriage to Mary Jane Dallow in 1893 produced a son and daughter. Goodall took pride in his physical prowess, and in four successive seasons from 1893-94 did not miss a League match for Derby. He later assisted a number of clubs and after a short stint as player-manager at Glossop North

End played his final game for Wolves in December 1905 aged 40. Making Derby his base, he left football to forge a new career as a performing strong man, touring the theatres of Britain, Europe and America with his son Richard as assistant – in his signature turn 'Walking the Hoop' he navigated the inner circumference of a giant upturned metal ring. The gravity-defying act received sensational reviews, earning him the sobriquet 'The Human Fly'. Typically he had made the entire apparatus in his own workshop at his Wolfa Street home. He continued performing into his fifties, and it was said that the strain hastened his end. After retiring he spent his later years in London – he had been living at 28, Southern Road, Fortis Green, when he collapsed and died aged 64 while out walking on the Finchley High Road. One of Derby County's greatest players – and surely the club's most colourful character – was returned to his adopted town and buried in Nottingham Road Cemetery.

Appearances: Pre-League, 10 apps 1887-88, 2 goals. League era: 423 apps 1889-90 to 1902-03, 52 goals. Total: 433 apps 1887-88 to 1902-03, 54 goals

GORHAM Charles
Half-back

Born: Walkeringham, Nottinghamshire, 19 October 1861
Died: 142, Noel Street, Nottingham, 26 August 1922
Career: Derby Deaf and Dumb, Spondon, Derby County 1884, Leeds Town, Ilkeston Town, England Deaf XI

Gorham played a handful of first-team games in Derby's opening season, otherwise assisting Derby County Wanderers, before leaving the Midlands temporarily in 1885 to live in Yorkshire, working in Leeds and York and continuing to play both football and cricket. He is unique in Derby County history – their only deaf and dumb player. The son of country clergyman George Martyn Gorham – an Old Reptonian – Charles was born deaf and educated at Mr. J. Barber's private school in West Brompton, London, where he never acquired speech. He was remembered as 'a high-spirited and mischievous boy, devoted to games and very sociable.' After leaving school he took up draughtsmanship and came to work in Derby in the early 1880s, helping found both Derby and Nottingham Deaf football and cricket clubs. He later forged lasting links as a mission worker with the Derby School for the Deaf. As a pioneer of Deaf football he was captain of the first Deaf English XI which on 28 March 1891 drew 3-3 against Scotland in Glasgow, Gorham scoring the first English goal. As a talented cricketer he played for Spondon, Derby Midland, and the Yorkshire Gentlemen, the latter designated first-class games. He achieved both the hat-trick and a century. He was besides labelled 'an excellent cyclist and billiard player, while at shooting, cards and chess he can hold his own with the majority'. Although later styling himself 'a journeyman joiner' his most significant work was as an influential activist for the deaf community. Whilst editor of the 'Deaf and Dumb Times' from 1889 to 1891 he displayed great dynamism and was often outspoken, leading the way in helping found the British Deaf and Dumb

Association. After leaving Yorkshire in 1892 he took up residence in Ilkeston, before spending his last two decades in Nottingham. A lifelong bachelor, he maintained his mission work in the Derby area until his final days. After falling ill he returned to Yorkshire to convalesce with his sister Mary at the family home in Masham, but breathed his last at his Nottingham residence, dying aged 60 of pleurisy. Gorham remains one of Derby County's most interesting personalities, not least for demonstrating that success in football can be gained through no more than good vision, decent feet, a fine physique, and an acute brain.

Appearances: 7 apps 1884-85, 0 goals

GREAVES John Lineker
Centre-half

Born: Ecclesall Road, Ecclesall Bierlow, near Sheffield, Yorkshire, 16 May 1861
Died: Forest Hospital, Buckhurst Hill, Essex, 16 May 1930 (Estate value £4382. 15s 8d)
Career: Bakewell Town, Derby County 1886

J. L. Greaves was a popular figure in the strong Bakewell Town side of the mid-1880s, and when selected for Derbyshire in 1886 was praised for his 'fine tackling and overhead kicking'. Derby County borrowed his services once – in December 1886 he deputised for regular centre-half George Clifton. The son of brewer's clerk Daniel Greaves, he lost his father in boyhood. He became a journalist, moving to Bakewell in 1882 as correspondent for the *Derbyshire Times*. By the time he left in 1890 his weekly column 'Gleanings in the Peak' was considered an institution – for his efforts he was promoted to the Chesterfield office. Whilst still single he lived with his widowed mother, and stated at his leaving presentation that 'there is no woman I more admire in the entire world'. Perhaps that bore on his future – his 1891 marriage produced a son but ended in a bitter divorce five years later, luridly reported in the press. After working briefly for the *Mansfield Reporter* he remarried and lived in London, sometimes travelling to America and Canada. He died on his sixty-ninth birthday the year after losing his second wife. Although experiencing 'difficult times' and beset by evident character flaws Greaves had a definite lyrical side – both a talented wordsmith and fine tenor singer who performed several times at Matlock Pavilion. Nor did his creativity end there – in 1887 he invented and patented the 'Speedy' rapid-opening envelope. A poetic tribute penned during his football pomp provides a lasting epitaph: 'Sharp J. L. Greaves, half-back, alert, and eager for the fray. The ball kicked-off, he dashes forth, his courage to display. And here and there and everywhere, he follows in the trail – and like the *Times* of Derbyshire is never known to fail.'

Appearances: 1 app 1886-87, 0 goals

GROOME Alfred
Full-back and half-back

Born: Derby, 1864
Died: The Lord Nelson, The Wardwick, Derby, 4 February 1893 (Estate value £75. 10s)
Career: St. Luke's, St. Werburgh's, Derby County 1887

Alf Groome – sometimes styled Groom – played only three first-team games in two seasons, one in the company of older brother Harry. Between times he was a pivotal member of the Derby County Wanderers, and extremely popular. The son of Henry Groome – landlord of the Lord Nelson in The Wardwick – he became an upholsterer by trade. With a number of others in the reserves he shared a love of music. In Groome's case a particularly diverse one – for twenty years a member of St. Werburgh's church choir, but also a regular performer with the Macaw Minstrels negro troupe, a popular entertainment form in Victorian times. His tragic death at the age of 28 followed a severe chill – he took to bed in the Lord Nelson right opposite his church in an attempt to recuperate, but died of pneumonia within a week leaving a young widow. A remarkably well-attended funeral demonstrated the esteem in which he was widely held – he was buried in Uttoxeter Road cemetery amidst moving scenes. His grave recorded that 'He had a soul full of music and a heart full of kindness'. A substantial memorial fund enabled a specially-commissioned stained glass window to be placed in his honour in St. Werburgh's, alas now redundant as a place of worship.

Appearances: 3 apps 1886-87 to 1887-88, 0 goals

GROOME Henry
Outside-right

Born: Derby, 1862
Died: 27, Wolfa Street, Derby, 25 January 1923 (Estate value £210.)
Career: St. Luke's, St. Werburgh's, Derby County 1887

'Harry' Groome – sometimes Groom – was like his younger brother Alf an enthusiastic member of the Derby County Wanderers. He was promoted only sporadically to the first team, once in the same line-up as Alf, when he marked the occasion with a goal. Also adept at athletics and cycling, he excelled at the annual Derby County Sports when fellow players George Bakewell and Harry Lowles invariably provided keen opposition. The son of Henry Groome senior, landlord of the Lord Nelson in The Wardwick, he trained as a stonemason but became manager of the Nelson when his father died, and later licensee of the Royal Oak in the Market Place. After the turn of the century he diversified into the bottling and selling of mineral water, acquiring Robinsons of Gerard Street then moving the business to Mansfield Road before later selling it to Burrows and Sturgess. He died at home aged 61 leaving a widow and son.

Appearances: 7 apps 1886-87 to 1887-88, 2 goals

GWYNNE Reverend Llewellyn Henry
Centre forward

Born: Kilvey, near Swansea, Wales, 11 June 1863
Died: St. Margaret's Hospital, Epping, Surrey, 3 December 1857 (Estate value £23,438. 2s 8d)
Career: Clapham Rovers, Derby County 1887, Brailsford, Nottingham St. Andrew's, Nottingham Emmanuel

Arguably no Derby County player achieved more in the wider sphere of life than Welsh-born Llewellyn Henry Gwynne, who between 1920 and 1946 ministered in North Africa as the first Bishop of Egypt and Sudan. His frequent use of air travel to cover his vast diocese earned him the nickname 'The Flying Bishop'. When he died his football star had long dimmed, but such was his esteem as a religious leader that 1,300 attended his thanksgiving service in Westminster Abbey. When a young curate of St. Chads Church, he led the Derby County attack on seven occasions during 1887-88, otherwise assisting the reserves. He is one of the few to have a game named in his honour. In 'Gwynne's Match' on 24 December 1887 Eckington Works were humbled 7-2 in the Derbyshire Senior Cup. Perhaps the true spirit of Christmas visited him, for a festive County Ground congregation saw 'the rampaging cleric' net four and lend a hand in two. During his brief tenure his strong and direct approach impressed, and on 14 January 1888 he was rewarded with the captaincy against Long Eaton Rangers, finishing his stint a few games later with a rare average of more than a goal a game. Although Gwynne remained a strict amateur, the Church authorities questioned the ethics of him playing with paid professionals, but he quizzically maintained his influence to be 'all for the general good' since 'no player ever swore in my presence'. The fifth child of schoolmaster Richard Gwynne, he was first taught at his father's small school in Kilvey, before advancing to nearby Swansea Grammar School, where he proved a decent rugby player and good cricketer. When aged nineteen he took a temporary teaching post in Beverley, Yorkshire, to help support his parents, but being devoutly religious they were keen for 'Henry' to enter the Church – to that end he enrolled at St. John's Theological College in Highbury, North London, where he embraced association football and sometimes assisted the crack amateur side Clapham Rovers. Ordained in 1886 aged 23, his first appointment brought him to Derby. A passionate advocate of 'muscular Christianity' – the creed promoting character development through sporting pursuits – he set up and coached the St. Chad's Church Football Club. Among his charges in the junior St. Chad's Choir team was a pale 12-year-old 'discovery' – the Rams' future star Steve Bloomer. In 1890 Gwynne was sent to a curacy at St. Andrew's, Nottingham, and in 1892 appointed vicar of the neighbouring parish of Emmanuel – he continued to play football and in 1895 co-founded Notts Magdala FC. He also founded a cricket club and played to a good standard with Notts Amateurs. In 1899 he made a life-changing decision, responding to a call for missionary workers to go to North Africa. Gwynne became Archdeacon for the Sudan in 1904, and in 1908 was consecrated Bishop of Khartoum. During World War One he served in France as a high-rank army chaplain, returning to the Sudan in 1919, and a year later was appointed Bishop of Egypt and the Sudan. From his base in Cairo he served until returning to England in 1946, aged 83. Lasting physical testimonies to his influence in Africa are the cathedrals in Cairo and Khartoum both built at Gwynne's behest. A confirmed bachelor, and devout teetotaller to boot, he spent his final years in Epping, Surrey, where he died aged 94. Few might have guessed that 70 years previously the archetypal 'aged cleric' was plundering goals for Derby County – along with H. S. Wansbrough, Gwynne is one of two Bishops to play for Derby, but the only one in football history to have bagged a 'double brace' on Christmas Eve. His ashes are buried in Khartoum Cathedral.

Appearances: 7 apps 1887-88, 8 goals

HALES George William
Right-back

Born: Kings Cliffe, Northamptonshire, 1867
Died: General Hospital, Nottingham, 2 June 1935
Career: Breaston, Derby County 1886

Derby County were short in defence when they tried out Breaston's young full-back at home to Liverpool Ramblers in September 1886. The *Long Eaton Advertiser* observed: 'The village favourite brought with him quite an entourage, the County Ground regulars being much amused at the antics of his followers, who hooted and clamoured in a most extraordinary manner each time the ball came near him.' The game itself also proved remarkable, Derby securing a 13-0 victory which remains their biggest ever. But the *Advertiser* pulled no punches in declaring Hales 'not at all of the right calibre to secure a regular place' – indeed he never played again. The son of a Midland Railway pointsman, he moved to Breaston in infancy and spent his working life in the lace trade. In 1886 he married local girl Lois Plackett – related to the Breaston clan who supplied Henry and Laurence to Derby – she died in 1890 after presenting George with twins. He later remarried and had a second family. George Hales remains a perfect example of one whose big opportunity rendered meagre returns, although in donning the shirt just once he achieved what generations of Derby County followers have only dreamed of. He had been living with his son at 102 Bridge Street, Long Eaton, when he was admitted to hospital, where he died aged 68 knowing that he had played his own small part in Derby's record triumph.

Appearances: 1 app 1886-87, 0 goals

HALL J
Outside-right

Born: Inconclusive
Died: Inconclusive

One-gamer Hall was 'borrowed on the ground' for the woeful 8-0 reverse at Sheffield Wednesday on Christmas Eve 1887 when Derby arrived two men short. The problem arose because Derby had to play Eckington in a Derbyshire Cup replay on the same day. No further details of stand-in J. Hall are known.

Appearances: 1 app 1887-88, 0 goals

HARDY Thomas Conry
Inside-right

Born: Long Eaton, Derbyshire, 1867
Died: 15 Lawson Avenue, Long Eaton, Derbyshire, 7 June 1889 (Estate value £137. 14s 11d)
Career: Long Eaton Rangers, Derby County 1887, Long Eaton Rangers

Tom Hardy had only one game with Derby County, but was an established favourite with his home side Long Eaton Rangers. The son of lacemaker William Hardy, he followed his father into the trade. Hardy was said to be 'a fine example of a clean-living lad' who 'never lost his temper on the football field, and moved about with an imperturbable serenity'. This held good even when serious ill-health struck him. 'He played many games for Rangers when far from fit, but appeared cheerful under the most distressing circumstances'. This was no idle observation, for it came in Hardy's obituary – aged 21 and still a bachelor, he was the first Derby County player to pass away. Many lined the streets of Long Eaton for his emotional funeral – afterwards the *Long Eaton Advertiser* observed: 'Tom Hardy suffered intense pain but complained not once. Indeed only his close family were aware of his illness right to the last – this was the calibre of a true sportsman and a genuine hero.'

Appearances: 1 app 1887-88, 0 goals

HARRISON J.
Inside-right

Born: Inconclusive
Died: Inconclusive
Career: Derby County 1884

Harrison remains one of the few mystery men in Derby's early history. When he played his solitary game in the fourth ever fixture the *Derby Daily Telegraph* labelled him 'the Old Carthusian' – although the Charterhouse School register seems not to yield 'the right Harrison' it is likely he was indeed educated there, possibly for only a short time. On Boxing Day 1884 he also played against Derby for Hendon when the visitors were short-handed. Despite the existence of a strong candidate, his identity remains open. Notwithstanding this, the inside-forward's sole Derby outing scarcely troubled the opposition, the *Derby Daily Telegraph* dismissively asserting that 'Harrison was worse than useless'.

Appearances: 1 app 1884-85, 0 goals

HARVEY Frank
Full-back

Born: Duffield, Derbyshire, 1862
Died: 36, King Alfred Street, Derby, 5 December 1904 (Estate value £863 3s 2d)
Career: Derby Town, St. Luke's, Derby County 1884

Frank Harvey played in Derby's opening game, but bowed out after seven appearances. The son of Thomas Whilton Harvey – a Milford-born miller and later general sales agent – Frank had been sent to Derby to live with an aunt after his mother died when he was only 12. By his late teens he was a clerk with the Midland Railway and playing football for the old-established Derby Town club. By the time newly-formed Derby County called on his services he was a regular with St. Luke's, continuing with them after his brief County sojourn. Whilst with Saints he also played once for Sheffield Wednesday 'against' Derby – helping them out in January 1886 when Wednesday arrived two men short. His Luke's team-mate Will Shipley, who had also played in Derby's first game, filled the other Wednesday vacancy. It was said that Frank's older brother Whilton might also have joined Derby County, but he died aged 25 only weeks before the opening fixture, mourned as 'the best forward Derbyshire has ever had'. Derby's first game must have carried great poignancy for Frank – it says something for his spirit that he was later remembered as 'the comical man of the side, always up to some sort of fun'. He too was denied a long life. At his death aged 42 he left a wife and two children.

Appearances: 7 apps 1884-85, 0 goals

HENSON George
Forward

Born: Inconclusive
Died: Inconclusive
Career: Derby Junction, Derby County 1887

Along with brother John an established member of the old Derby Junction side which vied with Derby County for local supremacy. In the event the younger club County lured both brothers away. By 1886-87 they were increasingly helping Derby County Wanderers. George played once for the full side, at Ashbourne St. Oswald's in October 1887 when Derby had to fulfil two 'first-team' fixtures in a single day. The existence of two sets of Henson brothers of viable age – both George and John and both employed in foundry-related work – makes conclusive donation of the shirt impossible on existing evidence. Foremost candidates are the Hensons who lived for three decades in Abbey Street, within traditional 'Juncs' territory.

Appearances: 1 app 1887-88, 0 goals

HENSON John
Outside-left

Born: Inconclusive
Died: Inconclusive
Career: Derby Junction, Derby County 1887

John and George – labelled in reports 'the brothers Henson' – were well-established in the Derby Junction side by 1885-86, but the following season increasingly appeared for Derby County Wanderers. In January 1887 John was twice promoted to the first team as cover for 'Lol' Plackett, but was unable to supplant him. Conclusive identity cannot be attributed on current findings – see previous entry – but seductive candidates are the Henson brothers who lived for three decades in Abbey Street close to 'Juncs' territory. The alternative possibles lived in the Whitecross Street and Kedleston Road area.

Appearances: 2 apps 1886-87, 0 goals

HICKINBOTTOM Albert George
Outside-left

Born: Derby, 9 October 1867
Died: Manor House Hospital, Golder's Green, Middlesex, 23 September 1927
Career: Darley Abbey, Derby County 1886, Derby Midland

Widely known by his pet-name 'Sammy', generally listed 'S. Hickinbottom'. Younger brother of Derby's long-serving Ernie – one of nine children of Darley Abbey mill worker Thomas Hickinbottom. Like Ernie he started with Darley Abbey, assisted Derby County, and then moved to Derby Midland. But whilst Ernie picked up again with Derby in the League era – most loyally after they absorbed the Midland club – 'Sammy' was unable to break through to the same extent. He played just 5 times, all pre-League, being largely kept out by 'Lol' Plackett and Tommy Needham, but otherwise proved a useful member of the reserve side. A signal fitter on the railways, he lived initially in Shaftesbury Crescent, but by 1901 had moved with his wife and family to Rotherham, then finally to 38 Woodheys Road, Neasden, northwest London. He died aged 59 pre-deceasing Ernie by a full twelve years.

Appearances: 5 apps 1885-86 to 1886-87, 1 goal

HICKINBOTTOM Ernest Thomas
Half-back and outside-left

Born: Darley Abbey, Derbyshire, 1865
Died: The Baseball Ground, Derby, 2 September 1939
Career: Darley Abbey, Derby County 1884, Derby Midland, Derby County

Ernie became a legend at Derby County in two distinct spells spanning the club's first decade. After defecting from Darley Abbey he played most of the first two seasons, but several times helped out his native Abbots at very short notice, not always endearing himself to the Derby committee. In the next five campaigns he played only once for Derby, attaching himself instead to their great rivals Derby Midland, where he became captain. Only when Midland were absorbed by Derby in 1891 and their players acquired did 'Hicky' return, assisting in three League campaigns before bowing out in March 1894. Very speedy, he was initially a half-back, but often played left-wing in his first spell, reverting to half-back in his second. Although quite lightweight, he was bony and muscular, earning a reputation as a hard player. Defender Jimmy Methven recalled that 'good old 'Hicky' was apt to use his cranium for more than heading the ball'. Another observer noted 'his undying spirit, labouring tirelessly to the very end even if the cause was lost.' His younger brother 'Sammy' also played occasionally for Derby. One of nine children of Darley Abbey mill worker Thomas Hickinbottom, Ernie began work as a smith's labourer, later becoming a riveter and bridge repairer with the Midland Railway. Married without children he had been living at 8 Bloom Street when at the age of 74 he collapsed and died at the Baseball Ground while watching the Rams play the final League game before World War Two. The circumstances poignantly symbolised the passing of the 'old guard' – yet few who saw 'an old man' stretchered along the touchline as play continued would realise its significance. When the League resumed in 1946-47 a new era dawned, the 'early days' consigned to history, only latterly 'reclaimed'.

Appearances: Pre-League: 52 apps 1884-85 to 1885-86, 12 goals. League era: 53 apps 1888-89 to 1893-94, 0 goals. Total: 105 apps 1884-85 to 1893-94, 12 goals

HILL Charles
Goalkeeper

Born: Derby, 1868
Died: Derby, 19 June 1901
Career: Trent College, Derby County 1885

'Charlie' Hill – sometimes styled Charles Edward Hill – became Derby's sixth goalkeeper when still at school in Long Eaton. Trent College labelled him 'a sure and active goalkeeper who understands the game and does the right thing.' Tall and athletic, he appeared as 'Brown' on his first try-out, and soon became Derby's most regular keeper of 1884-85 even though sometimes kept out by 'scholastic duties'. But the first four games of 1885-86 proved his final stint – he moved to London and trained in medicine, marrying and having two children while still a student. Failing to follow up his training, he returned to Derby to join his father Henry's lucrative business as a scrap metal merchant and 'general dealer'. Life then delivered an unexpected turn – in 1896 Hill suffered the untimely death of his wife, followed not long afterwards by the loss of his father. Left with two young children but financially bolstered he remarried in 1899 to Eliza Eugenia Wild some ten years his junior, but only after paying the significant sum of £250 for 'breach of promise' to another Derby girl, the court observing that 'he is not as steady in his habits as he ought to have been.' During this turbulent time Hill joined the Derbyshire Yeomanry Cavalry, becoming a corporal, and when the call for Boer War volunteers was raised in 1900 he joined the Derbyshire Company of the Imperial Yeomanry, seeing active service in South Africa before being invalided home. Maintaining links with the Yeomanry, he had just returned from a training camp in Bakewell when the final drama in an eventful life occurred. Hill and 'Eugenia' had been living at the Central Hotel in Derby Market Place, their relationship said by the press to be 'close but stormy', when late on the night of 19 June 1901, after an evening spent in local hostelries, they were both recovered drowned from the River Derwent near Exeter Bridge – Hill was 32 and Eugenia 21. An inquest returned open verdicts, but suggestions were made that Eugenia may have taken to the waters first and strong swimmer Hill had tried to save her, perhaps hitting his head on a stone when plunging in. The tragic pair share a gravestone in Nottingham Road cemetery.

Appearances: 16 apps 1884-85 to 1885-86, goals conceded 20

HODGES Alfred
Inside-left

Born: Findern, Derbyshire, 1866
Died: Gordon Hotel, Snow Hill, Birmingham, Warwickshire, 8 November 1900 (Estate value £525. 6s)
Career: Derby Whitworth, Derby County 1885

Hodges occasionally assisted Derby County Wanderers and had one first-team outing away to Repton School, but otherwise confined himself to good local teams. He also played for the short-lived Derby County Rugby Club. The son of William Henry Hodges – keen sportsman and highly respected accountant and Director at the Midland Railway Co. – Alfred was educated at Loughborough Grammar School and Cheltenham College before qualifying as a solicitor in 1889. In 1896 when living with his parents at Ash Tree House, Osmaston Road, he married the family's somewhat younger maid 'Nellie' – Mickleover girl Millicent Ellen Watson – cementing the match 'quietly' in Chorlton, Lancashire. The couple moved to Birmingham where Hodges set up practice – but his time there ended tragically. On 7 November 1900 he booked into the Gordon Hotel where next morning he failed to appear at breakfast. He was discovered unconscious in his room having taken a dangerous quantity of laudanum and attempts at revival failed. An inquest returned a verdict of 'suicide while in an unsound state of mind' – the press stating 'he had been depressed owing to the death of his mother and the suicide of his brother, and also had health worries'. His residence at the time of death was 49 Whitehall Road, Handsworth – aged 34 he left a wife and two children.

Appearances: 1 app 1884-85, 0 goals

HODGKINSON G
Inside-right

Born: Inconclusive
Died: Inconclusive
Career: Derwent Wanderers, Derby County 1887

One of the Derby County Wanderers but played only once for the first team, when on 22 October 1887 the club was obliged to fulfil two senior fixtures in a single day. Likely to be George Hodgkinson, but his full identity remains uncertain, several of that name unable to be distinguished conclusively.

Appearances: 1 app 1886-87, 0 goals

HUNT William
Goalkeeper

Born: Inconclusive
Died: Inconclusive
Career: Derby Whitworth, Derby Junction, Derby County 1884

'Bodger' Hunt was Derby's third goalkeeper, hastily engaged after the club's seventh game in which L. F. Gillett let in seven against Walsall Town. Hunt had suffered a nasty shoulder break playing for Derby and District in March 1884, but showed great resilience to recover. He came with good credentials from both Derby Junction and Derby Whitworth – the latter a talented hybrid team of pupils, old boys or invited 'associates' of the Whitworth School – but was himself dropped after five games following shaky displays at Darwen and Halliwell, both expressly remarked upon by the Derby press. He had one last outing in 1885-86 but otherwise assisted the reserves. His full identity has yet to emerge – thought to be William, there were several Hunts of that name who cannot be conclusively distinguished.

Appearances: 6 apps 1884-85 to 1885-86, goals conceded 14

HUTCHINSON Frederick Charles Mahon
Half-back

Born: Derby, 1868
Died: Derby, 1918
Career: Osmaston Rectory School, Liverpool Ramblers, Derby County 1886

'F. C. M.' was the younger brother of T. E. M. Hutchinson, playing twice to his much older sibling's once. In his early student days while a member of Liverpool Ramblers – mostly ex-public schoolboys – he assisted Derby at Everton in the opening game of 1886-87. Two weeks later with 'T. E. M.' he was back in the Liverpool Ramblers side which travelled to Derby to be beaten 13-0. He played once more for the Derby first team but was otherwise confined to the supporting ranks of Wanderers and Rovers. Son of George Teesdale Hutchinson, rector of Osmaston-by-Derby, he attended the Osmaston Rectory School and established his football credentials there. He was also a useful member of Osmaston Cricket Club. In 1891 he styled himself 'medical student' but nothing has been unearthed of his further life except that it ended in his native Derby aged 50.

Appearances: 2 apps 1886-87, 0 goals

HUTCHINSON Thomas Edward Mundy
Outside-left

Born: Derby, 1856
Died: 30 Talbot Road, Winton, Bournemouth, then in Hampshire, 17 May 1953 (Estate value £9,952. 3s)
Career: Liverpool Ramblers, Derby County 1885

Listed only as 'Hutchinson of Liverpool Ramblers' – although two other candidates (one his brother 'F. C. M.', the other William Haines Hutchinson of Derby School) could conceivably fit that bill, process of elimination strongly suggests the designated player is T. E. M. Hutchinson. He was living in the north-west and attached to 'gentleman amateur' team Liverpool Ramblers when he made his sole appearance for Derby County, filling in for the injured 'Jammer' Smith at Blackburn Olympic in December 1885. The following season with his brother 'F. C. M.' – who played twice for Derby – he was in the Liverpool Ramblers side beaten 13-0 by Derby at the County Ground. The son of George Teesdale Hutchinson, the curate and later rector of Osmaston-by-Derby, 'T. E. M.' went to Derby School before gaining his B.A. at Trinity College, Dublin. Ordained in 1887 at Chester Cathedral, he was vicar of Rock Ferry on Merseyside (1887-91) before becoming his father's curate at Osmaston. An all-round sportsman, he played golf for Derbyshire in the 1890s. Leaving Derby in 1902 he became vicar of Horfield, Bristol, remaining until at least 1911. He was then in his fifties, but little is known of his later life bar an impressive longevity – he died on the south coast aged 96.

Appearances: 1 app 1885-86, 0 goals

ILIFFE Frank Ernest
Left-back

Born: Derby, 1868
Died: 23, South Park Street, Chatteris, Cambridgeshire, 3 December 1925 (Estate value £1235 8s. 5d)
Career: Trent College, Derby County 1887, Derby Constitutional

Frank Iliffe was one of several young men from medical backgrounds who assisted Derby County in early years. Son of Derby doctor and surgeon Frank Iliffe of The Wardwick and later Curzon Street, he first showed promise in schools football for the unbeaten Trent College side of 1884-85 which also included Charles Hill, soon to be Derby's goalkeeper. School records labelled Iliffe 'a vigorous back, fast, but apt to kick rather wildly'. He became a loyal member of the tight-knit group serving Derby County Wanderers and Derby County Rovers – the reserve and third team. His sole first-team outing – in a side largely reserves – was a 3-2 win at Grantham in 1886-87. He was also a good local cricketer. After time as a medical student Iliffe styled himself 'dispenser of medicine'. His long bachelor years were ended in 1908 when at the age of 40 he married a 23-year-old bride in Derby. The couple settled in her home town of Chatteris,

Cambridgeshire. Of their two sons, one was lost at the age of eight. Frank Iliffe died aged 57.

Appearances: 1 app 1886-87, 0 goals

JACKSON Harry
Centre-forward

Born: Nottingham, 23 April 1864
Died: 32, Lenton Boulevard, Nottingham, 29 May 1899
Career: Sneinton Wanderers, Notts County, Derby County 1887, Notts County, Nottingham Forest

Starting serious football with Notts County, centre-forward Harry Jackson earned the sobriquet 'The Wizard of Goalscorers'. After making his Notts debut 'against' Derby County in 1884-85 he notched up a remarkable record – by the time Derby secured his services in March 1887 he had scored 82 goals for Notts in 80 appearances. On first trying out for Derby he used the enigmatic pseudonym R. T. 'Cameron', but was soon unmasked, the *Long Eaton Advertiser* crooning that 'right well did Jackson acquit himself'. But Derby retained his services for only two games before he decided to resume playing in Nottingham – maintaining his goal-a-game average Jackson naturally scored twice in his brief Derby stay. He played serious football only sporadically from then on, and proved less prolific, but on leaving Notts County after 5 Football League appearances he was credited with 96 goals in 123 games. In 1889-90 he played once for Nottingham Forest – a 9-0 defeat at Darwen – before fading from the scene. The son of commercial traveller Charles Jackson, he built up a successful business as a monumental sculptor and 'mural architect' with a works in Nottingham at Lenton Boulevard. Married with one son, he continued to be well-known on the sporting scene – a keen shooter, talented cricketer and 'prominent in boating circles'. He holds a unique but unenviable place in the Derby County annals – the first player to take his own life, using his own gun at home whilst his wife was in another room. The circumstances were bizarre – hitherto healthy and happy he became increasingly agitated one Saturday night after playing cricket. A telegraph wire had been erected outside his house, and when he suffered mild chest discomfort while trying to get to sleep he became convinced that the electric current was invading his body. After the same thing happened on Sunday night his anxiety turned rapidly to paranoia – he shot himself early on the Monday morning. An inquest returned a verdict of 'suicide whilst in an unsound state of mind'. He was 35.

Appearances: 2 apps 1886-87, 2 goals

'JONES' F.
See BAKEWELL George

F. 'Jones' was the pseudonym used by regular winger George Bakewell at home to Notts County on 26 September 1885. Notts were unfazed and emerged 3-0 winners. The deception was possibly a weak attempt to mask his identity at a time the Nottingham club coveted his services. In the event Bakewell stayed loyal to Derby before finally joining Notts County in 1891.

KELSALL Walter Leonard
Left-half

Born: Burslem, Staffordshire, 1864
Died: 5 Avonside, Hampton, Evesham, Worcestershire, 19 June 1922
Career: Alvaston & Boulton Olympic, Derby County 1884, Brailsford

W. L. Kelsall was playing with Alvaston when he threw in his lot with the newly-formed Derby County in 1884 – possibly recruited that summer on a cricket field, since he played both with and against Derby's first 'signing' Haydn Morley, a prime mover in gathering together the club's initial band of players. Kelsall played mainly for Derby County Wanderers but was given nine outings in the first team, all but one in the opening season. He was one of a number from the business and professional classes who gave such a diverse social mix to Derby's early line-ups. The son of cobalt merchant and colour manufacturer Edwin Stanway Kelsall – of Hamil House, Burslem – he came to Derby in the early 1880s. In 1890 Kelsall married Lucy Beatrice Bemrose, from the well-known Derby printing family. He became a bank clerk, and by 1901 had moved to the Chesterfield area as manager of the town's London City & Midland Bank. He continued to involve himself in sport, playing cricket for Chesterfield Wednesday – he had been good enough to once play for the Derbyshire Club and Ground XI. His marriage bore two sons but ended in acrimonious divorce in 1906 after his wife's allegations of maltreatment and excessive drinking were upheld – all luridly reported in the press. She soon remarried to Ernest Morley brother of Haydn. Unable to continue in banking Kelsall had by then moved away and changed direction entirely – acquiring a business partner he began trading as a market gardener and artificial manure merchant in Evesham, Worcestershire, but a split soon occurred. Kelsall continued to sell fertiliser and grow fruit on his own account, spending his later days in lodgings in Evesham. He had been living at 51a High Street when he died aged 57 in the infirmary wing of the Evesham Union Workhouse.

Appearances: 9 apps 1884-85 to 1886-87, 0 goals

KEYS John
Inside-right

Born: Derby, 1865
Died: 88, Vauxhall Road, Liverpool, 5 March 1890
Career: Derby County 1886, Everton, Everton Athletic

The son of Derby publican William Keys – landlord of the Seven Stars in Leaper Street – 'Jack' Keys was tried out in Derby County's final fixture of 1885-86 against an XI of Derby. He did well enough to feature over the following two seasons but was unable to command a regular place – for an inside-forward he failed to score enough goals. Along with two other Derby players – Frank Sugg and Harry Warmby – Keys graduated to Everton for the inaugural Football League season, playing once in their third League game. Warmby was by then his brother-in-law, having married Keys' sister Lydia. In 1889-90 Keys transferred his allegiance to Everton Athletic and became a great favourite. But his health began to fail, and in a match against Wigan Central he suffered an injury which proved fatal within a fortnight. He died at the home of his widowed mother. Aged 24 and still a bachelor he was buried at Anfield Cemetery.

Appearances: 19 apps 1885-86 to 1887-88, 2 goals

KNOX James Jenkinson
Inside-right

Born: Bakewell, Derbyshire, 1866
Died: 'Redlands', East Molesey, Surrey, 25 December 1898 (Estate value £604)
Career: Cambridge University, Bakewell Town, Derby County 1885, United Hospitals, Corinthians, Surbiton Hill

One of two Bakewell Town players used by Derby County – the other being J. L. Greaves. J. J. Knox made his debut on Boxing Day 1885 and became an admirable forward stand-in over two seasons. Derby might have benefited more from his evident talent – in 12 games he finished on the losing side only twice – but like his Cambridge colleague Spilsbury his availability was limited by both his studies and commitments to other sides. The son of physician and surgeon John Knox, of Church House, Bakewell, he was sent in his early teens to the Royal Medical Benevolent College, Surrey, and also spent some time at Staveley Grammar School, excelling in both academia and sport. After entering Cambridge in 1883 he won his football blue, gained a BA and MA, and qualified as a doctor and surgeon, setting up practice at East Molesey, Surrey. Whilst earlier assisting both Bakewell and Derby he was named as reserve for England against Ireland in 1886. A year later he was elected captain of the United Hospitals XI, and on appearing for the celebrated Corinthians was labelled 'one of the best-known Surrey County players'. In 1888 he was on the injury list with an unusual complaint – an infected finger resulting from a cut sustained during an autopsy. Given his physical prowess and healing profession, his own end proved tragic and ironic in equal portion. He died 'suddenly at home' on Christmas Day 1898 – aged only 32 he left a wife and daughter.

Appearances: 12 apps 1885-86 to 1886-87, 6 goals

LATHAM Arthur
Right-back and centre-half

Born: Coventry, Warwickshire, 23 January 1863
Died: Derbyshire Royal Infirmary, Derby, 8 November 1929 (Estate value £685. 5s 6d)
Career: Derby Junction, Derby Town, Derby St. Luke's, Derby Midland, Derby County 1884

Poached by Derby County from the strong Derby Midland side, he had previously done duty with Junction, Derby Town and St. Luke's. As such he was considered a highly experienced catch, and did not disappoint. Always conspicuous for 'pulling his knickers right above his waist' he turned out sporadically in the first two seasons – intermittently again assisting 'Juncs' – but fully committed himself from 1886-87, a season which embraced his temporary conversion from full-back to centre-half. Apt to creep upfield unnoticed, he scored the occasional goal, and was said to 'recount such moments for years afterwards to anyone who would listen'. He also recalled his amazement at 'receiving fifteen shillings expenses for a single game in the amateur era.' Latham lasted well into the League age, making the right-back spot his own before bowing out in 1891-92. After taking charge of the reserves, he became the club's long-serving trainer throughout the Steve Bloomer era, and on several occasions was 'sponge man' for England. In April 1902 he was Derby's emergency goalkeeper at Blackburn Rovers when chosen keeper Tom Harrison failed to turn up. Latham retired as Derby trainer in 1919 after being associated with the club for 35 years – he then took up a similar position at Norwich City, where former Derby player Major Frank Buckley was secretary-manager. The son of silk weaver Thomas Latham, the family came to Derby when Arthur was an infant. Both father and son later followed the trade of painter and decorator. Of Arthur's 8 children, a son Walter of the Leicestershire Regiment was killed in World War One in 1915. Latham moved back to Derby after his spell at Norwich, and at the time of his death aged 66 had been living in Pybus Street.

Appearances: Pre-League: 79 apps 1884-85 to 1887-88, 3 goals. League era: 51 apps 1888-89 to 1891-92 (plus 1901-02), 1 goal. Total: 130 apps 1884-85 to 1891-92 (plus 1901-02), 4 goals.

LAWRENCE Samuel Eaton
Left-back

Born: Burton-on-Trent, Staffordshire, 1866
Died: 11, Reservoir Road, Burton-on-Trent, Staffordshire, 23 February 1963 (Estate value £3,323 6s)
Career: Burton Strollers, Burton Wanderers, Derby County 1886, Burton Alma

When regular full-back Haydn Morley joined Notts County early in 1886-87, Derby County were in dire need of a solid replacement. Barely a week later Sam Lawrence of Burton Wanderers accepted Derby's invitation – he quickly impressed and became their regular left-back for two seasons, one of the few pre-Leaguers captured from the Burton area. His bearded countenance and strong physique proved an influential presence, his trademark 'ponderous clearances' often relieving the defence when calm assurance was most needed. His main fault was 'getting too far up the field and leaving the rearguard exposed' – forward ambitions rewarded by only a single goal, a freak punted return 'from almost sixty yards'. Lawrence remained an amateur but in a late-life interview revealed his 'expenses' had been 5 shillings a game, confirmation of the 'open secret' that useful sums were given even to 'unpaid' players. The son of brewery clerk Frederick Lawrence, he followed his father into the same profession. His marriage produced a son and daughter, but son Percy was killed in World War One in 1918. Lawrence himself proved a long survivor – his death in 1963 marked the closing of an era, the last of the pre-League players to fade. Aged 97 he is thought to be the longest-lived Derby County player – legendary management duo Brian Clough and Peter Taylor arrived at the Baseball Ground only four years after his passing.

Appearances: 56 apps 1886-87 to 1887-88, 1 goal

LAWSON Edward Kelso Lennox
Left-back

Born: Hartshorne, Derbyshire, 1859
Died: 'The Cottage', Dartmouth, Devon, 28 March, 1910 (Estate value £361. 15s 9d)
Career: Derby County 1886

E. K. Lawson was a reliable member of Derby County Wanderers, but made only three first team appearances. He deputised once for Haydn Morley and twice for Sam Lawrence, men of such calibre that Lawson was unable to supplant either. None of his games ended in victory, although two were drawn. The son of Edward Weekes Lawson – Crimean War veteran and Deputy Chief Constable of the Derbyshire Police Force – he attended Trent College in Long Eaton before going into banking. He became manager of the Uttoxeter and Ashbourne Union Bank Ltd. in Swadlincote, where he was also Honorary Superintendent of the Swadlincote Fire Brigade. He was a talented tennis player and had other eclectic interests – besides being an active Freemason and Secretary of the Church Gresley Horticultural Society, his Airedale Terriers took second prize in the inaugural show of the Burton-on-Trent Canine Society! He died aged 50 in Devon leaving a wife and three sons.

Appearances: 3 apps 1885-86 to 1886-87, 0 goals

LEES John
Centre-forward

Born: Castle Donington, Leicestershire, 1864
Died: 28, Frederick Street, Long Eaton, Derbyshire, 1936
Career: Castle Donington Town, Sawley Rangers, Derby County 1887, Long Eaton Rangers

Son of Midland Railway labourer George Lees, he captained his native Castle Donington Town in 1886-87. A plumber by trade, Lees relocated to Borrowash and began assisting nearby Sawley Rangers in 1887-88. Early that season he was given a run by Derby County after William 'Tich' Smith's return to Long Eaton Rangers left a void in the forward ranks. Although showing flashes of promise, only one of Lees' first four games was won, and he failed to score in any. He gave way to the rampaging cleric Reverend Gwynne, but plugged away in the reserves and again made the first team later that campaign, going on to figure in the first two seasons of the League era. In 1890-91 he led the attack for Long Eaton Rangers. Married with nine children, he ended his days in Long Eaton, dying there aged 72.

Appearances: Pre-League: 8 apps 1887-88, 1 goal. League era: 10 apps 1888-89 to 1889-90, 2 goals. Total: 18 apps, 1887-88 to 1889-90, 3 goals

LEVERS William Henry
Left-half

Born: East Bridgford, Nottinghamshire, 1862
Died: 'The Thatch', Duffield Road, Allestree, Derby, 31 October 1940 (Estate value £26,936 11s 8d)
Career: Derby County 1886

Son of corn merchant Thomas Levers, he moved to Derby early in the 1880s as a travelling salesman for the Derby grocery chain run by Giles Austin, forerunner to the Austin Hodgkinson group. A loyal Derby County reserve, he enjoyed only two first-team outings when the ranks were depleted. He was Vice-President of Derby

Constitutional Cricket Club, stalwart of the Beaconsfield Club billiards team, Town Councillor and committed freemason. When Derby County became a Limited Company in 1896 he stood as a guarantor – he had been successful in business, and in 1929 received a £1000 legacy from Giles Austin for his efforts. He subsequently carried on business as Lever & Co. Tea Merchants on Lodge Lane. Married with a son and daughter, by his middle years he was residing comfortably in Belper Road, later retiring to Allestree where he died aged 78 leaving a notably large estate.

Appearances: 2 apps 1886-87, 0 goals

LOCKER William
Outside-left

Born: Long Eaton, Derbyshire, 16 February 1866
Died: Kingsway Hospital, Derby, 15 August 1952 (Estate value £2,591 16s 9d)
Career: Long Eaton Rangers, Derby County 1887, Long Eaton Rangers, Stoke, Notts County

'Billy' Locker is one of the small elite to achieve the 'Derby Double' – playing football for Derby County and cricket for Derbyshire. His sole football outing came in December 1887 as an emergency stand-in 'found on the ground' – he was otherwise a regular for Long Eaton Rangers. Later as a right-hand bat for Derbyshire (1894 to 1903) he averaged 17.03 in 16 matches, with a top score of 76. He also played cricket for Derby Midland – team mate and fellow 'Derby Double' Levi Wright wrote that Locker 'took the finest catch I ever saw, when the famous Gilbert Jessop skied one to the boundary'. Locker had one game with Stoke in November 1889, but his best time in football came after signing for Notts County in June 1890 for £2 a week. In 1890-91 he scored 14 goals in 27 games and played in Notts' losing FA Cup Final side against Blackburn Rovers. Described as 'fast and most energetic, seldom brilliant, but having the most useful quality a player can possess, the knack of scoring goals' – he came close to international recognition, appearing for the North against the South at Sunderland in 1889, and chosen as England reserve against Ireland. The son of lace maker William Locker senior, he entered the same trade at the age of 15, working his way into management at a company best-known for its hair-nets – for years on end he sent one every Christmas to Levi Wright's wife! A lifelong bachelor, he worked until he was 75, and also immersed himself in civic life, spending 14 years on the Long Eaton Council, and two as its Chairman. After declining into dementia he died aged 86 in Derby's Kingsway Hospital – one of the select pre-League band to live beyond Derby's 1946 FA Cup win.

Appearances: 1 app 1887-88, 0 goals

LOWLES Harry
Left-back

Born: Hunterston, Cheshire, 5 December 1863
Died: 24 Statham Street, Derby, 2 October 1944 (Estate value £4,117 10s 10d)
Career: Darley Abbey, Derby County 1886, Derby St. Luke's, Derby Midland

Son of coachman John Lowles, the family moved to the East Midlands when Harry was still at school. When he first began work he boarded in West Row in Darley Abbey, where he established himself in the strong village side which furnished Derby County with several good players. He became a reliable member of Derby County Wanderers and provided cover in the first-team on seven occasions over two seasons. He later played for St. Luke's and Derby Midland. Lowles lived for many years in Statham Street and in later life was an active member of the West End Bowls Club. He started as a clerk at the Midland Railway when he was fourteen, and was a chief clerk when he retired in 1926 after 49 years service. Married with four children, he enjoyed a good retirement before his death aged 80 during the war years, living not quite long enough to see Derby County lift the FA Cup in 1946.

Appearances: 7 apps 1886-87 to 1887-88, 0 goals

LUNTLEY James
Goalkeeper

Born: Croydon, Surrey, 10 February 1859
Died: Park Road, Chilwell, Nottinghamshire, 21 January 1904 (Estate value £306. 3s 3d)
Career: Nottingham Forest, Derby County 1885, Nottingham Waverley, Beeston

Along with his brothers Walter and Edwin – the latter 'Ted' twice playing for England – James Luntley made his name at Nottingham Forest. Originally a left-winger, between 1883 and 1886 he filled most positions, and was the Forest goalkeeper when he made a single emergency appearance 'between the sticks' for Derby County. On 23 November 1885 his brother Walter had been selected to play away at Sheffield Wednesday, but had to cry off. After he sent James instead the *Derby Daily Telegraph* commented – 'and a right good replacement he proved to be'. Derby emerged 8-2 winners. James kept playing at a lesser level into his thirties, returning to the outfield. The brothers were the sons of artist James Luntley (1826-87) an accomplished provincial portrait painter who had exhibited at the Royal Academy – James junior sat for him but did not share his father's talent with the brush. In 1879 he enlisted in the army, serving with the 7th Dragoon Guards – he left in 1882 with the rank of corporal. Thereafter he began trading as a lace manufacturer but died aged 44 leaving a widow and four children. He is buried in Beeston Cemetery.

Appearances: 1 app 1885-86, goals conceded 2.

LUNTLEY Walter William
Goalkeeper

Born: Chapel Street, Croydon, Surrey, 12 January 1856
Died: Port Erin, Isle of Man, 22 May 1940
Career: Nottingham Forest, Beeston, Derby County 1884

Between 1877 and 1883 Luntley was a favourite at Nottingham Forest, where his younger brothers Edwin and James also made their names. Originally a half-back and full-back, he converted to goalkeeper in his mid-twenties, and was the fourth of nine custodians used by Derby County in their opening season. The relative 'veteran' played only twice in that campaign, but quickly impressed the *Derby Daily Telegraph*: 'Luntley has a long reach, a steady eye, a strong arm and a cool head, qualities which combined with a due amount of activity are all the requisites of a successful goalkeeper.' In a longer stint the following season, he enjoyed a spell of five games without conceding, and not until his ninth overall appearance did he taste defeat. Luntley would surely have played more, but commitments to his lace-making business restricted his availability. He continued to play at a lesser level, turning out for Beeston into the early 1890s. The son of accomplished portrait painter James Luntley (1826-87), he came to Beeston as an infant, spending his boyhood at Station Villas adjacent the Victoria Hotel. He later lived in Nottingham with his wife and two children. Said to be 'a brilliant player in six-a-side contests' – then a popular recreation – he was also a speedy track runner and 'very ready steeplechaser', later President of the Northern Counties Amateur Athletic Association. In addition he was Vice-President of Beeston Victoria Angling Club and a captain of Bulwell Forest Golf Club. His brother James kept goal once for Derby County – making the Luntleys the only goalkeeping brothers in the club's history. Walter considerably outlived both James and 'Ted' – he died aged 84 whilst visiting his daughter in the Isle of Man. His burial there marked the loss of a true pioneer from football's amateur dawn.

Appearances: 21 apps 1884-85 to 1885-86, goals conceded 29

MARSHALL Joseph
Goalkeeper

Born: Ripley, Derbyshire, 24 April 1862
Died: The Victoria Hotel, Cowley Street, Derby, 15 January 1913 (Estate value £1265. 12s 11d)
Career: Staveley, Chesterfield Spital, Accrington, Derby County 1887, Derby Junction

Joe Marshall was 'one of the finest goalkeepers in the country' when he joined Derby County, having already made his mark with Staveley and in brief dalliances with Spital and Accrington. Also a talented cricketer, he moved to Derby after contracting to play the summer game for Vulcan Ironworks, and between 1887 and 1890 played six matches for Derbyshire, two designated 'first-class'. It was said that 'his talents merited his reaching the very top rank at both sports, but that somehow eluded him, perhaps on account of his happy-go-lucky approach.' Although letting in 8 on his debut, Marshall survived to share duties in 1887-88 with Harry Bestwick, and the following season kept goal in Derby's first Football League game. He played 15 more but was beaten far too regularly, and the following campaign withdrew to Derby Junction. Inconsistency was his fatal flaw, it being recalled that 'he had a remarkable habit of performing prodigies of valour one minute and of giving away the show hopelessly the next, letting in some real ladylike efforts.' But he remained a great crowd favourite and ever the showman – 'one of his regular tricks was to duck under an advancing forward and throw him over his back, but with such innocence that referees seldom admonished him.' A native of Ripley, son of engine driver John Marshall, he began as a stoker, but in Derby ultimately became 'mine host' at several popular hostelries – the Canal Tavern, Liversage Arms, Plough Inn, and finally the Victoria Hotel, where he died aged only 50. Twice married, he left a widow and children and a host of admirers. An obituary observed – 'Everyone who knows Joe Marshall will regret his death, for he was a good fellow and has died without an enemy.' He is buried in Uttoxeter Road Cemetery.

Appearances: Pre-League: 8 apps 1887-88, goals conceded 22. League era: 16 apps 1888-89, goals conceded 48. Total: 24 apps 1887-88 to 1888-89, goals conceded 70

MATTHEWS James
Goalkeeper

Born: Kilsby, Northamptonshire, 1857
Died: 202 Crewe Street, Derby, 30 October 1939
Career: Derby Midland, Derby Junction, Derby County 1884, Derby Junction

Jim Matthews kept goal for Derby Midland in the season before Derby County were formed. Then in Derby's inaugural campaign he was the regular goalkeeper for Derby Junction, but filled in once for Derby in an emergency over the Christmas period –

Walter Luntley had cried off at the last moment. The son of agricultural labourer William Matthews, he came to Derby with several of his brothers in the 1870s in search of work, a familiar migratory route. In his late teens he got a job as a carriage cleaner with the Midland Railway, and was later a rivet-maker. By his forties he was a bricklayer's labourer and also running a grocery shop with his wife at 33 Lower Dale Road. One of his sons 'Billy' Matthews played one game for Derby County in 1912 having previously starred as a productive inside-forward at Aston Villa and Notts County – Billy died aged only 33 while landlord of The Roebuck Inn at Melbourne. His father by contrast reached 81.

Appearances: 1 app 1884-85, goals conceded 2.

MAYCROFT David
Half-back

Born: Newcastle-under-Lyme, Staffordshire, 1860
Died: Grantham, 1933
Career: Melbourne Town, Derby Junction, Derby County 1884

Along with George Springthorpe, one of two men from Melbourne Town tried out in the opening season, having previously had a spell as a forward with Derby Junction. Maycroft's debut in Derby's seventh game proved harrowing – the 7-0 home defeat to Walsall Town in the FA Cup. At a time when the team was constantly reshuffled in a bid to find the right blend, Maycroft played only once more, this time tasting victory, before resuming his more secure place with Melbourne Town. Rather more workaday than some of the 'white collar' men who formed a significant part of Derby's early ranks, he was the son of engine fitter John Maycroft. He lived in Kings Newton and Melbourne before a short hop to Coalville in the 1890s, but finally left the area for Grantham, working variously as an engine driver and in foundry work. Of his eight children two in particular had contrasting fortunes – his 19-year-old son Maurice was killed at the Battle of Loos in 1915, but his youngest daughter Caroline died in 2006 aged 100. Maycroft lived to be 72.

Appearances: 2 apps 1884-85, 0 goals

MONK Isaac
Centre-forward and half-back

Born: Derby, 1865
Died: Derbyshire Royal Infirmary, Derby, 12 May 1930 (Estate value £235. 5s 5d)
Career: Derby County 1886

'Ike' Monk – sometimes styled Monks – made two winning appearances at inside-right towards the end of 1885-86 before establishing himself at centre-forward when George Evans withdrew from the scene. Between spells in the reserves, Monk proved a versatile option, deputising in 1887-88 as right-half and playing centre-half for the first three games of the inaugural League campaign. His finest hour was at centre-forward in an FA Cup tie at Staveley in October 1887 – Derby trailed 1-0 with only a few minutes to go before Monk bagged a brace to steal a famous victory. The win gave Derby a psychological edge over their older north Derbyshire rivals in establishing ultimate supremacy in the county. By 1892 the original Staveley FC had disbanded. The son of John Monk, landlord of the Hare and Hounds in Erasmus Street, Isaac became a steam engine fitter, continuing to live in Erasmus Street and then nearby Darwin Terrace with his wife and seven children. The couple were living at 17 Park Street when Isaac died in hospital aged 65.

Appearances: Pre-league: 23 apps 1885-86 to 1887-88, 7 goals. League era: 4 apps 1888-89, 0 goals. Total: 27 apps 1885-86 to 1888-89, 7 goals

MOORE Henry Bernard
Goalkeeper

Born: Stanton Ford School, Curbar, Derbyshire, 1848
Died: Gordon Road, Borrowash, Derbyshire, 24 October 1922 (Estate value £1290. 0s 4d)
Career: Ockbrook & Borrowash, Derby County 1884

Sporting full whiskers and beard 'Harry' Moore was the trusty veteran keeper of Ockbrook & Borrowash when he made his debut for Derby County in their historic first win – at Repton School on the Tuesday afternoon of 28 October 1884 – when first-choice keeper Gillett was unable to play. Aged 36 he was comfortably the oldest debutant of the early days, and has the singular distinction of being the earliest-born of all Derby County players. Whilst considered reliable, his only other outing a month later tarnished his statistics. Derby crashed 7-0 to Derby Junction, the committee afterwards trying to get the result expunged on the grounds that 'we were not at full strength'. Moore also played a few times for Derby County Wanderers. Born at the Peak District school run by his mother and father Edward and Harriet – headmaster and schoolmistress respectively – a solid education equipped him with an eye for business. As a young man he moved to Borrowash near Derby and set up as a wheelwright, later diversifying his interests into undertaker, cab proprietor, haulier and general 'all-rounder'. The company H. B. Moore became a prosperous concern and its founder a well-known local character affably serving the area's transport needs. Married with three sons, his Borrowash residence for many years was 'Sunnyside' on Nottingham Road. Derby County's 'first-born' died aged 74 and is buried in Borrowash at the Old Cemetery.

Appearances: 2 apps 1884-85, goals conceded 9.

MORLEY Haydn Arthur
Full-back and half-back

Born: 43, Regent Street, Derby, 26 November 1860
Died: Cannonfields, Outseats, near Hathersage, Derbyshire, 15 May 1953 (Estate value £155. 14s 3d)
Career: Repton School, Derby Whitworth, Derby Town, Derby St. Luke's, Derby Midland, Derby County 1884, Notts County, Derby County 1889, Sheffield Wednesday, Loughborough Town, Casuals, Derby Junction, Derby Amateurs

Son of Derby County founder William Morley – the ebullient Haydn was the first player to pledge his allegiance to the club, having already served both Derby Town and Derby Midland. This set the tone, and during the summer of 1884 the young solicitor acted as unofficial 'recruitment officer', exercising his infectious enthusiasm to attract the best talent to the fledgling side – several key men were unashamedly 'poached' from local rivals, engendering much ill-feeling. One of two players to serve on the original committee, captain for the first game, and for two seasons a driving force – but four games into the 1886-87 campaign he resigned from the team amid some acrimony after 'falling out with members of the committee' and 'creating rifts among the players.' Snapped up by Notts County, he still assisted Derby in odd games – after 47 appearances for Notts he officially rejoined Derby in 1888-89, adding four League games to his tally. A committed amateur, Morley fully exercised his freedom to 'play for anyone' – assisting many more clubs than those listed, a host of Derbyshire sides used him at least once. In 1889-90 he graduated to The Wednesday – a great Sheffield favourite and captain in their 1890 FA Cup Final defeat by Blackburn Rovers. Dubbed a 'Pocket Hercules', his diminutive stature belied a big personality and gutsy style – a pen-picture recalled: 'Little Morley was a pale fellow, apparently without much strength, and with no weight for tackling, yet this 'bit of a chit' proved himself a smart full-back. A good kick, and speedy, he was largely a tactical player, and timed his rushes for the ball to a nicety.' He first shone at Repton School (1873-80) but was then considered a better cricketer – later playing twice for Derbyshire (1884 and 1891) and with good local sides including Derby Midland and Belper Meadows. After leaving Repton he qualified as a solicitor, practising and living in Derby before removing to Sheffield around 1895, conducting his business Haydn Arthur Morley and Co. at 26, Paradise Square. By all accounts a hearty reveller fully embracing the freedom of bachelorhood, he eventually married in 1908 when aged 47, his bride 28-year-old Sheffield girl Katie Annie Broomhead – the couple had two daughters and a son. This added to a much earlier namesake son born in 1893 – to unmarried mother Ellen Richardson, daughter of Derby County secretary Sam Richardson. That episode created quite a stir and was instrumental in Morley moving to Sheffield to start afresh. In later life he moved out of the city to nearby Hathersage – he set up the village bowls club and ran a brass band there. Recorded as a 'veritable Peter Pan', he attended his office into his nineties, only 'retiring' as a result of ill-fortune – a scratch on his foot became badly infected, leading to the amputation of a leg. Derby County's first 'signing' died aged 92 at the home of his son – along with father William and brother 'W. T.' the third nonagenarian of the remarkable Morley dynasty which was so influential in the club's early days.

Appearances: Pre-League: 72 apps 1884-85 to 1887-88, 2 goals. League era: 6 apps 1888-89, 0 goals. Total: 78 apps 1884-85 to 1888-89, 2 goals

MOSS Gerald
Centre-forward

Born: Allahabad, India, 2 March 1868
Died: Hammersmith Hospital, London, 6 July 1936
Career: Derby School, Bakewell, Derby County 1887

Gerald Moss was still at Derby School when given a number of outings at centre-forward in 1886-87. He was captain of football, rowing and rifles, in the school cricket XI, and a good athlete. His Derby County performances were said to be of the 'curate's egg' variety – good in parts – so while often playing admirably he never fully convinced that he had the quality to sustain a place. In five games leading the attack he scored one goal. Moss also assisted the reserves and other Derbyshire sides but his army career curtailed his time in Derby. Born in India the son of Thomas Moss, of the Indian Civil Service, Gerald spent part of his boyhood in York, and in November 1887 enlisted in the York and Lancaster Regiment. His service record proved exemplary – he attained the rank of Sergeant in four years but seems never to have been commissioned as an Officer, finishing as a Sergeant Instructor in India before leaving the army in 1905. He returned to live in London where he worked in a clerical and accounting capacity. Seemingly never married, he had been living at 221 Hammersmith Road, London, when he died in hospital aged 68.

Appearances: 5 apps 1886-87, 1 goal

MUSSON Charles Walter
Goalkeeper (as borrowed stand-in, normally half-back)

Born: Bedworth, Warwickshire, 1859
Died: Green Lane Farm, Rawmarsh, Rotherham, 16 December 1920 (Estate value £1646 13s.)
Career: Effingham Brass Works, Rotherham Town

Rotherham Town captain 'Walter' Musson was the unlikely stand-in goalkeeper for a midweek game at Sheffield Wednesday in December 1886. Derby arrived a man short after regular keeper Harry Bestwick cried off at the last moment – Rotherham's half-back Musson had gone to watch, but agreed to stand between the posts, doing well enough for Derby to emerge with a 2-2 draw. Also in the Derby side that day was Musson's former Rotherham team-mate Harry Warmby. Musson perchance had gone to meet his old friend – the two had also played together for Effingham Brass Works where both had been 'brass buffers'. Warmby moved to Derby, but Musson gave long service to Rotherham Town – the son of coalminer Charles Musson, he fathered ten children, and died aged 61 leaving quite a healthy estate.
Appearances: 1 app 1886-87, goals conceded 2

NASH Richard Wilkinson
Forward

Born: Upton Lea, near Slough, Buckinghamshire, 3 January 1864
Died: 'Allestree', Harestone Valley Road, Caterham Valley, Surrey, 29 March 1941 (Estate value £17,069. 17s 11d)
Career: Derby County 1884, Old Etonians, Casuals, Slough

Old Etonian R. W. Nash – by profession a civil engineer – came to work in Derby in the early 1880s. He had returned to Buckinghamshire by 1890, but left a distinctive mark on the Derby sporting scene, proving a great enthusiast and popular figure. After his debut in the club's fourth game the *Derby Daily Telegraph* bluntly observed that 'Nash was almost useless'. Yet later they said: 'Nash is proving himself a useful man, and we hope to see more of him'. In the event he appeared sporadically over three seasons, bagging a fair return of goals. Nash was one of the small band of 'toffs' assisting Derby County in their formative years – but when League football began in 1888 he took sanctuary in the gentlemen sides Old Etonians and Casuals. After returning south he also played for the newly-formed Slough Town FC and at both football and cricket for Buckinghamshire. The son of gentleman farmer Henry Fleetwood Nash, he married in 1893 and produced two children, but lost his wife Ethel soon after the birth of their only daughter. Although only 37 he is thought to have remained a widower for forty years – he spent time in Brazil in the 1920s, but settled in Surrey. In his Derby days he played cricket for Allestree, evidently retaining a lasting affection for that youthful time, for he died aged 77 at the Surrey home he had named 'Allestree'.
Appearances: 20 apps 1884-85 to 1887-88, 7 goals

NEEDHAM Thomas
Outside-left

Born: Derby, 18 April 1867
Died: 8 Beech Gardens, Alvaston, Derby, 24 February 1956 (Estate value £286. 5s 1d)
Career: Darley Abbey, Derby County 1886, Burton Swifts

One of a number of players lured by Derby County from Darley Abbey – as a consequence the old village club's demise was hastened, while the younger but 'bigger' club flourished. Tommy Needham was mainly a left-sided forward but filled in wherever needed. Labelled 'baby-faced' and 'very conscientious' he made his debut in 1885-86 but only established himself two seasons later, when he played all but seven games and scored 14 goals, including a Christmas Eve hat-trick. He became one of the relatively few pre-Leaguers to survive into the League age, staying with Derby until 1889-90. Thereafter he assisted Burton Swifts. The son of labourer Thomas Needham senior, the family lived initially in Leaper Street, but Tommy moved to Darley Abbey as a boy with his widowed mother. He began work as a 'printer's lad' but became a railway porter and ended as a railway foreman. He was twice married with three children – his first wife died aged 26. Needham himself lived to a fine age – after Derby County won the FA Cup in 1946 he enjoyed a further ten years, signing off aged 88.

Appearances: Pre-League: 45 apps 1885-86 to 1887-88, 21 goals. League era: 16 apps 1888-89 to 1889-90, 3 goals. Total: 61 apps 1885-86 to 1889-90, 24 goals

NICHOLLS Hubert
Full-back and half-back

Born: Champion Hill, Camberwell, Surrey, 20 May 1858
Died: 'Cranleigh', Longton, Stoke-on-Trent, Staffordshire, 1 July 1925 (Estate value £12,023. 6s 11d)
Career: Cambridge University, Swifts, Derby County 1884, Blackwell Colliery

The *Derby Daily Telegraph* announced with some enthusiasm in November 1884 that 'Nicholls of Swifts is about to take up his residence in Derby'. Swifts were a crack gentlemen's side based near Slough, and Nicholls had earlier won his blue at Cambridge University, where he played in the St. John's College XI with Derby County colleague Percy Exham. He had little trouble winning a place at Derby and was roundly praised – 'makes very few mistakes and is wonderfully cool and steady'. But his commitments to the medical profession restricted his involvement to sporadic outings over three seasons. During his time in Derbyshire, Nicholls also became associated with Blackwell Colliery, where he was designated Assistant Surgeon, and on occasion added a touch of class to the colliery team. The son of army outfitter John Nicholls, he earned his BA and MA at Cambridge, and qualified as a doctor and surgeon. In 1890 he married Edith Frances Foulds, daughter of a Derby doctor, and set up practise in Longton, Stoke-on-Trent. He was Justice of the Peace for Stoke for some years. He died at his home 'Cranleigh' aged 67, survived by his wife and two of three offspring, leaving a healthy estate.

Appearances: 11 apps 1884-85 to 1886-87, 0 goals

OTHER A. N.

On only two occasions did match reports resort to 'A. N. Other' in their recorded line-ups — goalkeeper against Repton School on 12 February 1885, and right-back against Gainsborough Trinity on 28 January 1888, both selections remaining eternal mystery men.

OTTEWELL F.
Outside-right

Born: Inconclusive
Died: Inconclusive
Career: St. Alkmund's, Derby Whitworth, St. Werburgh's, Derby County 1887

Made his sole senior appearance on Christmas Eve 1887 when Derby were obliged to fulfil two 'first-team' fixtures on the same day. An adaptable player he otherwise helped the reserves and third team. Since several Ottewells were active in football locally, a definite identity cannot be allocated on current evidence.

Appearances: 1 app 1887-88, 0 goals

PARRY Francis Herbert
Half-back

Born: Walmer, Kent, 6 September 1866
Died: The Golf Hotel, Woodhall Spa, Lincolnshire, 11 September 1924 (Estate value £1424. 18s 6d)
Career: Derby County 1884

F. H. Parry helped out four times in the opening season but was otherwise part of the reserves pool, as was his younger brother Charles de Courcy Parry. He was also a good cricketer with Derby Friars, Spondon and Mickleover. His family came to Nottingham when Parry was still an infant, thence to Derby where his father Captain Francis J. Parry, a former Royal Marine, became Chief Constable of Nottinghamshire and

Derbyshire. Parry's teenage home was The Lodge, Mickleover, and at Repton School he boarded in the same house as later Derby team mate Benjamin Spilsbury. Married with one son, Parry forged a good management career with the Bass brewery, residing at Geary House, Bretby, then High Street, Burton-on-Trent, with a clutch of servants. His wife hailed from Lincolnshire, the county in which Parry died aged only 58. Brother Charles became Chief Constable of Cumberland and Westmorland and was awarded the CBE. Charles's 'wayward adventurer' son Charles Norman – Parry's nephew – achieved gruesome celebrity in 1920 as the young pursuant said to have shot dead the 'most wanted' World War One deserter Percy Toplis, the infamous 'Monocled Mutineer'.

Appearances: 4 apps 1884-85, 0 goals

PARSONS William Edward
Goalkeeper

Born: Thayetmyo, Central Burma, 23 October 1864
Died: Bakewell Street, Derby, 10 March 1917
Career: Derby St. Luke's, Derby County 1885, Derby St. Luke's, Lincoln City

Born in Burma where his father Sergeant William Parsons – 2nd Battalion of the 19th regiment – was serving in the army, Parsons came to England at the age of twelve and lost his father three years later. In his late teens he attached himself to the established St. Luke's club, and was their goalkeeper for several seasons before Derby County was formed. Enigmatically known as 'Spoff' he proved extremely loyal to St. Luke's, appearing only four times for Derby purely to help them out. An observer recalled: 'Goalkeeper was a real problem to the County in the early days. They desperately wanted Parsons from the start, and it was common knowledge the committee offered him good inducements, but 'Spoff' was proof to all their blandishments, showing most admirable loyalty to the Saints on account of his deeply religious conviction. Time and again he was chaired shoulder-high from their Peet Street ground after performing miracles. He never looked very strong, but he was by far the best goalkeeper in the district, and very adept with his feet. He often kept goal in long white cricket trousers.' Alas he let in four on his Derby debut. Perversely Parsons did part from St. Luke's in 1891-92 – making 18 appearances for Lincoln City – but remained firmly linked to the club, and to the church as a Sunday school teacher. Married with three children, he worked as a compositor at the Bemrose Printing Works, and was an auditor for the Derby Typographical Society. As such it was fitting that his death made the 'Stop Press' of the *Derby Daily Telegraph*: 'Parsons succumbed aged 52 earlier today to appendicitis and pneumonia. His death will excite much regret amongst all who admired his sterling character, but especially those who recall his brilliant achievements between the posts. It is a pathetic fact that an old comrade Jack Robinson – the former Derby County and England goalkeeper – called at his home this very afternoon, only to be told his friend had just died.' 'Spoff' Parsons is honoured by a fine brass plaque in St. Luke's church.

Appearances: 4 apps 1884-85 to 1887-88, goals conceded 5

PEARCE Cornelius
Forward

Born: Grimsby, Lincolnshire, 1866
Died: 35, Tiverton Street, New Cleethorpes, Lincolnshire, 19 December 1923 (Estate value £982. 9s 3d)
Career: Grimsby Town, Derby County 1887, Derby Midland

The story of 'Neal' Pearce is a perfect example of how the potential rewards of the 'new' game professional football persuaded countless young men to leave their home towns in search of something better. When professionalism was legalised in 1885 Pearce was young and single – and this son of Grimsby fish merchant George Pearce seemed anxious not to follow in his father's footsteps. He began work as an ironmonger's apprentice, but also enjoyed football. Pearce was a reserve at Grimsby Town when Derby County visited in 1887 for a pre-season six-a-side contest. They borrowed his services for the day, won the tournament, and promptly signed him on. He began in the reserves and later had a good but fleeting spell in the first team – none of his five games were lost. He might have played more but for a bizarre incident which probably hastened his departure. Against Wolves in the penultimate game of 1887-88 Pearce had been asked to 'stand by' in case he was needed. In the event he wasn't, but Pearce insisted on taking the field, and flatly refused to leave. As the game began, Derby had twelve men on the arena. Play was soon stopped, but fifteen minutes elapsed before Pearce was frog-marched off by the constabulary, having already ignored the avuncular appeals of club President William Monk Jervis. Pearce was said to have 'left the field with a crestfallen air' – perhaps he realised the game was up. He never played for Derby again – after the odd outing for Derby Midland he returned to Grimsby where almost inevitably he became a fish merchant. He also married and had two children. He did though retain a lifelong interest in Derby County and for many seasons later would greet them whenever they played in Grimsby, invariably being the butt of good-natured chaff concerning his long-remembered misdemeanour. He was also listed as a League referee and linesman in 1912. His parable as a player still resonates in today's game – thwarted ambition through failure to 'make the grade' is as common as ever it was. He died in Cleethorpes aged 58 although his recorded address at the time was in Blackpool – his grave in Cleethorpes cemetery carries the enigmatic inscription 'In memory of my dear friend Neal Pearce'.

Appearances: 5 apps 1887-88, 3 goals

PEEL H.
Left-back

Born: Staveley, Derbyshire, probably 1863
Died: Staveley, Derbyshire, probably 1914
Career: Staveley, Derby County 1884

Peel was established in his native Staveley side when he made his sole Derby appearance in the fourth game of the opening season. This was after three straight losses, the committee having been urged by correspondents in the Derby newspapers to 'look further into the county for talent' – the first instance of supporter pressure being applied. Ending on the losing side he resumed with Staveley and became one of their early stars. Listed only as 'H. Peel' his identity is not quite cast iron, but the strong likelihood is that he is Ernest Harry Peel (1863-1914) the son of foundry worker John Peel. 'Harry' worked at the Staveley Ironworks as a pattern maker and was father to nine children. He died aged 51 in the town of his birth.

Appearances: 1 app 1884-85, 0 goals

PITMAN Reuben John
Goalkeeper

Born: Derby, 30 April 1864
Died: 296, Stockbrook Street, Derby, 30 December 1932
Career: Derby County 1887

What he lacked in stature Pitman recouped in bravery. A cameo stated: 'A player of much pluck which he at times carries to the point of recklessness, giving the impression that he would rather be 'kicked to death' than concede a goal. His habit of falling on the ball and curling up around it has brought him many hard knocks from forwards none too particular about their methods in trying to part him from it.' Largely a reserve, he assisted the firsts periodically until the second League campaign. One of few to have a game named in his honour, 'Pitman's Match' marked his 'extraordinary performance' in a Cup tie at Aston Villa on 16 February 1889. Although Derby lost 5-3 he was said to have performed 'perfect heroics time and again in an absolute quagmire.' The legend gained momentum, and at the time of his death the *Derby Daily Telegraph* somewhat over-gilded the narrative: 'In the famous game against Villa it was said that without Pitman, Derby would have had at least 40 goals scored against them.' But in the course of time the ball passed him rather too often – and in his final two games he let in ten. One of five children of painter and decorator Hugh John Pitman, he followed his father's profession. His own marriage also produced a large family. Pitman's life was far from easy, but the manner of his demise aged 68 sums up his stoicism. After falling and fracturing a thigh he refused to see a doctor, insisting it was not troubling him. He continued to get about but died of pneumonia 6 weeks later, the coroner remarking upon his 'extraordinary courage in the face of great pain'. A daughter added: 'He was one of those men who would never admit anything could hurt him'. He is buried at Nottingham Road Cemetery.

Appearances: Pre-League: 8 apps 1886-87 to 1887-88, goals conceded 15. League era: 7 apps 1888-89 to 1889-90, goals conceded 20. Total: 15 apps 1886-87 to 1889-90, goals conceded 35.

PLACKETT Laurence
Outside-left

Born: Breaston, Derbyshire, 16 January 1869
Died: 'The Rosery', Wilsthorpe Road, Breaston, Derbyshire, 28 February 1939 (Estate value £1443. 6s 7d))
Career: Long Eaton Alexandra, Derby County 1886, Breaston, Nottingham Forest

'Lol' Plackett made his debut in the final game of 1885-86 and became a regular the next season, although sometimes assisting his native Breaston in key games. He was later the first Derby County player to complete an ever present season in the Football League. He scored twice in Derby's opening League game at Bolton Wanderers and was at outside or inside-left throughout 1888-89. But the relentless nature of the 'new football' appeared to take its toll. In June 1889 he wrote to the committee that he could not play in 1889-90 as he was unable to leave his employment, and besides felt 'that I cannot stand the strain of another season's programme of League matches'. The rationale might be questionable, for he joined Nottingham Forest instead – although in fairness they were not then members of the Football League. Plackett scored twice for Forest in nine Football Alliance games. The son of lace manufacturer Henry Plackett, he came from a well-known Breaston family renowned for their sporting prowess – at one time an entire Plackett XI was got together for a cricket match. Laurence worked as a clerk in the Corporation Accounts Department, and lived his entire life in Breaston. His younger brother Henry also played in Derby's opening League season before moving to Nottingham Forest. Both were keen cricketers, and 'Lol' a renowned athlete with Breaston Harriers. He died at home aged 70 shortly before the Second World War, leaving a wife and only son. Brother Henry lived until 1948.

Appearances: Pre-League: 55 apps 1885-86 to 1887-88, 15 goals. League era: 24 apps 1888-89, 8 goals. Total: 79 apps 1885-86 to 1888-89, 23 goals

135

RADFORD Joseph Edwin
Centre-forward

Born: Derby, 1863
Died: Blackpool, Lancashire, 1941
Career: Derby Junction, Derby County 1887

Son of cabinet-maker Joseph Radford senior, he became first a joiner and later a general builder. While living in Freehold Street in the 1880s he was a regular for the nearby Junction Street side during its heyday as a powerful force. Joe Radford led the Derby County attack only once, in a draw at Rotherham Town in November 1887. After marrying in 1883 he had two daughters, and by his forties had moved to Blackpool as a builder, his wife Ellen running a boarding-house there. In 1912 the family sailed for Boston, United States, but returned to England within a year. Radford died back in Blackpool aged 78.

Appearances: 1 app 1886-87, 0 goals

ROULSTONE Walter
Left-half

Born: Devonshire Street, Derby, 1867
Died: 74 Bondgate, Castle Donington, Leicestershire, 20 February 1953
Career: Sawley Rangers, Derby County 1887, Heanor Town, Castle Donington Town

One of a trio who began with Sawley Rangers – the others were Amos 'Jammer' Smith and Albert Williamson – before giving sterling service to Derby County. 'Roddy' Roulstone played only one pre-League season, but became the first real stalwart of the League era. Known for his tough-tackling and dogged approach, he missed only one game in the first three League campaigns and was the first to complete 100 League appearances for Derby County. After his final game in December 1894 he had a spell with Heanor Town, but ultimately lent his considerable experience to his local club Castle Donington Town, who he captained in 1899-1900. His older brother Frank played once for Derby in the opening League season, and a younger brother Arthur counted Loughborough Town, Kettering, Leicester Fosse and Ilkeston United among his clubs. The son of Reuben Roulstone, the family graduated to Castle Donington in Walter's boyhood, and he became both an honorary native and revered elder there. Generations of Roulstones had been basket-makers – after learning the skills as a child, Walter spent his entire working life in the family business and shop. Married with seven children, he resided in Bondgate for over 60 years, living long enough to know that his former club had won the FA Cup in 1946 – he died seven years later aged 86 having lost his wife Emily only six weeks earlier. The most enduring testimony to his effectiveness as a player was that delivered many years earlier by the England international winger Billy Bassett – 'I would sooner meet any half in the game than the wild man Roulstone. He frightens me to death'

Appearances: Pre-League: 31 apps 1887-88, 0 goals. League era: 125 apps 1888-89 to 1894-95, 4 goals. Total: 156 apps 1887-88 to 1894-95, 4 goals

SELVEY Walter
Inside-forward

Born: Derby, 4 December 1865
Died: 19, Becher Street, Derby, 1 November 1944
Career: Derby Midland, Derby County 1887, Derby Junction

The son of Joseph Selvey, a forgeman in the railway industry, Walter followed a similar route, serving over four decades as a springmaker in the Carriage and Wagon department of Midland Railway. He played initially for the strong works team Derby Midland which pre-dated Derby County, but like others from that rival club was tempted to change his shirt. Having become established in the Derby County Wanderers he was given a first-team chance in December 1887. Whilst other reserves squandered their opportunities, Selvey impressed and was given an extended run – he scored 6 times by the end of the season, forming a good understanding with newly-arrived centre-forward Archie Goodall. He played once in the following first League season before transferring his allegiance to another local rival Derby Junction. His older brother Scotch also played one League game. Selvey kept close to Derby County after his playing days – with his wife and two daughters he lived for some time at 180 Shaftesbury Crescent right by the Baseball Ground, remaining in that area until his death from bronchial pneumonia aged 78.

Appearances: Pre-League: 19 apps 1887-88, 6 goals: League era: 1 app 1888-89, 0 goals: Total: 20 apps 1887-88 to 1888-89, 6 goals

SHEPHERD W
Inside-left

Born: Inconclusive
Died: Inconclusive
Career: Derby County 1884

Shepherd assisted the reserves occasionally but played only one senior game, Derby's first ever victory, the 3-2 win at Repton School on 28 October 1884. Several W. Shepherds were playing locally and his identity remains elusive. He may have been William Shepherd the Heanor Templars captain having a try-out, but the case remains open.

Appearances: 1 app 1884-85, 0 goals

SHERWIN Charles
Inside-right

Born: Boulton, Derby, 15 February 1854
Died: Alvaston, Derby, 5 January 1895
Career: Derby County 1884

Charles Sherwin played two games in the forward line in the inaugural season, as did his much younger brother Percy, although on different occasions. They did play together for the enthusiastic band which formed the reserves side Derby County Wanderers. Like Percy, Charles was unable to make the best of his first-team chance, but outdid his brother by bagging a goal in a 4-2 win at Wirksworth in the Derbyshire Cup. The son of farmer and builder William Sherwin, Charles lived on the family farm on London Road until his marriage. He worked as a smith, builder and later wheelwright – all related to his father's business. He died aged 40 leaving a widow and two children.

Appearances: 2 apps 1884-85, 1 goal

SHERWIN Percy Reginald
Outside-left

Born: Boulton, Derby, 13 August 1863
Died: The Cottage Hospital, Ashby-de-la Zouch, Leicestershire, 28 October 1935 (Estate value £352)
Career: Derby County 1884

Both Percy Sherwin and his older brother Charles made two full appearances in the Derby forward line, but on separate occasions. They did appear together for the reserves team Derby County Wanderers. Percy's chance came early in the opening season when he deputised on the left-wing for Charlie Ward. Indeed Ward soon departed the scene, and Sherwin might have made the position his own, but failed to impress sufficiently. Instead half-back Ernie Hickinbottom was tried there and proved a revelation, securing the left-wing spot for the remainder of that season. Sherwin was the son of farmer and builder William Sherwin of London Road, Boulton, close to Alvaston. He worked on the family farm well into his forties, by that time married with a daughter. In his younger days he had been a noted local athlete and good club cricketer for Alvaston. In common with several of the Wanderers clan he shared a love of music and other gentle pursuits – a member of the Alvaston musical and horticultural societies, and warden of Boulton Parish Church. In later years he moved to Elms Farm, Newbold, Leicestershire, but died nearby in hospital aged 72.

Appearances: 2 apps 1884-85, 0 goals

SHIPLEY William
Half-back and forward

Born: Derby, 1860
Died: The Woolsack, 164 Parliament Street, Derby, 3 November 1892
Career: Victoria Street Congregational, St. Luke's, Derby County 1884, St. Luke's

'Will' Shipley played in the historic opening fixture, but thereafter made only one further appearance, neither game being won. His flirtation with Derby County proved merely an interlude to his staunch commitment to the much older-established St. Luke's club, for whom he was already playing when Derby County was formed. Whilst with 'Saints' he also played one game 'against' Derby County for Sheffield Wednesday, agreeing to help Wednesday out when they arrived two men short in January 1886. The son of gimp maker William Shipley senior, he became an accounts clerk, and from 1891 served as joint auditor of the Derbyshire FA. With his wife Lucy Coxon he was also licensee of The Woolsack in Parliament Street. All seemed 'set fair' until Will's sad early death in 1892 – aged only 32 he left a widow and no children. At the next meeting of the Derbyshire FA a vote of condolence was unanimously passed.

Appearances: 2 apps 1884-85, 0 goals

SINTON James
Outside-right

Born: Hampstead Road, St. Pancras, London, Middlesex, 1866
Died: 54, Luton Road, Harpenden, Hertfordshire, 3 September 1956 (Estate value £3,883. 2s)
Career: Derby County 1887

The St. Pancras birthplace is an apt one – James Sinton came to Derby as an infant when his railway clerk father James senior moved with the Midland Railway. He became a reliable member of the reserves but represented the senior side only once, when Derby had to fulfil two 'first team' fixtures in a single day. Rather than face Bolton Wanderers at the County Ground, Sinton was given the supposedly easier task of visiting Ashbourne St. Oswalds for a Derbyshire Cup tie, but Derby's effective second string was soundly beaten. He had followed his father into the Midland Railway but in January 1888 resigned his position as a clerk in the Goods Department to pursue a vocation for music. He moved to Dresden, Germany, to take up an appointment with a firm of musical instrument makers. The experience proved fruitful – on returning to England he married in 1893 and managed a wholesale musical instrument business in Ealing, later running his own similar firm in Bournemouth before returning to the London area. His marriage produced four children. Sinton proved one of the longest survivors of the pre-League era – after losing his wife he died just 8 months later at the age of 90.

Appearances: 1 app 1887-88, 0 goals

SMITH Amos
Inside-left

Born: Sawley, Derbyshire, 13 September 1857
Died: 16, Bonsall Street, Long Eaton, Derbyshire, 6 December 1940
Career: Sawley Rangers, Long Eaton Rangers, Derby County 1884, Sawley Rangers, Long Eaton Rangers

'Jammer' Smith was the first popular hero at Derby County, a predecessor to Steve Bloomer a decade later. After starting in his teens with his native Sawley, he became a high-scoring favourite with Long Eaton Rangers, where he acquired his enigmatic nickname. Soon after marrying Elizabeth Carter in Melbourne in the summer of 1884 he played in Derby's historic first game on his 27th birthday. No one in the opening season made more appearances – he missed only two games, finishing top-scorer with 17 goals in 33 outings. In the third fixture at Notts County he was the scorer of the club's first away goal. After adding a further 18 strikes in 1885-86 – playing in all but 7 games – he returned to his roots, dividing his loyalties between Sawley and Long Eaton Rangers, at the latter enjoying a second heyday into his thirties. A broken leg early in 1890-91 hastened the end of a fine career, but he made a final token appearance in February 1893 for Long Eaton Athletic – the Rangers reserve side – as an emergency stand-in. The son of farm labourer William Smith, he added a robust rusticity to an early Derby forward-line which included the lofty Cambridge University duo Spilsbury and Chevallier. Although only small he was stocky and said to be 'hard as nails, rarely succumbing to injury'. One supporter recalled: 'Jammer Smith was a highly-popular figure who had a style and personality all his own. Of immense spirit and energy, he was neither fast nor at all a clever ball-player, but had a wonderful knack of getting into position for any opening that might present itself in front of goal. He benefited a lot from the right-wing screw crosses of George Bakewell – often there to send the ball home, he employed his head with such formidable accuracy that the cleverest goalkeepers were liable to be beaten.' Away from football Smith spent his entire working life in the lace trade – after starting in his early teens he was employed for many years by Daykins of Long Eaton. He had already lost his wife and several of eight children when he died aged 83 in the street he had lived in for over 50 years. Derby County's first cult hero is buried in Long Eaton Cemetery.

Appearances: 63 apps 1884-85 to 1885-86, 36 goals

SMITH George Henry
Left-back

Born: Locomotive Inn, Long Eaton, Derbyshire, 1865
Died: 'Invergarry', 3, Briar Gate, Long Eaton, Derbyshire, 15 October 1933 (Estate value £9,429. 1s 1d)
Career: Long Eaton Rovers, Long Eaton Alexandra, Long Eaton Rangers, Derby County 1886, Long Eaton Rangers

George 'Loco' Smith was one of three Smiths from Long Eaton Rangers who assisted Derby County, each distinguished at Rangers by their nicknames – the others being his brother 'Tich' and the celebrated 'Jammer'. George got his moniker through spending the first 25 years of his life at the Locomotive Inn, where his father William was landlord. In common with quite a few others he never really 'joined' Derby County, playing only one game in November 1886 as cover for the injured Sam Lawrence. Otherwise he was a Long Eaton Rangers man through and through, among his high-spots a famous Birmingham Cup Final win over West Bromwich Albion in 1887 – a triumph shared with 'Tich' and 'Jammer'. He was in the lace-making trade for over 40 years before retiring in 1925. A great cricket enthusiast, he played for Long Eaton Zingari and the Conservative Club, and was later a subscriber to Sandiacre and Derbyshire County Cricket Club. Still known as 'Loco' in advancing years, he had been ill for six weeks when he died aged 68 leaving a widow, two sons, a daughter, and for the time a very healthy estate.

Appearances: 1 app 1886-87, 0 goals

SMITH William
Forward

Born: Locomotive Inn, Long Eaton, Derbyshire, 30 March 1869
Died: The Barley Mow, Weekday Cross, Nottingham, 27 September 1907 (Estate value £331. 0s 9d)
Career: Long Eaton Rangers, Derby County 1887, Long Eaton Rangers, Derby Junction, Notts Rangers, Notts County, Nottingham Forest, Long Eaton Rangers, Notts County, Loughborough Town, Lincoln City, Burton Swifts

Man of many clubs 'Tich' Smith stood at only 5 feet 6 inches but proved a real handful for countless bigger defenders. Like his brother George 'Loco' his first loyalty lay with his local side Long Eaton Rangers, but he left them to begin a brief productive spell with Derby in January 1887 – aged just seventeen he scored 7 in his first nine games and was labelled 'a rattling good youth'. He then returned to Long Eaton before one final run out for Derby early in 1887-88. He also played once for Derby Junction in September 1888. In due course he embraced the professional game, flitting around the

East Midlands clubs to notch 122 Football League appearances for Notts County, Nottingham Forest, Loughborough Town and Lincoln City. He ended a fine career at Burton Swifts in his early thirties. On 19 December 1891 he played for England in an 'unofficial' international against Canada at Kennington Oval, scoring 4 in a 6-1 victory. The same season he helped Nottingham Forest become Football Alliance champions. The son of William Smith senior – progressively railway guard, publican and lace manufacturer – 'Tich' also entered the lace trade before taking on a series of licensed premises. He was mine host at the New Inn in Long Eaton, and finally the Barley Mow in Nottingham, where he died aged only 38. He left a widow and three daughters including twins, one of the latter living in three centuries to reach 105. He was buried in Long Eaton Cemetery.

Appearances: 13 apps 1886-87 to 1887-88, 7 goals

SPILSBURY Benjamin Ward
Inside-forward

Born: 'The Longlands', Findern, Derbyshire, 1 August 1864
Died: North Vancouver, British Columbia, Canada, 15 August 1938 (Estate value £2,519. 0s 9d)
Career: Repton School, Cambridge University, Cambridge University Wanderers, Derby County 1884, Brentwood, Corinthians, England (3 caps, 5 goals)

England international Ben Spilsbury was the first 'big name' at Derby County – routinely dubbed 'the illustrious 'Cantab'' he assisted his home club only when tacit commitments to Cambridge University, Corinthians, and occasionally Brentwood allowed. This led to periodic allegations that he 'chooses his matches to suit himself', but his contribution to Derby County was invaluable, not least in raising the new club's profile in influential circles. A 'powerful forward with a stinging shot', he played in Derby's historic opening game and in the second scored the club's first recorded goal. Over five seasons he established a prolific scoring rate, and was the first Derby player to bag four in a game. Often elected captain, he endured long enough to play and score in a solitary League match before moving to Canada. One of nine children of his namesake father the Reverend B. W. Spilsbury – wealthy landowner and vicar of Findern – he was educated first at Rossall School near Fleetwood, Lancashire, then from 1876 to 1883 at Repton, where he excelled at football, cricket, and athletics. On going to Jesus College, Cambridge, in October 1883, he gained his soccer Blue (1884-87) and captained the University side in his final season. He also won his athletics Blue and emerged with a BA. In 1889 he travelled to the wilds of Canada hoping to make his fortune from virgin land development – but the pioneering life proved tough and unrewarding, and by 1901 he had returned to the family home in Findern, single and far from wealthy. In 1906 aged 41 he married Scots-born Edith Jessie Barnsfather, eight years his junior, and soon returned to Canada where this time he progressed well in the real estate and insurance business – the couple had four children. Spilsbury died there aged 74 but is commemorated on the grave of his father at Findern's All Saints' Church. His wife lived until 1965 aged 93, and his descendants still reside in Canada.

Appearances: Pre-League: 43 apps 1884-85 to 1887-88, 31 goals. League era: 2 apps 1888-89, 1 goal. Total: 45 apps 1884-85 to 1888-89, 32 goals.

SPRINGTHORPE George
Forward

Born: Heanor, Derbyshire, 3 July 1864
Died: 63, Arthur Street, Derby, 5 December 1937 (Estate value £653. 5s)
Career: Nottingham Imperial, Hyson Green, Basford Rovers, Melbourne Town, Derby Junction, Derby County 1884, Derby Midland

The Melbourne Town captain appeared twice in the inaugural season, but after scoring in an 8-0 thrashing of Stafford Road wasn't selected further. The son of lace manufacturer Robert Springthorpe, he spent his teenage years in Nottingham and began playing there for local sides. After the family moved to Melbourne in 1883, George soon made a mark in the Melbourne forward-line and was reported to have been playing 'so well that he must soon attract the interest of bigger clubs'. Both Junction and Midland also gave him a try. He worked in his father's business and in 1887 married a Kings Newton girl – six children followed. Both father and son moved to Derby after their Melbourne business premises at Victoria Mill were destroyed by fire in 1890 – only partially insured, Robert Springthorpe suffered big losses. He managed to start afresh in Derby but was declared bankrupt in 1894. George remained in the lace trade until retirement. He died at home aged 73 – his grave is in Derby's Uttoxeter Road Cemetery.

Appearances: 2 apps 1884-85, 1 goal

STALEY Arthur Norton
Half-back

Born: Darley Abbey, Derby, 1863
Died: Derbyshire Royal Infirmary, Derby, 20 February 1896
Career: Darley Abbey, Derby County 1887, Derby Midland

Diminutive half-back whose time at Derby County was like several others sandwiched between spells at Darley Abbey and Derby Midland. Staley played sporadically over two seasons, but otherwise appeared in the reserves. In December 1887 he also made a single unlikely appearance for Casuals, agreeing to help out the 'gents' against Derby when they turned up a man light. The son of railway porter Robert Staley, he was working as a core maker in an iron foundry when in 1891 his father, by then a foreman for the Midland Railway, suffered a fatal accident – hit by an express train while inspecting the line at Bedford. Arthur had by then married Emily Gibson and the couple's only son Arthur Robert was born in 1893. Staley became assistant trainer at Derby County, and was well-liked by the players, who gave him the nickname 'Energetic'. But he died aged only 33 in tragic circumstances later related by player Jimmy Methven: 'In 1895-96 we had gone into special training at Ashover Hydro for a big cup-tie. On our second day Arthur was informed by wire that his young boy was dangerously ill, and he was asked to return home quickly. In order to catch his train he ran all the way to the station, a good distance, and got overheated. He travelled with the compartment window down and contracted a chill, which developed into pneumonia, and he passed away within a fortnight.' His son recovered but was himself destined to die aged only 42.

Appearances: 13 apps 1886-87 to 1887-88, 1 goal

STORER William
Full-back and later forward

Born: Butterley Hill, Ripley, Derbyshire, 25 January 1867
Died: 12, Belgrave Street, Derby, 28 February 1912 (Estate value £759 8s 8d)
Career: Chesterfield Spital Olympic, Ripley Town, Derby County 1888, Derby Midland, Derby County 1891, Loughborough Town, Glossop North End

'Bill' Storer was most famous as a Derbyshire and England cricketer, but also a versatile footballer with a tough reputation. In 1888 a Sheffield newspaper observed that 'Storer played one of the most unsportsmanlike games we have ever seen' – as such he was routinely the target for opposing supporters' wrath. The son of engine smith John Storer, he became a turner's apprentice in his early teens. Already an established full-back, he first assisted Derby County in 1887-88 as cover for Lawrence and Latham, but later joined Derby Midland after gaining employment in the Midland Railway Signals Department – as was then common practice, the job offer was brazenly linked to his sporting prowess. When Midland were absorbed by Derby in 1891 Storer came with the package – by then playing as a forward, his second Derby stint spanned two League seasons – appearing in all five forward positions he scored regularly. As a cricketer he served Derbyshire from 1887 to 1905 and played in six Tests 1897-99. Famed as a wicketkeeper he was also a fine bat and competent leg-spinner, scoring 12,966 runs in all first-class cricket at an average of 28.87, and taking 214 wickets for Derbyshire. Among many claims to fame, he was the first professional to score two centuries in a match, against Yorkshire at Derby in 1896, a feat hitherto achieved only by amateurs. Married with six children, he had a spell as a licensee after the turn of the century, but began to suffer ill health, dying at home aged only 45. Storer's younger brother Harry played cricket for Derbyshire and was goalkeeper for Arsenal and Liverpool, whilst his nephew Harry junior later completed the Storer dynasty in even finer style – Derbyshire cricketer, England and Derby County footballer, and also the club's manager.

Appearances: Pre-League: 5 apps 1887-88, 0 goals. League era: 27 apps 1891-92 to 1892-93, 11 goals. Total: 32 apps 1887-88 to 1892-93, 11 goals

SUGG Frank Howe
Centre-half

Born: Ilkeston, Derbyshire, 11 January 1862
Died: Waterloo, Liverpool, 29 May 1933
Career: Derby County 1884, Burnley, Sheffield Wednesday, Bolton Wanderers, Everton, Lancashire Nomads

The son of Hubert Henri Sugg an Ilkeston solicitor, the family moved to Sheffield when Frank was an infant. At the age of 9 he suffered the untimely loss of his father. After attending Sheffield Grammar School he became a solicitor's clerk before taking up both football and cricket professionally and later founding a successful sports outfitting company. Standing an imposing six feet with a powerful physique, he was a big personality and popular figure. Domiciled in Derby when the club was formed, he assisted the team throughout the opening season and was several times captain. Initially a centre-half, he switched to centre-forward for a number of games, and against Stafford Road on 15 November 1884 scored Derby County's first ever hat-trick. But once professionalism was legalised Sugg ruthlessly 'played the field' and took up good offers from several leading clubs. He captained both Burnley and Sheffield Wednesday and was Everton's centre-forward in the inaugural Football League season. A fine cricketer, he unusually played for three counties – Yorkshire in 1883, his native Derbyshire 1884-86, and Lancashire 1887-89 – scoring 11,859 runs in 305 matches at a healthy average of 24.45. One of only four Test cricketers to play for Derby County, he was selected twice for England against Australia in 1888. In 1926 and 1927 he was a first-class umpire. Along with older brother Walter, who also played cricket for Derbyshire, he founded the Sugg & Co. retail sports chain which finally closed its doors only in 2001. Frank was a true all-round sportsman – weightlifter, long-distance swimmer, finalist in the Liverpool amateur billiards championships, a prodigious shot-putter, record holder for throwing the cricket ball, and the winner of countless prizes for rifle shooting and bowls. Married with four children, his colourful and productive life ended at home aged 71 just eight days after the death of his brother Walter.

Appearances: 30 apps 1884-85, 6 goals

TAYLOR Edgar Stephen Henry
Centre-half

Born: Long Eaton, 1867
Died: 94, Park Road, Peterborough, Cambridgeshire, 28 January 1916
Career: Long Eaton Alexandra, Long Eaton Rangers, Derby County 1886, Long Eaton Rangers

E. H. Taylor was one of the Long Eaton Rangers clan so well-used by Derby County, although he filled in only once for George Clifton, also a Rangers man. His one outing was a 3-0 defeat at Aston Villa in November 1886. Thereafter he continued with Rangers. The son of joiner and builder Charles Taylor, he was a lace-maker in Long Eaton from the age of 14. After marrying a builder's daughter in Peterborough in 1895 he settled there, his wife running a boarding house and Edgar working as an insurance agent and later a clerk at a florists and fruiterers. The couple had five children. In his twenties Taylor had been considered a leading cyclist, the Long Eaton track being a noted centre in the 1880s and 1890s – he was particularly adept in tricycle racing. After contracting an infection he died of kidney failure aged 48.

Appearances: 1 app 1886-87, 0 goals

WALKER John
Forward and half-back

Born: Inconclusive
Died: Inconclusive
Career: Derby St. Luke's, Derby County 1885, Derby Midland, Derby Junction, Derby County 1889

'Johnny' Walker spread himself around, enjoying spells with all four of Derby's leading clubs. He played three times for Derby County in their first campaign, but didn't appear again until the League era, when he was used sparingly over two seasons. Between times he gave good service to Midland and 'Juncs', being in the famous Junction side that in 1887-88 knocked Blackburn Rovers out of the FA Cup on the Arboretum Field. In January 1889 he was on the 'injured list' with a complaint not often encountered – 'ill with typhoid fever'. Walker played his last game for Derby in January 1891, but at the start of 1896-97 became the club's assistant trainer under Arthur Latham, filling the post for at least two seasons. The Derby press labelled him 'a well-known local footballer', yet strangely his full identity remains uncertain, the name John Walker a very common one. He is known to have been a good local cricketer, often assisting Derby Midland.

Appearances: Pre-League: 3 apps 1884-85, 0 goals. League era: 13 apps 1889-90 to 1890-91, 0 goals. Total: 16 apps 1884-85 to 1890-91, 0 goals

WANSBROUGH Horace Septimus
Left-half

Born: Westbury on Trym, Bristol, Gloucestershire, 1865
Died: 'Stopham Lodge', Tongdean Avenue, Hove, Sussex, 8 November 1939 (Estate value £5367. 1s 4d)
Career: Derby School, Duffield, Hendon, Derby County 1885

A rare naval presence in the Rams' ranks. After playing for Derby School from 1881 he began assisting Derby County reserves as soon as the club was formed, also helping out short-handed Hendon on their Christmas 1884 tour of the Midlands. He was promoted to the Derby first team only once – the penultimate game of 1884-85 lost at home to Chesterfield Spital. A good all-round sportsman, he rowed for Derby School, played tennis for Derbyshire, and in later years made his mark in the English Croquet Championships. The son of Henry Wansbrough of Bristol – wholesale stationer and paper manufacturer – he suffered the loss of his mother in only his second year, when she died giving birth to her ninth child. Independent from an early age, he lived with an older brother at 'The Villa' in Little Eaton while attending Derby School, his father primarily remaining at his business in Bristol. After gaining his BA at Durham (1888) Septimus trained for the clergy. Following his curacy at St. Paul's, Wimbledon Park, he was appointed Chaplain in Her Majesty's Fleet in 1893, subsequently serving on *HMS Howe*, *Benbow*, *Majestic* and *Warspite*. His naval travels earned him some unlikely honours – winner in 1894 of the Royal Malta Golf Club Cup, and in 1900 playing cricket for Devon v Cornwall at Plymouth. He was based in barracks at Portsmouth for a number of years but ultimately curtailed his naval links. In 1920 he was inducted Bishop of Taunton and appointed rector of Bradford-on-Tone, Somerset. From 1926 he was Rector of Stopham near Hove, where he died aged 74. A lifelong bachelor, he remains with H. L. Gwynne one of two Bishops to have played for Derby County.

Appearances: 1 app 1884-85, 0 goals

WARD Charles Albert
Outside-left

Born: Derby, 2 May 1864
Died: 16, Reginald Street, Derby, 18 February 1935 (Estate value £1083. 10s)
Career: Derby Town, Derby Midland, Derby County 1884, Derby Midland

Winger Charlie Ward played for Derby Town in 1881-82, and subsequently Derby Midland, before he was secured by Derby County for their first ever game. He scored on his second outing – the club's first home match – but perhaps uneasy about defecting from his employers' team, he returned to Midland after only 9 games, despite impressive performances. The son of railway inspector John Ward, he became a railway clerk at 14, serving the Midland Railway and its successor London Midland Scottish for 47 years. When he retired in 1925 he was Head of the General and Accounts Office earning over £700 per annum. In his youth Ward had been a noted sprinter, and later won his county cap for bowls. Also a keen member of the Derby Choral Union and the Lyric Opera Company. For 17 years he served in the 1st Battalion the Derbyshire Volunteers, retiring with the rank of Sergeant. Ward maintained close interest in Derby County into his late years, and was one of the few survivors from the first season to attend the club's Golden Jubilee Dinner in 1934 – a surviving menu carries his proud signature 'C. A. Ward 1884'. He died aged 70 just a few months later leaving a widow and two sons.

Appearances: 10 apps 1884-85, 3 goals

WARMBY William Henry
Left-half

Born: Rotherham, Yorkshire, 1863
Died: 28, Southwell Road, Sheffield, Yorkshire, 19 May 1916 (Estate value £94. 3s 6d)
Career: Effingham Brass Works, Rotherham, Derby St. Luke's, Derby County 1884, Everton, Everton Athletic

Having played a number of games for Rotherham in 1883-84 'Harry' Warmby secured a place in Derby's historic 'first eleven' but next played when the opening campaign was almost over. In the interim he remained loyal to St. Luke's bar the odd 'scamper' with Midland, but committed himself to Derby for 1885-86. Thereafter he missed only 3 games in three seasons before signing professional with Everton in June 1888. He became licensee of the Strawberry Hotel close to Anfield, then Everton's home. After playing once in the first Football League season, he moved to Everton Athletic in 1889-90, suffering a broken collar bone towards the end of the season. Transferred to Athletic with him was ex-Derby and Everton player 'Jack' Keys – the two were brothers-in-law, Warmby marrying Keys' sister Lydia in 1886. After she died in 1899 leaving him with two daughters, Warmby remarried and settled in Sheffield as a steam engine maker. The son of pattern maker Henry Warmby, he had been a 'buffer' at the Effingham Brass Works in Rotherham, moving to Derby in the early 1880s. Warmby adopted the air of the 'modern footballer' well ahead of time – the *Derby Daily Telegraph* once labelled him 'that aesthetic youth who seems to believe he can do what he likes'. On arriving at Everton he complained bitterly when they refused to pay his moving expenses, and the club's minute books record several misdemeanours. He died aged 53 survived by his second wife and their three exotically-named sons – Byron Winston, Adrian Rufus, and Noel Elvyn. All lived into the late-1970s having seen their father's former team Derby County win two League Championships.

Appearances: 118 apps 1884-85 to 1887-88, 3 goals

WESTON Walter
Full-back and half-back

Born: 22, Parker Street, Derby, 25 December 1860
Died: 57, Iverna Court, Kensington, London, 27 March 1940 (Estate value £1,220. 11s 11d)
Career: Derby School, Clare College Cambridge, Derby County 1885

Walter Weston appeared six times in the opening season, twice replacing his younger brother Willie and playing three times with him. Walter played against Derby County prior to his debut – helping out short-handed Hendon on Boxing Day 1884. Willie faced him as Derby ran out 3-1 winners. One of eight sons of Derby elastic webbing manufacturer John Weston, the family lived for some time at Mile Ash House in Darley Abbey, but experienced mixed fortunes. Walter displayed great sporting prowess at Derby School – in the football and cricket teams, a fine rower, and holder of the school record for the mile – 4 minutes 47 seconds. At Clare College, Cambridge, he gained his BA (1883) followed by an MA (1887). After ordination into the Church of England he soon embarked on missionary ventures to the Far East, being appointed British Chaplain at Kobe, Japan, in 1888. While there he conquered many peaks as an amateur mountaineer, and through his well-praised books was credited with popularising the activity. For this he was dubbed in Japan the 'Father of Mountaineering' – latterly recognised by the erection there of both a statue and memorial plaque. He was the first honorary member of the Japanese Alpine Club and a Fellow of the Royal Geographical Society. On returning to England in 1895 he took the curacy of Christ Church, Wimbledon, and in 1902 married Frances Emily Fox, daughter of the eminent civil engineer Sir Francis Fox (1844-1927) from a celebrated Derby family. The couple had no children. Reverend Weston returned to Japan a number of times, continuing to chronicle his travels. He also spent five years as the vicar of Ewell, Surrey, and engaged in much charitable work. In his seventies he was made President of the Old Derbeian Society – and after losing his wife in 1937 financed the restoration of the school chapel in her memory. When he died aged 79 at his Kensington apartment the school held a memorial service in his honour. His ashes were interred at Putney Vale Cemetery.

Appearances: 6 apps 1884-85, 0 goals

WESTON William Arthur
Right-back

Born: Derby, 25 January 1863
Died: Inconclusive, possibly United States
Career: Derby School, Derby County 1884

'Willie' Weston came into the side just before Christmas in the opening season, after the club's initial right-back Reg Evans ceased playing. He dominated the position for the rest of the campaign, but in subsequent seasons played mostly in the reserves, appearing only occasionally for the first team. His brother the Reverend Walter also assisted Derby at full-back. The son of elastic webbing manufacturer John Weston – whose firm Weston and Thompson had a mill on Parliament Street – he was sent to the Guignes School in north-central France before entering Derby School in 1877. Both brothers played football for Derby School right into their twenties, it being accepted practice for ex-pupils or masters to assist the boys. Both also graced the cricket team. Willie became a clerk in the elastic factory, which ultimately foundered. Like his brother he succumbed to the urge to travel. On 25 January 1893 – his thirtieth birthday – he sailed from Liverpool for New York describing himself as a 'gardener'. In 1902 the Derby School Register recorded him 'sheep farming, near Boston, U.S.A.' but there are no conclusive 'sightings' thereafter. 'W. A.' remains tantalisingly elusive, one of the few prominent early players who cannot be tracked to his grave.

Appearances: 24 apps 1884-85 to 1887-88, 0 goals

WILLIAMSON Albert
Half-back and full-back

Born: Sawley, Derbyshire, 14 April 1866
Died: The Grove, Shardlow, Derbyshire, 26 January 1951
Career: Sawley Rangers, Derby County 1884

Along with Sawley compatriot Amos 'Jammer' Smith, Williamson added some down-to-earth rusticity to the eclectic early line-ups. He played in the opening fixture but then resumed with Sawley Rangers before attaching himself firmly to Derby ten games later. The son of farm labourer William Williamson, he was said to be 'a real countryman, who affected the broad Derbyshire drawl of his native village to the very end'. He amassed over 150 games, and as a mark of his loyalty a benefit was played in February 1890 between Derby County and Derby Junction – Williamson received a cheque for £70. He bowed out in 1890-91. A pen-picture recalled: 'He possessed a long reach and could take the ball in all sorts of awkward positions. His tackling and placing were very accurate, but his form varied from first-class to extremely moderate, and he was never so good on poor pitches, so most of his best games were at the County Ground. He was a loyal servant, but didn't always appear to throw himself heart and soul into the game, especially when things were going the wrong way.' On 16 April 1886 he had become one of the first Derby players given his marching orders, for kicking Cursham of Notts County, which he protested was 'not deliberate'! Williamson worked in the lace trade and lived in Sawley all his life – married in 1890, his only son Private William Edward Williamson of the York and Lancaster Regiment was killed in France in February 1916, aged 19. In contrast, Albert was a guest of honour at the Derby County Golden Jubilee Dinner in 1934, and lived to see the Rams lift the FA Cup in 1946. He had been living at 8 Blandford Avenue, New Sawley, when he died in hospital aged 84.

Appearances: Pre-league: 129 apps 1884-85 to 1887-88, 5 goals. League era: 44 apps 1888-89 to 1890-91, 0 goals. Total: 173 apps 1884-85 to 1890-91, 5 goals

WILSHAW Samuel
Inside-left

Born: Staveley, Derbyshire, 1864
Died: Chesterfield area, 1937
Career: Staveley, Derby County 1887, Staveley

Described as 'a slim-built youth with perfect control', Sammy Wilshaw was considered hot property as the 1887-88 campaign approached. Derby County insisted they were signing him – Staveley flatly denied he was going. In the event Derby won the day – Wilshaw wore the 'chocolate and blue' in the opening game, and was soon partnering 'the illustrious 'Cantab' Spilsbury' in the forward line, an interesting social contrast. But he made only 12 appearances, and despite a good scoring rate, an informed observer suggested he was both a big disappointment and Derby's first 'bad boy' – 'The committee were elated when they secured his services, but he turned out to be the equivalent of 'Dead Sea Fruit'. He hardly did himself justice in a single game, and some of his performances were so shockingly bad, he had in the end to be dropped, and go back from whence he came. The secret of his failure was that he got surrounded in Derby with companions of the most foolish description, who pandered to his 'notorious weakness' to such an extent that he was ruined for first-class football'. Wilshaw's particularly tough background placed him in a relative minority in Derby's early ranks – the son of coal miner and later road labourer William Wilshaw, he was the archetypal 'ordinary working lad' of the type who a decade later came to greater prominence in the professional game. He was initially an iron moulder at the Staveley Works, but by his thirties was a miner at the coal face. Married with family, he died aged 72.

Appearances: 12 apps 1887-88, 6 goals

'WILSON' J.
See WALKER John

Born: Inconclusive
Died: Inconclusive
Career: Derby County 1885

The mysterious 'Wilson' was listed once in the opening season. The inverted commas either suggest a pseudonym or the reporter's uncertainty concerning a player he was unfamiliar with. Since 'J. Wilson's' home debut was immediately followed by the appearance of another newcomer J. Walker, it seems likely that 'Wilson' was a reporter's error for Walker, the two being one and the same.

WOOD John Brooks
Centre-forward

Born: Habrough, Lincolnshire, 16 December 1869
Died: Winchester, Hampshire, 24 October 1901 (Estate value £7,590. 12s. 11d)
Career: Derby School, Derby County 1884

After attending Brigg Grammar School in his native Lincolnshire, J. B. Wood entered Derby School in 1882 and established himself as a sporting prodigy – in the Football XI aged 14 and captain of cricket a year later. He was well accustomed to playing with and against adult footballers, it being accepted convention for a School XI to comprise pupils, masters and Old Boys together, and to fulfil fixtures against senior clubs. That being the case, Derby County felt comfortable to draw on his services in an emergency when he was seventeen days short of his fifteenth birthday, labelled in the match report 'Wood of Derby School'. This makes him Derby County's youngest ever first-team player. Alas his sole outing proved a chastening experience – missing five key players Derby were defeated 7-0 by Junction on 29 November 1884, the first meeting between the bitter local rivals. The Derby committee sought to have the result annulled on grounds that 'the team was not representative of our true strength'. Although failing, they quietly expunged the fixture from the end-of-season list given to the press, effectively creating a 'Phantom Game'. Son of Lincolnshire farmer William Wood and his wife Anne Brooks, after leaving Derby School he helped run the family farms. In 1894 he married comfortably-off widow Kate Farebrother, daughter of a ship-owner. Six years his senior she already had 3 children. No issue of his own were added. He later diversified from farming – at the time of his death aged only 31 he was designated 'of Winchester, a brewer'. Derby County's '14-year-old debutant' left a healthy estate and a singular football record.

Apps: 1 app 1884-85, 0 goals

WRIGHT Levi George
Full-back and half-back

Born: The Armoury, New Road, Oxford, 15 January 1862
Died: 42, Derby Lane, Normanton, Derby, 11 January 1953 (Estate value £1009. 13s 6d)
Career: St. Anne's Church, Derby Midland, Derby Junction, Notts County, Derby County 1887

L. G. Wright was a legendary figure in Derbyshire cricket but also a fine footballer. The son of Enos Wright – a Sergeant in the militia – he came to Derby in January 1881 to take up the post of Assistant Master at St. Anne's School, but soon joined the Midland Railway as a clerk, enjoying a long career there. When Midland Football Club was formed in 1881 Wright was one of the first members, staying loyal to them well after Derby County came into existence, although playing the odd game for Junction. He willingly assisted the short-lived Derby County Rugby Club but donned Derby 'soccer' colours only once in the pre-League era – two days before his debut in April 1887 he had played 'against' Derby in his sole outing for Notts County as a 'found on the ground' stand-in. He reverted to Midland until the inaugural League season, then adding four more games to his Derby tally, the last as centre-forward. Wright suffered defeat in all of his five appearances, but was a better player than this suggests, regularly selected full-back for the North of England, and considered first stand-in for the full international side, although never getting his cap. He was a noted Derbyshire batsman from 1883 to 1909, in two seasons captain – in all first-class matches he scored 15,166 at an average of 26.10. In later years he was a revered character at the Arboretum Bowls Club, playing into his eighties, the *Derby Telegraph* dubbing him 'the 'Grand Old Man' of Derbyshire sport, an approachable Methuselah who will share a chat with anyone.' Married with three children, his only son Sergeant Walter Brooks Wright of the Derbyshire Yeomanry died aged 24 in 1915 from wounds suffered at Gallipoli. In contrast 'L. G.' reached 90 – father and son share a grave in Normanton Cemetery.

Appearances: Pre-League: 1 app 1886-87, 0 goals. League era: 4 apps 1888-89, 1 goal. Total: 5 apps 1886-87 to 1888-89, 1 goal

THANK YOU!

Many individuals and organisations have helped to bring this book to fruition, some in just a small way, others with much greater impact altogether. And a further group anonymously – the growing band of archivists who have digitised countless thousands of newspapers, books and genealogical records, making them available online for researchers, remain entirely unknown to me. Yet collectively I owe them a huge debt of gratitude for making my task not just an easier one, but indeed possible at all. Of the helpers I do know, each and every one has been greatly appreciated, whatever their contribution, and in the spirit of equality I would like to acknowledge them all alphabetically.

Malcolm Bailey (Charterhouse), Philip Beetham, Keith Breakwell (Long Eaton), British Library, Andy Brown (Thomas Brown), publisher Tony Brown for embracing the project and creating the finished product, Bob Budd (cover design), Rob Cavallini, Freddie Chalk (Butterflies CC), Jan Cobb (Old Reptonians), Patrick Cobb (Butterflies CC), Anthony Cobbold (J. B. T. Chevallier), Maxwell Craven, Wendy Daunt (Charles Gorham), Gary Delaney, Derby Local Studies Library, Kalwinder Singh Dhindsa, Andy Ellis for key photographs and other early knowledge, Terry Fletcher, Eric Gaskell (William Morley), Alan Gifford (Ben Spilsbury), Barry Chevallier Guild (J. B. T. Chevallier), Joy Hales (*Derbyshire Life & Countryside*), Dave Harris (Midland Railway Study Centre), Kate Ibbitson for continued understanding and all-round support, Long Eaton Library, Bryan Lowe (Morley family), Kathy Lucero (Willie Weston), Alan Luntley (Luntley brothers), Ann Luntley (Luntley brothers), Mike McKenna (Long Eaton), Andy Mitchell, Gerald Mortimer for his kind foreword, and whose Derby County writings inspired the idea, Paul Mortimer (Rams Trust), Tony Overton (Midland Railway), Philip Paine, Robert Pass (George Evans), David Pinney (Trent College archivist), David Potter, Richard Quantrill, Ann Randell (Trent College), Lyn Richardson (Sam Richardson), George Shardlow (shirt research and cover images), Tobias Shardlow (shirt research and cover images), Barrie Sheard (Derby School), Barbara Springthorpe (George Springthorpe), Ian Stals (early images), Paul Stevens (Repton School archivist), Alan Thompson (Repton Village History Group), Alan Villiers (Long Eaton), Hannah Walker.

Should I have inadvertently overlooked anyone please accept my further thanks and sincere apologies.

Peter Seddon
Derby
September 2013

APPENDIX: DERBY COUNTY LINE-UPS 1884-85 TO 1887-88

1884-85

			P1	P2	P3	P4	P5	P6	P7	P8	P9	P10	P11
Sep 13	Great Lever	0-6	Gillett LF	Evans RL	Harvey F	Williamson A	Morley HA	Warmby WH	Bakewell G	Shipley W	Spilsbury BW	Smith A	Ward CA
27	Blackburn Olympic	3-4	Gillett LF	Evans RL	Morley HA	Exham PG	Birch-Thorpe CE	Hickinbottom E	Bakewell G	Spilsbury BW	Chevallier JBT	Smith A	Ward CA
Oct 2	Notts County	1-3	Gillett LF	Latham A	Evans RL	Harvey F	Exham PG	Sugg FH	Hickinbottom E	Spilsbury BW	Chevallier JBT	Smith A	Ward CA
25	Stoke Town	0-2	Gillett LF	Harvey F	Peel EH	Exham PG	Sugg FH	Hickinbottom E	Bakewell G	Harrison J	Chevallier JBT	Smith A	Nash RW
28	Repton School	3-2	Moore HB	Douglas FSK	Morley HA	Nash RW	Exham PG	Gorham C	Bakewell G	Smith A	Chevallier JBT	Shepherd W	Ward CA
Nov 1	St. Luke's (DC)	3-1	Gillett LF	Evans RL	Harvey F	Exham PG	Sugg FH	Gorham C	Bakewell G	Spilsbury BW	Chevallier JBT	Smith A	Ward CA
8	Walsall Town (FAC)	0-7	Gillett LF	Evans RL	Harvey F	Gorham C	Maycroft D	Exham PG	Bakewell G	Chatterton W	Sugg FH	Smith A	Ward CA
15	Stafford Road	3-0	Hunt W	Evans RL	Latham A	Morley HA	Gorham C	Frost J	Bakewell G	Nash RW	Sugg FH	Smith A	Ward CA
22	Great Lever	0-3	Hunt W	Latham A	Davies WT	Morley HA	Exham PG	Nicholls H	Bakewell G	Chevallier JBT	Sugg FH	Smith A	Hickinbottom E
29	Junction Street	0-7	Moore HB	Gorham C	Davies WT	Parry FH	Exham PG	Bellamy W	Evans H	Nash RW	Wood JB	Chevallier JBT	Ward CA
Dec 6	Wirksworth (DC)	4-2	Hunt W	Evans RL	Harvey F	Maycroft D	Sugg FH	Gorham C	Bakewell G	Sherwin C	Springthorpe G	Smith A	Ward CA
13	Darwen	3-3	Hunt W	Davies WT	Burgess	Morley HA	Sugg FH	Williamson A	Bakewell G	Hickinbottom E	Cooper L	Smith A	Sherwin P
15	Haliwell	1-4	Hunt W	Davies WT	Latham A	Morley HA	Sugg FH	Williamson A	Bakewell G	Hickinbottom E	Cooper L	Smith A	Sherwin P
20	Lockwood Brothers	2-1	Luntley W	Weston WA	Morley HA	Gorham C	Sugg FH	Kelsall WL	Bakewell G	Cooper L	Hickinbottom E	Hickinbottom E	Ward CA
26	Hendon	3-1	Luntley W	Weston WA	Morley HA	Williamson A	Sugg FH	Parry FH	Cooper L	Hickinbottom E	Spilsbury BW	Cochrane AHJ	Smith A
27	Casuals	1-2	Matthews J	Weston WA	Morley HA	Williamson A	Sugg FH	Hickinbottom E	Bakewell G	Cooper L	Spilsbury BW	Briggs J	Smith A
29	Haliwell	1-1	Brown	Weston WA	Latham A	Williamson A	Morley HA	Shipley W	Bakewell G	Cooper L	Sugg FH	Hickinbottom E	Smith A
Jan 3	Walsall Town	1-0	Hill C	Morley HA	Weston W	Williamson A	Sugg FH	Parry FH	Bakewell G	Spilsbury BW	Cooper L	Hickinbottom E	Smith A
7	Cambridge Univ.	4-4	Farquharson EB	Weston WA	Morley HA	Williamson A	Sugg FH	Weston W	Bakewell G	Cooper L	Cochrane AHJ	Hickinbottom E	Smith A
17	Darley Abbey	1-0	Hill C	Weston WA	Weston W	Parry FH	Morley HA	Williamson A	Bakewell G	Sherwin C	Sugg FH	Smith A	Kelsall WL
24	Long Eaton Rangers	1-1	Farquharson EB	Weston WA	Morley HA	Williamson A	Weston W	Harvey F	Bakewell G	Cooper L	Sugg FH	Smith A	Hickinbottom E
31	Nottingham Forest	6-1	Hill C	Flowers J	Morley HA	Williamson A	Sugg FH	Kelsall WL	Bakewell G	Cooper L	Chevallier JBT	Smith A	Hickinbottom E
Feb 2	Blackburn Rovers	3-4	Parsons WE	Weston WA	Latham A	Williamson A	Sugg FH	Sugg FH	Bakewell G	Cooper L	Nash RW	Smith A	Hickinbottom E
7	Stafford Road	8-0	Hill C	Weston WA	Morley HA	Williamson A	Sugg FH	Kelsall WL	Bakewell G	Nash RW	Chevallier JBT	Smith A	Springthorpe G
12	Repton School	4-1	AN Other	Weston WA	Morley HA	Gorham C	Sugg FH	Exham PG	Chatterton W	Nash RW	Chevallier JBT	Hodges A	Briggs J
14	Junction Street (DCC)	0-0	Hill C	Weston WA	Morley HA	Williamson A	Sugg FH	Hickinbottom E	Bakewell G	Cooper L	Chevallier JBT	Smith A	Nash RW
21	Bolton Wanderers	1-4	Bromage E	Weston WA	Morley HA	Williamson A	Sugg FH	Kelsall WL	Bakewell G	Cooper L	Walker J	Smith A	Hickinbottom E
Mar 3	Junction Street (DCC)	1-1	Hill C	Weston WA	Morley HA	Williamson A	Sugg FH	Wilson	Cooper L	Spilsbury BW	Chevallier JBT	Smith A	Hickinbottom E
16	Lockwood Brothers	5-0	Bromage E	Weston WA	Morley HA	Williamson A	Sugg FH	Kelsall WL	Walker J	Cooper L	Chatterton W	Smith A	Hickinbottom E
21	Stoke Town	1-1	Bromage E	Weston WA	Morley HA	Williamson A	Sugg FH	Kelsall WL	Bakewell G	Cooper L	Chatterton W	Smith A	Hickinbottom E
28	Junction Street (DCC)	4-0	Hill C	Weston W	Morley HA	Williamson A	Sugg FH	Kelsall WL	Bakewell G	Cooper L	Chatterton W	Smith A	Hickinbottom E
Apr 6	Nottingham Forest	1-1	Hill C	Warmby WH	Morley HA	Williamson A	Cubley FE	Hickinbottom E	Bakewell G	Nash RW	Chevallier JBT	Smith A	Cochrane AHJ
7	Corinthians	3-3	Hill C	Warmby WH	Morley HA	Williamson A	Sugg FH	Hickinbottom E	Bakewell G	Cooper L	Chatterton W	Smith A	Cochrane AHJ
11	Spital (DCC)	1-2	Hill C	Weston WA	Morley HA	Williamson A	Sugg FH	Wansbrough HS	Bakewell G	Cooper L	Chatterton W	Smith A	Hickinbottom E
25	Notts County	2-0	Hill C	Flowers J	Morley HA	Williamson A	Sugg FH	Warmby WH	Bakewell G	Cooper L	Chevallier JBT	Smith A	Hickinbottom E

Dec 29: C Hill played as "Brown" in this game
Mar 3: J Walker played as "Wilson"

1885-86

Date	Opponent	Score	P1	P2	P3	P4	P5	P6	P7	P8	P9	P10	P11
Sep 19	Stoke	2-3	Hill C	Morley HA	Warmby WH	Cooper GF	Williamson A	Flowers G	Flowers J	Spilsbury BW	Smith A	Cooper L	Hickinbottom E
26	Notts County	0-3	Hill C	Williamson A	Morley HA	Cooper GF	Flowers J	Warmby WH	Jones F	Spilsbury BW	Evans G	Cooper L	Smith A
Oct 3	Stafford Road	5-1	Hill C	Williamson A	Flowers J	Nicholls H	Morley HA	Warmby WH	Bakewell G	Cooper L	Evans G	Smith A	Cooper GF
10	Aston Villa	2-4	Hill C	Williamson A	Morley HA	Cooper GF	Flowers J	Warmby WH	Bakewell G	Cooper L	Evans G	Smith A	Nash RW
17	Sheffield	5-2	Luntley W	Williamson A	Morley HA	Nicholls H	Flowers J	Warmby WH	Bakewell G	Cooper L	Evans G	Smith A	Nash RW
24	Wolves	0-0	Luntley W	Williamson A	Morley HA	Cooper GF	Flowers J	Warmby WH	Bakewell G	Cooper L	Evans G	Smith A	Nash RW
31	Birmingham St Georges (FAC)	3-0	Luntley W	Williamson A	Morley HA	Nicholls H	Nicholls H	Warmby WH	Bakewell G	Spilsbury BW	Evans G	Smith A	Nash RW
Nov 7	Small Heath Alliance	6-0	Luntley W	Morley HA	Nicholls H	Cooper GF	Nash RW	Warmby WH	Bakewell G	Cooper L	Evans G	Smith A	Hickinbottom E
14	Aston Villa (FAC)	2-0	Luntley W	Williamson A	Morley HA	Cooper GF	Flowers J	Warmby WH	Bakewell G	Spilsbury BW	Evans G	Smith A	Cooper L
21	Brentwood	3-0	Luntley W	Williamson A	Morley HA	Cooper GF	Flowers J	Warmby WH	Bakewell G	Nash RW	Evans G	Cooper L	Smith A
23	Sheffield Wednesday	8-2	Luntley J	Williamson A	Morley HA	Cooper GF	Flowers J	Warmby WH	Bakewell G	Cooper L	Spilsbury BW	Hickinbottom E	Smith A
26	Blackburn Rovers	2-3	Bestwick TH	Williamson A	Morley HA	Cooper GF	Flowers J	Warmby WH	Bakewell G	Cooper L	Evans G	Hickinbottom E	Smith A
Dec 5	Nottingham Forest	1-2	Luntley W	Morley HA	Nicholls H	Williamson A	Cooper GF	Warmby WH	Bakewell G	Cooper L	Evans G	Smith A	Hickinbottom E
12	Small Heath Alliance	2-4	Luntley W	Williamson A	Morley HA	Cooper GF	Nicholls H	Warmby WH	Bakewell G	Spilsbury BW	Evans G	Cooper L	Smith A
19	Blackburn Olympic	0-3	Bestwick TH	Williamson A	Morley HA	Cooper GF	Flowers J	Warmby WH	Bakewell G	Cooper L	Evans G	Hickinbottom E	Hutchinson TEM
26	Casuals	2-1	Luntley W	Williamson A	Morley HA	Cooper GF	Flowers J	Warmby WH	Bakewell G	Knox JJ	Evans G	Hickinbottom E	Cooper L
28	Blackburn Rovers	1-1	Luntley W	Flowers J	Williamson A	Cooper GF	Morley HA	Warmby WH	Cooper L	Knox JJ	Evans G	Hickinbottom E	Smith A
Jan 1	Bolton Wanderers	1-1	Bestwick TH	Williamson A	Morley HA	Cooper GF	Flowers J	Warmby WH	Bakewell G	Spilsbury BW	Evans G	Hickinbottom E	Cooper L
9	Nottingham Forest	1-0	Bestwick TH	Williamson A	Warmby WH	Williamson A	Morley HA	Warmby WH	Bakewell G	Knox JJ	Evans G	Cooper L	Knox JJ
16	Sheffield	3-3	Luntley W	Williamson A	Morley HA	Cooper GF	Flowers J	Hickinbottom E	Bakewell G	Spilsbury BW	Evans G	Hickinbottom E	Smith A
23	Sheffield Wednesday	7-0	Bestwick TH	Williamson A	Morley HA	Cooper GF	Flowers J	Warmby WH	Bakewell G	Cooper L	Evans G	Smith A	Nash RW
30	Notts County	3-7	Bestwick TH	Williamson A	Morley HA	Cooper GF	Flowers J	Warmby WH	Bakewell G	Cooper L	Evans G	Nash RW	Smith A
Feb 6	Preston North End	1-6	Luntley W	Williamson A	Morley HA	Williamson A	Flowers J	Warmby WH	Bakewell G	Cooper L	Evans G	Hickinbottom E	Smith A
17	Cambridge University	1-0	Luntley W	Williamson A	Flowers J	Warmby WH	Morley HA	Cooper GF	Bakewell G	Knox JJ	Evans G	Cooper L	Hickinbottom E
20	Stoke	4-1	Luntley W	Williamson A	Warmby WH	Cooper GF	Flowers J	Hickinbottom E	Bakewell G	Knox JJ	Evans G	Cooper L	Cooper L
22	Aston Villa	1-2	Luntley W	Williamson A	Latham A	Cooper GF	Flowers J	Warmby WH	Bakewell G	Cooper L	Hickinbottom E	Smith A	Needham T
27	Stafford Road	2-0	Luntley W	Williamson A	Morley HA	Cooper GF	Flowers J	Warmby WH	Bakewell G	Cooper L	Evans G	Smith A	Hickinbottom E
Mar 13	Bolton Wanderers	0-7	Bestwick TH	Williamson A	Warmby WH	Cooper GF	Flowers J	Hickinbottom E	Bakewell G	Cooper L	Evans G	Smith A	Hickinbottom A
20	Aston Villa	3-3	Luntley W	Williamson A	Morley HA	Cooper GF	Flowers J	Warmby WH	Bakewell G	Cooper L	Evans G	Smith A	Hickinbottom E
27	Blackburn Olympic	2-1	Luntley W	Williamson A	Morley HA	Warmby WH	Flowers J	Hickinbottom E	Bakewell G	Cooper L	Evans G	Smith A	Cooper L
Apr 3	Long Eaton Rangers	3-1	Luntley W	Williamson A	Morley HA	Warmby WH	Flowers J	Hickinbottom E	Bakewell G	Monk I	Evans G	Smith A	Cooper L
16	Notts County (DCC)	4-1	Bromage E	Latham A	Morley HA	Williamson A	Flowers J	Hickinbottom E	Bakewell G	Knox JJ	Evans G	Smith A	Cooper L
26	Northwich Victoria	3-0	Luntley W	Williamson A	Morley HA	Warmby WH	Flowers J	Hickinbottom E	Bakewell G	Knox JJ	Evans G	Smith A	Cooper L
27	Bolton Wanderers	1-1	Bestwick TH	Latham A	Morley HA	Williamson A	Flowers J	Hickinbottom E	Bakewell G	Needham T	Evans G	Smith A	Cooper L
May 1	Wolves	2-0	Bestwick TH	Latham A	Morley HA	Williamson A	Flowers J	Hickinbottom E	Bakewell G	Spilsbury BW	Evans G	Warmby WH	Cooper L
8	Bolton Wanderers (DCC)	0-2	Bestwick TH	Latham A	Morley HA	Williamson A	Flowers J	Hickinbottom E	Bakewell G	Monk I	Evans G	Smith A	Warmby WH
11	'Eleven of Derby'	2-2	Hunt W	Cooper GF	Lawson EK	Warmby WH	Flowers J	Hickinbottom E	Bakewell G	Keys J	Evans G	Plackett L	Cooper L

Sep 26: G Bakewell played as "F.Jones" in this game

1886-87

				P1	P2	P3	P4	P5	P6	P7	P8	P9	P10	P11
Sep	11	Everton	1-4	Bestwick TH	Latham A	Morley HA	Williamson A	Cooper GF	Warmby WH	Bakewell G	Hutchinson F	Evans G	Cooper L	Keys J
	18	Long Eaton Rangers	0-2	Bestwick TH	Latham A	Morley HA	Williamson A	Forman A	Warmby WH	Bakewell G	Spilsbury BW	Evans G	Cooper L	Plackett L
	25	Liverpool Ramblers	13-0	Bestwick TH	Hales G	Latham A	Williamson A	Morley HA	Warmby WH	Bakewell G	Spilsbury BW	Knox JJ	Cooper L	Plackett L
Oct	2	Sheffield	7-2	Bestwick TH	Bower H	Latham A	Williamson A	Morley HA	Warmby WH	Bakewell G	Spilsbury BW	Evans G	Cooper L	Plackett L
	9	Burton Wanderers (Birm. Cup)	6-1	Bestwick TH	Bower H	Latham A	Williamson A	Clifton G	Warmby WH	Bakewell G	Spilsbury BW	Evans G	Cooper L	Plackett L
	16	Sheffield Wednesday	3-0	Bestwick TH	Latham A	Lawrence SE	Williamson A	Clifton G	Warmby WH	Bakewell G	Chatterton W	Evans G	Cooper L	Plackett L
	23	Notts County	6-3	Bestwick TH	Latham A	Lawrence SE	Williamson A	Clifton G	Warmby WH	Bakewell G	Keys J	Evans G	Cooper L	Plackett L
	30	Aston Unity (FAC)	4-1	Bestwick TH	Latham A	Warmby WH	Williamson A	Clifton G	Hutchinson F	Bakewell G	Keys J	Evans G	Cooper L	Plackett L
Nov	3	Cambridge University	6-2	Bestwick TH	Latham A	Lawrence SE	Williamson A	Clifton G	Warmby WH	Bakewell G	Keys J	Evans G	Cooper L	Plackett L
	6	Corinthians	2-3	Bestwick TH	Latham A	Lawrence SE	Williamson A	Clifton G	Warmby WH	Bakewell G	Knox JJ	Evans G	Cooper L	Plackett L
	13	Stoke	2-2	Bestwick TH	Latham A	Lawrence SE	Williamson A	Clifton G	Warmby WH	Bakewell G	Keys J	Evans G	Cooper L	Plackett L
	15	Aston Villa	0-3	Bestwick TH	Latham A	Lawrence SE	Williamson A	Taylor EH	Warmby WH	Bakewell G	Keys J	Cropper W	Cooper L	Hickinbottom A
	20	Mitchell St. Georges (FAC)	1-2	Bestwick TH	Latham A	Williamson A	Bower H	Clifton G	Warmby WH	Bakewell G	Knox JJ	Cropper W	Cooper L	Plackett L
	22	Oxford University	0-0	Parsons WE	Latham A	Smith GH	Williamson A	Clifton G	Warmby WH	Bakewell G	Keys J	Cropper W	Cooper L	Plackett L
	27	Bolton Wanderers	0-2	Bestwick TH	Bower H	Lawrence SE	Williamson A	Clifton G	Warmby WH	Bakewell G	Keys J	Evans G	Cooper L	Plackett L
Dec	4	Aston Villa	0-3	Bestwick TH	Latham A	Lawrence SE	Williamson A	Clifton G	Warmby WH	Bakewell G	Keys J	Evans G	Cooper L	Plackett L
	6	Sheffield Wednesday	2-2	Musson CW	Latham A	Lawson EK	Williamson A	Greaves JL	Warmby WH	Bakewell G	Keys J	Chatterton W	Cooper L	Evans G
	11	West Brom. (Birm. Cup)	0-6	Bestwick TH	Latham A	Lawson EK	Williamson A	Clifton G	Warmby WH	Bakewell G	Chatterton W	Evans G	Cooper L	Plackett L
	15	Corinthians	0-5	Bestwick TH	Latham A	Weston WA	Williamson A	Clifton G	Warmby WH	Bakewell G	Keys J	Chatterton W	Cooper L	Evans G
	18	Aston Unity	2-0	Bestwick TH	Latham A	Lowles H	Williamson A	Clifton G	Warmby WH	Bakewell G	Chatterton W	Monk I	Cooper L	Plackett L
	27	Casuals	3-0	Bestwick TH	Latham A	Lowles H	Williamson A	Clifton G	Warmby WH	Bakewell G	Spilsbury BW	Monk I	Cooper L	Needham T
	28	Blackburn Rovers	2-0	Bestwick TH	Weston WA	Lawrence SE	Williamson A	Clifton G	Warmby WH	Bakewell G	Spilsbury BW	Monk I	Cooper L	Plackett L
	29	London Hotspur	2-1	Bestwick TH	Latham A	Weston WA	Williamson A	Clifton G	Warmby WH	Bakewell G	Keys J	Monk I	Cooper L	Plackett L
Jan	22	Grimsby Town	1-4	Bestwick TH	Weston WA	Lawrence SE	Williamson A	Clifton G	Warmby WH	Bakewell G	Spilsbury BW	Moss G	Hickinbottom A	Henson J
	24	Grantham	5-0	Pitman R	Weston WA	Lawrence SE	Williamson A	Latham A	Warmby WH	Bakewell G	Spilsbury BW	Moss G	Smith W	Henson J
	29	Derby St. Luke's	1-1	Bestwick TH	Latham A	Lawrence SE	Williamson A	Clifton G	Warmby WH	Bakewell G	Smith W	Moss G	Cooper L	Plackett L
Feb	5	Wolves	1-5	Bestwick TH	Weston WA	Lawrence SE	Williamson A	Latham A	Warmby WH	Groome H	Smith W	Evans G	Bakewell G	Needham T
	12	Long Eaton Rangers	1-1	Bestwick TH	Latham A	Lawrence SE	Williamson A	Clifton G	Warmby WH	Bakewell G	Smith W	Moss G	Cooper L	Plackett L
	19	Nottingham Forest	2-1	Bestwick TH	Weston WA	Lawrence SE	Williamson A	Latham A	Warmby WH	Bakewell G	Keys J	Smith W	Cooper L	Plackett L
	22	Wolves	3-1	Bestwick TH	Brown E	Lawrence SE	Williamson A	Latham A	Warmby WH	Bakewell G	Needham T	Smith W	Cooper L	Plackett L
	26	Cambridge University	1-1	Bestwick TH	Nicholls H	Lawrence SE	Williamson A	Latham A	Warmby WH	Bakewell G	Needham T	Smith W	Cooper L	Plackett L
	28	Oxford University	3-0	Parsons WE	Nicholls H	Lawrence SE	Williamson A	Latham A	Warmby WH	Bakewell G	Spilsbury BW	Smith W	Cooper L	Plackett L
Mar	5	Bolton Wanderers	3-0	Bestwick TH	Bassano H	Lawrence SE	Williamson A	Latham A	Warmby WH	Bakewell G	Needham T	Smith W	Cooper L	Plackett L
	7	Notts County	3-3	Bestwick TH	Bassano H	Lawrence SE	Williamson A	Latham A	Warmby WH	Bakewell G	Needham T	Monk I	Cooper L	Plackett L
	12	Nottingham Forest	1-2	Pitman R	Nicholls H	Lowles H	Brayshaw E	Latham A	Warmby WH	Bakewell G	Needham T	Monk I	Cooper L	Plackett L
	14	Grantham	3-2	Pitman R	Bassano H	Iliffe FE	Groome H	Staley A	Levers WH	Groome H	Keys J	Monk I	Needham T	Hickinbottom A
	19	Blackburn Rovers	2-1	Bestwick TH	Groome A	Lawrence SE	Williamson A	Kelsall WL	Warmby WH	Bakewell G	Spilsbury BW	Cameron RT	Cooper L	Plackett L
	19	Sheffield	3-5	Cupit S	Forman A	Lowles H	Brown T	Staley A	Levers WH	Keys J	Groome H	Monk I	Hickinbottom A	Needham T
Apr	2	Stoke	3-1	Bestwick TH	Nicholls H	Lawrence SE	Williamson A	Latham A	Warmby WH	Bakewell G	Spilsbury BW	Monk I	Cooper L	Plackett L
	9	Notts County	3-0	Bestwick TH	Brayshaw E	Lawrence SE	Williamson A	Latham A	Warmby WH	Bakewell G	Spilsbury BW	Smith W	Cooper L	Plackett L
	11	Dumbarton Athletic	0-2	Bestwick TH	Wright LG	Lawrence SE	Williamson A	Latham A	Warmby WH	Smith W	Hardy T	Moss G	Cooper L	Plackett L
	12	Corinthians	2-1	Bestwick TH	Morley HA	Lawrence SE	Staley A	Latham A	Warmby WH	Groome H	Smith W	Jackson H	Needham T	Plackett L
	16	Long Eaton Rangers (DCC)	5-3	Bestwick TH	Latham A	Lawrence SE	Williamson A	Staley A	Warmby WH	Groome H	Keys J	Monk I	Cooper L	Plackett L
	30	Small Heath Alliance (DCC)	3-0	Bestwick TH	Morley HA	Lawrence SE	Williamson A	Latham A	Warmby WH	Groome H	Spilsbury BW	Monk I	Cooper L	Needham T
May	14	Notts Rangers (DCC)	0-1	Bestwick TH	Morley HA	Lawrence SE	Williamson A	Latham A	Warmby WH	Bakewell G	Spilsbury BW	Monk I	Cooper L	Needham T

Feb 22: E Brayshaw played as "E Brown" in this game
Mar 19: H Jackson played as "RT Cameron"

1887-88

Date	Opponent	Score	P1	P2	P3	P4	P5	P6	P7	P8	P9	P10	P11
Sep 17	Grimsby Town	0-1	Parsons WE	Latham A	Morley HA	Williamson A	Staley A	Warmby WH	Groome H	Keys J	Monk I	Wilshaw S	Needham T
24	Preston North End	0-8	Marshall J	Latham A	Lawrence SE	Williamson A	Warmby WH	(only 10 men)	Bakewell G	Spilsbury BW	Smith W	Staley A	Needham T
Oct 1	Walsall Swifts	3-0	Marshall J	Latham A	Lawrence SE	Staley A	Williamson A	Roulstone W	Bakewell G	Spilsbury BW	Warmby WH	Wilshaw S	Plackett L
8	Derby Midland	1-2	Marshall J	Morley HA	Latham A	Williamson A	Warmby WH	Roulstone W	Bakewell G	Needham T	Spilsbury BW	Wilshaw S	Plackett L
15	Staveley (FAC)	2-1	Bestwick TH	Latham A	Lawrence SE	Williamson A	Roulstone W	Warmby WH	Bakewell G	Spilsbury BW	Monk I	Needham T	Plackett L
22	Bolton Wanderers	3-0	Bestwick TH	Latham A	Lawrence SE	Williamson A	Roulstone W	Warmby WH	Bakewell G	Spilsbury BW	Lees J	Wilshaw S	Plackett L
22	Ashbourne St. Oswald's (DC)	0-3	Pitman R	Lowles H	Cooper GF	Groome A	Staley A	Birch-Thorpe CE	Sinton J	Hodgkinson G	Lees J	Needham T	Henson G
29	Preston North End	1-5	Bestwick TH	Latham A	Lawrence SE	Williamson A	Warmby WH	Roulstone W	Bakewell G	Spilsbury BW	Monk I	Wilshaw S	Plackett L
Nov 5	Ecclesfield (FAC)	6-0	Bestwick TH	Morley HA	Lawrence SE	Williamson A	Roulstone W	Warmby WH	Bakewell G	Spilsbury BW	Lees J	Needham T	Plackett L
8	Rotherham Town	1-1	Pitman R	Latham A	Roulstone W	Warmby WH	Pearce C	Staley A	Keys J	Spilsbury BW	Nash RW	Needham T	Wilshaw S
19	Leek	2-1	Bestwick TH	Latham A	Lawrence SE	Williamson A	Warmby WH	Roulstone W	Bakewell G	Keys J	Radford J	Wilshaw S	Needham T
26	Owlerton (FAC)	6-2	Bestwick TH	Monk I	Lawrence SE	Williamson A	Roulstone W	Warmby WH	Bakewell G	Spilsbury BW	Nash RW	Plackett L	Needham T
Dec 3	Aston Villa	0-3	Bestwick TH	Latham A	Lawrence SE	Williamson A	Roulstone W	Warmby WH	Bakewell G	Spilsbury BW	Nash RW	Plackett L	Wilshaw S
10	Eckington (DC)	1-1	Pitman R	Weston WA	Lowles H	Monk I	Staley A	Birch-Thorpe CE	Bakewell G	Chatterton W	Lees J	Selvey W	Needham T
17	Staveley	2-1	Bestwick TH	Latham A	Lawrence SE	Williamson A	Warmby WH	Warmby WH	Bakewell G	Selvey W	Gwynne Rev. LH	Needham T	Wilshaw S
24	Sheffield Wednesday	0-8	Marshall J	Cooper W	Roulstone W	Williamson A	Warmby WH	Birch-Thorpe CE	Ottewell F	Hall J	Lees J	Bingham A	Wilshaw S
24	Eckington (DC)	7-2	Pitman R	Weston WA	Lowles H	Monk I	Latham A	Staley A	Chatterton W	Selvey W	Gwynne Rev. LH	Needham T	Plackett L
26	Casuals	5-1	Bestwick TH	Latham A	Lawrence SE	Monk I	Warmby WH	Roulstone W	Bakewell G	Selvey W	Chatterton W	Plackett L	Wilshaw S
27	Blackburn Rovers	2-0	Bestwick TH	Latham A	Lawrence SE	Monk I	Roulstone W	Warmby WH	Bakewell G	Staley A	Gwynne Rev. LH	Needham T	Locker W
Jan 7	Crewe Alexandra (FAC)	0-1	Bestwick TH	Latham A	Lawrence SE	Williamson A	Warmby WH	Roulstone W	Bakewell G	Spilsbury BW	Gwynne Rev. LH	Needham T	Plackett L
14	Long Eaton Rangers (DC)	1-4	Pitman R	Weston WA	Lawrence SE	Monk I	Warmby WH	Warmby WH	Chatterton W	Selvey W	Gwynne Rev. LH	Plackett L	Needham T
21	Warwickshire	4-1	Bestwick TH	Latham A	Roulstone W	Williamson A	Lawrence SE	Warmby WH	Bakewell G	Staley A	Gwynne Rev. LH	Needham T	Selvey W
28	Gainsborough Trinity	2-4	Bestwick TH	AN Other	Lawrence SE	Williamson A	Warmby WH	Warmby WH	Bakewell G	Selvey W	Chatterton W	Wilshaw S	Needham T
Feb 4	Derby Midland	3-1	Bestwick TH	Latham A	Lawrence SE	Williamson A	Warmby WH	Roulstone W	Bakewell G	Spilsbury BW	Chatterton W	Needham T	Plackett L
11	Aston Villa	0-5	Bestwick TH	Latham A	Lawrence SE	Williamson A	Warmby WH	Roulstone W	Bakewell G	Hardy T	Gwynne Rev. LH	Needham T	Selvey W
18	Notts County	3-2	Bestwick TH	Latham A	Lawrence SE	Williamson A	Warmby WH	Warmby WH	Bakewell G	Spilsbury BW	Goodall A	Needham T	Needham T
25	Grantham Town	2-0	Marshall J	Latham A	Lawrence SE	Williamson A	Booth HD	Warmby WH	Bakewell G	Pearce C	Gwynne Rev. LH	Selvey W	Needham T
Mar 3	Leek	4-0	Marshall J	Latham A	Lawrence SE	Williamson A	Booth HD	Warmby WH	Bakewell G	Selvey W	Lees J	Needham T	Pearce C
10	Bolton Wanderers	5-5	Bestwick TH	Latham A	Lawrence SE	Booth HD	Warmby WH	Roulstone W	Bakewell G	Pearce C	Goodall A	Needham T	Lees J
17	Everton	1-1	Bestwick TH	Latham A	Lawrence SE	Williamson A	Warmby WH	Warmby WH	Bakewell G	Pearce C	Lees J	Selvey W	Needham T
24	Derby Midland (DCC)	3-1	Bestwick TH	Latham A	Lawrence SE	Williamson A	Warmby WH	Roulstone W	Bakewell G	Selvey W	Goodall A	Selvey W	Plackett L
31	Notts County	3-0	Bestwick TH	Latham A	Storer W	Williamson A	Warmby WH	Roulstone W	Bakewell G	Selvey W	Goodall A	Needham T	Plackett L
Apr 2	Derby Junction	2-1	Bestwick TH	Latham A	Lawrence SE	Williamson A	Warmby WH	Roulstone W	Bakewell G	Selvey W	Goodall A	Needham T	Plackett L
3	Burnley	1-0	Bestwick TH	Storer W	Lawrence SE	Williamson A	Warmby WH	Roulstone W	Bakewell G	Selvey W	Goodall A	Needham T	Plackett L
14	Sheffield Wednesday	2-2	Bestwick TH	Storer W	Lawrence SE	Williamson A	Warmby WH	Roulstone W	Bakewell G	Selvey W	Goodall A	Needham T	Plackett L
21	Wolves	3-1	Marshall J	Storer W	Lawrence SE	Williamson A	Warmby WH	Roulstone W	Bakewell G	Selvey W	Goodall A	Lees J	Plackett L
28	Mitchell's St. Georges	2-3	Marshall J	Latham A	Storer W	Williamson A	Warmby WH	Roulstone W	Bakewell G	Selvey W	Goodall A	Needham T	Plackett L
May 21	Preston North End	0-0	Bosworth J	Latham A	Morley HA	Williamson A	Warmby WH	Roulstone W	Bakewell G	Cooper L	Goodall A	Needham T	Plackett L